The New Oxford Guide to Writing

THE NEW

Oxford Guide to Writing

Thomas S. Kane

OXFORD UNIVERSITY PRESS
New York · Oxford

Oxford University Press

Oxford   New York   Toronto
Delhi   Bombay   Calcutta   Madras   Karachi
Kuala Lumpur   Singapore   Hong Kong   Tokyo
Nairobi   Dar es Salaam   Cape Town
Melbourne   Auckland   Madrid

and associated companies in
Berlin   Ibadan

Copyright © 1988 by Thomas S. Kane

First published in 1988 by Oxford University Press, Inc.,
198 Madison Avenue, New York, New York 10016-4314

First issued as an Oxford University Press paperback, 1994

Oxford is a registered trademark of Oxford University Press

Library of Congress Cataloging-in-Publication
Kane, Thomas S.
The new Oxford guide to writing.
Includes index.
1. English language—Rhetoric.
2. English language—Grammar—1950–   . I. Title.
PE1408.K2728   1988   808'.042   87-28266
ISBN 0-19-504538-6
ISBN 0-19-509059-4 (pbk.)

Some examples and the Punctuation section were previously published in
The Oxford Guide to Writing: A Rhetoric and Handbook for College Students.

We gratefully acknowledge permission to reprint from the following works:

The American Earthquake by Edmund Wilson. Copyright © 1958 by
Edmund Wilson. Reprinted by permission of Farrar, Strauss and Giroux, Inc.

American Ways of Life by George R. Stewart. Reprinted by permission
of Doubleday, a division of Bantam, Doubleday, Dell Publishing Group, Inc.

The Autobiography of Bertrand Russell. Reprinted by permission
of Unwin Hyman Limited.

Jacobean Pageant, or The Court of King James I by G. P. V. Akrigg.
Copyright © 1962 by G. P. V. Akrigg. Reprinted by permission of
Harvard University Press and Hamish Hamilton, Ltd.

A Walker in the City by Alfred Kazin. Copyright © 1951, 1979 by
Alfred Kazin. Reprinted by permission of Harcourt Brace Jovanovich, Inc.

15 14 13

Printed in the United States of America

Acknowledgments

This book is based on *The Oxford Guide to Writing: A Rhetoric and Handbook for College Students,* and thanks are due once more to those who contributed to that book: my friend and colleague Leonard J. Peters; Professors Miriam Baker of Dowling College, David Hamilton of the University of Iowa, Robert Lyons and Sandra Schor of Queens College of the City University of New York, and Joseph Trimmer of Ball State University, all of whom read the manuscript and contributed perceptive comments; Ms. Cheryl Kupper, who copyedited that text with great thoroughness and care; and John W. Wright, my editor at the Oxford University Press.

For the present edition I am again grateful to Professor Leonard J. Peters and to John W. Wright. In addition I wish to thank William P. Sisler and Joan Bossert, my editors at Oxford University Press, who encouraged, criticized, and improved, as good editors do.

Kittery Point, Maine   T.S.K.
December 1987

Contents

The New Oxford Guide to Writing

Introduction

Two broad assumptions underlie this book: (1) that writing is a rational activity, and (2) that it is a valuable activity.

To say that writing is rational means nothing more than that it is an exercise of mind requiring the mastery of techniques anyone can learn. Obviously, there are limits: one cannot learn to write like Shakespeare or Charles Dickens. You can't become a genius by reading a book.

But you don't have to be a genius to write clear, effective English. You just have to understand what writing involves and to know how to handle words and sentences and paragraphs. *That* you can learn. If you do, you can communicate what you want to communicate in words other people can understand. This book will help by showing you what good writers do.

The second assumption is that writing is worth learning. It is of immediate practical benefit in almost any job or career. Certainly there are many jobs in which you can get along without being able to write clearly. If you know how to write, however, you will get along faster and farther.

There is another, more profound value to writing. We create ourselves by words. Before we are business people or lawyers or engineers or teachers, we are human beings. Our growth as human beings depends on our capacity to understand and to use language. Writing is a way of growing. No one would argue that being able to write will make you morally better. But it will make you more complex and more interesting—in a word, more human.

1

Subject, Reader, and Kinds of Writing

Choosing a Subject

Often, of course, you are not free to choose at all. You must compose a report for a business meeting or write on an assigned topic for an English class. The problem then becomes not *what* to write about but how to attack it, a question we'll discuss in Chapters 5 and 6.

When you can select a subject for yourself, it ought to interest you, and interest others as well, at least potentially. It should be within the range of your experience and skill, though it is best if it stretches you. It ought to be neither so vast that no one person can encompass it nor so narrow and trivial that no one cares.

Don't be afraid to express your own opinions and feelings. You are a vital part of the subject. No matter what the topic, you are really writing about how *you* understand it, how *you* feel about it. Good writing has personality. Readers enjoy sensing a mind at work, hearing a clear voice, responding to an unusual sensibility. If you have chosen a topic that is of general concern, and if genuine feeling and intelligence come through, you will be interesting. Interest lies not so much in a topic as in what a writer has made of it.

About Readers

You don't want to repel readers. This doesn't mean you have to flatter them or avoid saying something they may disagree with. It does mean you must respect them. Don't take their interest for granted or suppose that it is the readers' job to follow you. It's your job to guide them, to make their task as easy as the subject allows.

Ask yourself questions about your readers: What can I expect them to know and not know? What do they believe and value? How do I want to affect them by what I say? What attitudes and claims will meet with their approval? What will offend them? What objections may they have to my ideas, and how can I anticipate and counter those objections?

Readers may be annoyed if you overestimate their knowledge. Tossing off unusual words may seem a put-down, a way of saying, "I know more than you." On the other hand, laboring the obvious also implies a low opinion of readers: don't tell them what a wheel is; they know. It isn't easy to gauge your readers' level of knowledge or to sense their beliefs and values. Sensitivity to readers comes only with experience, and then imperfectly. Tact and respect, however, go a long way. Readers have egos too.

Kinds of Writing

The various effects a writer may wish to have on his or her readers—to inform, to persuade, to entertain—result in different kinds of prose. The most common is prose that informs, which, depending on what it is about, is called exposition, description, or narration.

Exposition explains. How things work—an internal combustion engine. Ideas—a theory of economics. Facts of everyday life—how many people get divorced. History—why Custer attacked at the Little Big Horn. Controversial issues laden with feelings—abortion, politics, religion. But whatever its subject, exposition reveals what a particular mind thinks or knows or believes. Exposition is constructed logically. It organizes around cause/effect, true/false, less/more, positive/negative, general/particular, assertion/denial. Its movement is signaled by connectives like *therefore, however, and so, besides, but, not only, more important, in fact, for example.*

Description deals with perceptions—most commonly visual perceptions. Its central problem is to arrange what we see into a significant pattern. Unlike the logic of exposition, the pattern is spatial: above/below, before/behind, right/left, and so on.

The subject of *narration* is a series of related events—a story. Its problem is twofold: to arrange the events in a sequence of time and to reveal their significance.

Persuasion seeks to alter how readers think or believe. It is usually about controversial topics and often appeals to reason in the form of *argument,* offering evidence or logical proof. Another form of persuasion is *satire,* which ridicules folly or evil, sometimes subtly, sometimes crudely and coarsely. Finally, persuasion may be in the form of *eloquence,* appealing to ideals and noble sentiments.

Writing that is primarily *entertaining* includes fiction, personal essays, sketches. Such prose will receive less attention here. It is certainly important, but it is more remote from everyday needs than exposition or persuasion.

For Practice

▷ List ten or twelve topics you might develop into a short essay. Think of topics that deal not so much with things, places, or how-to-do projects as with your opinions and beliefs. Pick subjects that interest you and are within your experience, yet challenging. Be specific: don't simply write "my job" but something like "what I like most (or hate most) about my job."

▷ Selecting one of the topics on your list, compose a paragraph about the readers for whom you might develop it. Consider how you wish to affect those readers, what you want them to understand and feel. Think about their general knowledge, values, attitudes, biases; whether they are your age or older or younger, come from a similar or a different background; and how you would like them to regard you.

CHAPTER 2

Strategy and Style

Purpose, the end you're aiming at, determines strategy and style. Strategy involves choice—selecting particular aspects of a topic to develop, deciding how to organize them, choosing this word rather than that, constructing various types of sentences, building paragraphs. Style is the result of strategy, the language that makes the strategy work.

Think of purpose, strategy, and style in terms of increasing abstractness. Style is immediate and obvious. It exists in the writing itself; it is the sum of the actual words, sentences, paragraphs. Strategy is more abstract, felt beneath the words as the immediate ends they serve. Purpose is even deeper, supporting strategy and involving not only what you write about but how you affect readers.

A brief example will clarify these overlapping concepts. It was written by a college student in a fifteen-minute classroom exercise. The several topics from which the students could choose were stated broadly—"marriage," "parents," "teachers," and so on—so that each writer had to think about restricting and organizing his or her composition. This student chose "marriage":

Why get married? Or if you are modern, why live together? Answer: Insecurity. "Man needs woman; woman needs man." However, this cliché fails to explain *need*. How do you need someone of the opposite sex? Sexually is an insufficient explanation. Other animals do not stay with a mate for more than one season; some not even that long. Companionship, although a better answer, is also an incomplete explanation. We all have several friends. Why make one friend so significant that he at least partially excludes the others? Because we want to "join our lives." But this desire for joining is far from "romantic"—it is selfish. We want someone to share our lives in order that we do not have to endure hardships alone.

The writer's purpose is not so much to tell us of what she thinks about marriage as to convince us that what she thinks is true. Her purpose, then, is persuasive, and it leads to particular strategies both of organization and of sentence style. Her organization is a refinement of a conventional question/answer strategy: a basic question ("Why get married?"); an initial, inadequate answer ("Insecurity"); a more precise question ("How do we need someone?"); a partial answer ("sex"); then a second partial answer ("companionship"); a final, more precise question ("Why make one friend so significant?"); and a concluding answer ("so that we do not have to endure hardships alone").

The persuasive purpose is also reflected in the writer's strategy of short emphatic sentences. They are convincing, and they establish an appropriate informal relationship with readers.

Finally, the student's purpose determines her strategy in approaching the subject and in presenting herself. About the topic, the writer is serious without becoming pompous. As for herself, she adopts an impersonal point of view, avoiding such expressions as "I think" or "it seems to me." On another occasion they might suggest a pleasing modesty; here they would weaken the force of her argument.

These strategies are effectively realized in the style: in the clear rhetorical questions, each immediately followed by a straightforward answer; and in the short uncomplicated sentences, echoing speech. (There are even two sentences that are grammatically incomplete—"Answer: Insecurity" and "Because we want to 'join our lives.' ") At the same time the sentences are sufficiently varied to achieve a strategy fundamental to all good prose—to get and hold the reader's attention.

Remember several things about strategy. First, it is many-sided. Any piece of prose displays not one but numerous strategies—of organization, of sentence structure, of word choice, of point of view, of tone. In effective writing these reinforce one another.

Second, no absolute one-to-one correspondence exists between strategy and purpose. A specific strategy may be adapted to various purposes. The question/answer mode of organizing, for example, is not confined to persuasion: it is often used in informative writing. Furthermore, a particular purpose may be served by different strategies. In our example the student's organization was not the only one possible. Another writer might have organized using a "list" strategy:

People get married for a variety of reasons. First . . . Second . . . Third . . . Finally . . .

Still another might have used a personal point of view, or taken a less serious approach, or assumed a more formal relationship with the reader.

Style

In its broadest sense "style" is the total of all the choices a writer makes concerning words and their arrangements. In this sense style may be good or bad—good if the choices are appropriate to the writer's purpose, bad if they are not. More narrowly, "style" has a positive, approving sense, as when we say that someone has "style" or praise a writer for his or her "style." More narrowly yet, the word may also designate a particular way of writing, unique to a person or characteristic of a group or profession: "Hemingway's style," "an academic style."

Here we use *style* to mean something between those extremes. It will be a positive term, and while we speak of errors in style, we don't speak of "bad styles." On the other hand, we understand "style" to include many ways of writing, each appropriate for some purposes, less so for others. There is no one style, some ideal manner of writing at which all of us should aim. Style is flexible, capable of almost endless variation. But one thing style is not: it is not a superficial fanciness brushed over the basic ideas. Rather than the gilding, style is the deep essence of writing.

For Practice

▷ Selecting one of the topics you listed at the end of Chapter 1, work up a paragraph of 150 to 200 words. Before you begin to write, think about possible strategies of organization and tone. *Organization* involves (1) how you analyze your topic, the parts into which you divide it, and (2) the order in which you present these parts and how you tie them together. *Tone* means (1) how you feel about your subject—angry, amused, objective, and so on; (2) how you regard your reader—in a formal or an informal relationship; and (3) how you present yourself.

When you have the paragraph in its final shape, on a separate sheet of paper compose several sentences explaining what strategies you followed in organizing your paragraph and in aiming for a particular tone, and why you thought these would be appropriate.

CHAPTER 3

Grammar, Usage, and Mechanics

Purpose, strategy, and style are decided by you. But the decision must be made within limits set by rules over which you have little control. The rules fall into three groups: grammar, usage, and mechanics.

Grammar

Grammar means the rules which structure our language. The sentence "She dresses beautifully" is grammatical. These variations are not:

Her dresses beautifully.
Dresses beautifully she.

The first breaks the rule that a pronoun must be in the subjective case when it is the subject of a verb. The second violates the conventional order of the English sentence: subject–verb–object. (That order is not invariable and may be altered, subject to other rules, but none of these permits the pattern: "Dresses beautifully she.")

Grammatical rules are *not* the pronouncements of teachers, editors, or other authorities. They are simply the way people speak and write, and if enough people begin to speak and write differently, the rules change.

Usage

Usage designates rules of a less basic and binding sort, concerning how we *should* use the language in certain situations. These sentences, for instance, violate formal usage:

She dresses beautiful.
She ain't got no dress.

Sentences like these are often heard in speech, but both break rules governing how educated people write. Formal usage dictates that when *beautiful* functions as an adverb it takes an *-ly* ending, that *ain't* and a double negative like *ain't got no* or *haven't got no* should be avoided.

Grammar and usage are often confused. Many people would argue that the sentences above are "ungrammatical." Our distinction, however, is more useful. Grammatical rules are implicit in the speech of all who use the language. Usage rules, on the other hand, stem from and change with social pressure. *Ain't*, for example, was once acceptable. The adverbial use of an adjective like *beautiful* was common in seventeenth-century prose. Chaucer and Shakespeare use double negatives for emphasis.

The fact that usage rules are less basic than grammatical ones, however, and even that they may seem arbitrary, does not lessen their force. Most of them contribute to clarity and economy of expression. Moreover, usage applies to all levels of purpose and strategy, to informal, colloquial styles as well as to formal ones. For example, grammatically incomplete sentences (or fragments), frowned upon in formal usage, are occasionally permissible and even valuable in informal composition. (Witness the two fragments in the student paragraph on marriage on page 8.) *So* is regarded in formal English as a subordinating conjunction which ought not to introduce a sentence. But in a colloquial style, it may work better than a more literary connective like *consequently* or *therefore*.

Mechanics

In composition *mechanics* refers to the appearance of words, to how they are spelled or arranged on paper. The fact that the first word of a paragraph is usually indented, for example, is a matter of mechanics. These sentences violate other rules of mechanics:

she dresses beautifully
She dresses beautifuly.

Conventions of writing require that a sentence begin with a capital letter and end with full-stop punctuation (period, question mark, or exclamation point). Conventions of spelling require that *beautifully* have two *l*s.

The rules gathered under the heading of mechanics attempt to make writing consistent and clear. They may seem arbitrary, but they have evolved from centuries of experience. Generally they represent, if not the only way of solving a problem, an economic and efficient way.

Along with mechanics we include punctuation, a very complicated subject and by no means purely mechanical. While some punctuation is cut-and-dried, much of it falls into the province of usage or style. Later, in the chapter on punctuation, we'll discuss the distinctions between mechanical and stylistic uses of commas, dashes, and so on.

Grammar, Usage, and Style

Grammar, usage, and mechanics establish the ground rules of writing, circumscribing what you are free to do. Within their limits, you select various strategies and work out those strategies in terms of words, sentences, paragraphs. The ground rules, however, are relatively inflexible, broken at your peril.

It is not always easy to draw the line between grammar and usage or between usage and style. Broadly, grammar is what you must do as a user of English; usage, what you should do as a writer of more or less formal (or informal) English; and style, what you elect to do to work out your strategies and realize your purposes.

"Her dresses beautifully," we said, represents an error in grammar, and "She dresses beautiful," a mistake in usage. "She dresses in a beautiful manner," however, is a lapse in style. The sentence breaks no rule of grammar or of usage, but it is not effective (assuming that the writer wants to stress the idea of "beauty"). The structure slurs the emphasis, which should be on the key word and which should close the statement—"She dresses beautifully."

Most of our difficulties with words and sentences involve style. For native speakers, grammar—in our sense—is not likely to be a serious problem. Usage (which includes much of what is popularly called "grammar") and mechanics are more troublesome. But generally these require simply that you learn clearly defined conventions. And having learned them, you will find that rather than being restrictive they free you to choose more effectively among the options available to you as a writer.

Style is less reducible to rule, and more open to argument. No one can prove "She dresses in a beautiful manner" is poorer than "She dresses beautifully." (One can even imagine a context in which the longer sentence would be preferable.) Even so, it violates a principle observed by good writers; use no more words than you must.

You may think of that principle as a "rule" of style. We shall discuss and illustrate that and other stylistic "rules," but remember: they are generalizations about what good writers do, not laws dictating what all writers must do.

I

The Writing Process

Writing in its broad sense—as distinct from simply putting words on paper—has three steps: thinking about it, doing it, and doing it again (and again and again, as often as time will allow and patience will endure).

The first step, "thinking," involves choosing a subject, exploring ways of developing it, and devising strategies of organization and style. The second step, "doing," is usually called "drafting"; and the third, "doing again," is "revising." The next several chapters take a brief look at these steps of the writing process.

First a warning. They're not really "steps," not in the usual sense anyway. You don't write by (1) doing all your thinking, (2) finishing a draft, and then (3) completing a revision. Actually you do all these things at once.

If that sounds mysterious, it's because writing is a complex activity. As you think about a topic you are already beginning to select words and construct sentences—in other words, to draft. As you draft and as you revise, the thinking goes on: you discover new ideas, realize you've gone down a dead end, discover an implication you hadn't seen before.

It's helpful to conceive of writing as a process having, in a broad and loose sense, three steps. But remember that you don't move from step to step in smooth and steady progress. You go back and forth. As you work on a composition you will be, at any given point, concentrating on one phase of writing. But always you are engaged with the process in its entirety.

CHAPTER 4

Looking for Subjects

People write for lots of reasons. Sometimes it's part of the job. A sales manager is asked to report on a new market, or an executive to discuss the feasibility of moving a plant to another state. A psychology student has to turn in a twenty-page term paper, or a member of an art club must prepare a two-page introduction to an exhibit.

In such cases the subject is given, and the first step is chiefly a matter of research, of finding information. Even the problem of organizing the information is often simplified by following a conventional plan, as with scientific papers or business letters. Which is not to dismiss such writing as easy. Being clear and concise is never easy. (To say nothing of being interesting!) But at least the writing process is structured and to that degree simplified.

At other times we write because we want to express something about ourselves, about what we've experienced or how we feel. Our minds turn inward, and writing is complicated by the double role we play. *I* am the subject, which somehow the *I* who writes must express in words. And there is a further complication. In personal writing, words are not simply an expression of the self; they help to create the self. In struggling to say what we are, we become what we say.

Such writing is perhaps the most rewarding kind. But it is also the most challenging and the most frustrating. We are thrown relentlessly upon our own resources. The subject is elusive, and the effect can be a kind of paralysis. And so people say, "I can't think of anything to write about."

That's strange, because life is fascinating. The solution is to open yourself to experience. To look around. To describe what you see and hear. To read. Reading takes you into other minds and enriches your own. A systematic way of enriching your ideas and experiences is to keep a commonplace book and a journal.

The Commonplace Book

A *commonplace book* is a record of things we have read or heard and want to remember: a proverb, a remark by a writer of unusual sensibility, a witty or a wise saying, or even something silly or foolish or crass:

Sincerity always hits me something like sleep. I mean, if you try to get it too hard, you won't.   W. H. Auden

Women have served all these centuries as looking glasses possessing the . . . power of reflecting the figure of a man at twice its natural size.   Virginia Woolf

I hate music—especially when it's played.   Jimmy Durante

Shrouds have no pockets.   English proverb

All this—and perhaps.   Yiddish proverb

To keep a commonplace book, set aside a looseleaf binder. When you hear or read something that strikes you, copy it, identifying the source. Leave space to add thoughts of your own. If you accumulate a lot of entries, you may want to make an index or to group passages according to subject.

A commonplace book will help your writing in several ways. It will be a storehouse of topics, of those elusive "things to write about." It will provide a body of quotations (occasional quotations add interest to your writing). It will improve your prose. (Simply copying well-expressed sentences is one way of learning to write.) Most important, keeping a commonplace book will give you new perceptions and ideas and feelings. It will help you grow.

The Journal

A *journal*—the word comes from French and originally meant "daily"—is a day-to-day record of what you see, hear, do, think, feel. A journal collects your own experiences and thoughts rather than quotations. But, of course, you may combine the two. If you add your own comments to the passages you copy into a commonplace book, you are also keeping a kind of journal.

Many professional writers use journals, and the habit is a good one for anybody interested in writing, even if he or she has no literary ambitions. Journals store perceptions, ideas, emotions, actions—all future material for essays or stories. *The Journals* of Henry Thoreau are a famous example, as are *A Writer's Diary* by Virginia Woolf, the *Notebooks* of the French novelist Albert Camus, and "A War-time Diary" by the English writer George Orwell.

A journal is not for others to read. So you don't have to worry about niceties of punctuation; you can use abbreviations and symbols like "&." But if a journal is really to help you develop as a writer, you've got to do more than compose trite commonplaces or mechanically list what happens each day. You have to look honestly and freshly at the world around you and at the self within. And *that* means you have to wrestle with words to tell what you see and what you feel:

July 25, Thursday. . . . Today: clear, flung, pine-chills, orange needles underfoot.
    I myself am the vessel of tragic experience. I muse not enough on the mysteries of Oedipus—I, weary, resolving the best and bringing, out of my sloth, envy and weakness, my own ruins. What do the gods ask? I must dress, rise, and send my body out.   Sylvia Plath

But journals do not have to be so extraordinary in their sensibility or introspection. Few people are that perceptive. The essential thing is that a journal captures *your* experience and feelings. Here is another, different example, also fresh and revealing. The writer, Rockwell Stensrud, kept a journal as he accompanied an old-time cattle drive staged in 1975 as part of the Bicentennial celebration:

Very strict unspoken rules of cowboy behavior—get as drunk as you want the night before, but you'd better be able to get up the next morning at 4:30, or you're not living by the code of respectability. Range codes more severe than high-society ideas of manners—and perhaps more necessary out here. What these cowboys respect more than anything is ability to carry one's own weight, to perform, to get the job done well—these are the traditions that make this quest of theirs possible.

CHAPTER 5

Exploring for Topics

Before beginning a draft, you need to explore a subject, looking for topics. (*Subject* refers to the main focus of a composition; *topic* to specific aspects of the subject. The subject of this book is writing. Within that subject grammar, sentence style, and so on, are topics. Any topic, of course, can itself be analyzed into subtopics.)

Some people like to work through a subject systematically, uncovering topics by asking questions. Others prefer a less structured, less analytical approach, a kind of brainstorming. They just begin to write, rapidly and loosely, letting ideas tumble out in free association. Then they edit what they've done, discarding some topics, selecting others for further development.

Neither way is "right"—or rather both are right. Which you use depends on your habits of mind, how much you already know about a subject, and of course the subject itself. If you are writing about something that is easily analyzed—why one candidate should be elected, for instance, rather than some other—and if you've already thought a good deal about the matter, the analytical, questioning approach is better. But if your subject is more nebulous—your feelings about war, say—and you have not thought long and hard, you may get stuck if you try systematic analysis. It might be better to scribble, to get ideas on paper, any ideas, however farfetched, in whatever order.

Finding Topics by Asking Questions

What happened?
How?
When?

Why? What caused it? What were the reasons?
How can the subject be defined?
What does it imply or entail?
What limits should be set to it?
Are there exceptions and qualifications?
What examples are there?
Can the subject be analyzed into parts or aspects?
Can these parts be grouped in any way?
What is the subject similar to?
What is it different from?
Has it advantages or virtues?
Has it disadvantages or defects?
What have other people said about it?

These are general questions, of course; and they are not the only ones you might ask. Particular subjects will suggest others. Nor will all of these questions be equally applicable in every case. But usually five or six will lead to topics.

Suppose, for example, you are interested in how young adults (20 to 30) in the 1990s differ from similar people in the 1960s. Try asking questions. Consider definition. What do you mean by "differ"? Differ how? In dress style? Eating habits? Political loyalties? Life style? Attitudes toward love, sex, marriage? Toward success, work, money?

Already you have topics, perhaps too many. Another question suggests itself: Which of these topics do I want to focus on? Or, put another way: How shall I limit the subject? The choice would not be purely arbitrary; it would depend partly on your interests and partly on your ambitions. In a book you might cover all these topics. In a ten-page paper only one or two or three. We'll imagine a short paper and focus on love, sex, and marriage.

Now you have three major topics. How to organize them? Sex, love, and marriage seems a reasonable order. Next, each topic needs to be explored, which you do by again asking questions. How do the attitudes of the sixties and the nineties differ? Why? Examples?—from friends, popular culture (songs, advertisements, magazine articles, films), literature, sociological studies? Can you find useful quotations or stories or movies that support your points? Are there virtues in the attitudes of the nineties? Disadvantages? How do you evaluate those of the sixties? Was a comparable generational shift in values evident in other places and other times?

You're not going to get answers off the top of your head. But at least you know what you're looking for. You can begin to collect information, interviewing friends, studying magazines and movies and television shows, reading novels and stories, looking into scholarly studies of changing social attitudes.

You've got a lot to write about.

Finding Topics by Free Writing
or Brainstorming

Free writing simply means getting ideas on paper as fast as you can. The trick is to let feelings and ideas pour forth. Jot down anything that occurs to you, without worrying about order or even making much sense. Keep going; to pause is to risk getting stuck, like a car in snow. Move the pencil, writing whatever pops into mind. Don't be afraid of making mistakes or of saying something foolish. You probably will. So what? You're writing for yourself, and if you won't risk saying something foolish, you're not likely to say anything wise.

Here's how you might explore the different attitudes of the 1990s and the 1960s on sex, love, and marriage:

Sex—less permissive today. Herpes? AIDS? More conservative morality? Just a generational reaction, a swing of the pendulum?

Cooler about love and marriage. Less romantic. Harry and Ellen. Maybe feminism. If they have a chance at careers—prestige, money—women are harder-headed about marriage. Maybe more demanding about men, less willing to accept them on men's own terms. Maybe men leery of modern women.

Economics? It's a tougher world. Fewer good jobs, more competition. Everything costs—education, cars, housing, kids.

Materialism. Young people seem more materialistic. Concerned with money, worldly success. They want to make it. Be millionaires by thirty. Admiration for winners, fear being losers.

Less idealistic? Do disillusion and cynicism push toward self-interest? But people in their twenties today aren't really cynical and disillusioned. Never been idealistic enough. They don't have to learn the lesson of *The Big Chill*. They grew up in it.

Such jottings are not finely reasoned judgments. Many of the ideas are speculative and hastily generalized; some are probably biased. Still, topics have surfaced. The next task would be to look at them closely, rejecting some, choosing others; and then to gather information.

Thus both methods of exploration have led to topics, the rudiments of an essay. But notice that while they cover the same general subject, they have led in rather different directions. The analytical questions have stressed *what*—the nature of the changes in attitude; the free writing has stressed *why*—the reasons for the changes.

These different emphases were not planned. They just happened. And that suggests an important fact: it is profitable to use both methods to explore for topics. Questions have the advantage of focusing your attention. But a focused attention sees only what is under the lens, and that is a severe limitation. Brainstorming can be wasteful, leading in too many directions. But it is more likely to extend a subject in unforeseen ways and to make unexpected connections.

The two methods, then, are complementary, not antithetical. Temperamentally, you may prefer one or the other. But it's wise to try both.

For Practice

▷ Below is a series of provocative quotations. Select one that appeals to you and explore it for topics. You don't have to agree with the idea. The goal is just to get your thoughts on paper.

First, fill one or two pages with free writing. Put down *everything* that comes to mind. Then try the more analytical approach of asking questions. (A variation of this exercise is to work with several friends; group brainstorming can be more productive than working alone.)

Beware of all enterprises that require new clothes.   Thoreau

Know thyself.   Greek maxim

"Know thyself?" If I knew myself I'd run away.   Goethe

The business of America is business.   Calvin Coolidge

Business underlies everything in our national life, including our spiritual life.
                                                                    Woodrow Wilson

In love always one person gives and the other takes.   French proverb

Sex is something I really don't understand too hot. You never know *where* the hell you are. I keep making up these sex rules for myself, and then I break them right away.
                                                                    J. D. Salinger

No man but a blockhead ever writes, except for money.   Samuel Johnson

He's really awfully fond of colored people. Well, he says himself, he wouldn't have white servants.
                                                                    Dorothy Parker

If we wanted to be happy it would be easy; but we want to be happier than other people, which is almost always difficult, since we think them happier than they are.
                                                                    Montesquieu

Wrest once the law to your authority:
To do a great right, do a little wrong.
                    Shakespeare

A lawyer has no business with the justice or injustice of the cause which he undertakes, unless his client asks his opinion, and then he is bound to give it honestly. The justice or injustice of the cause is to be decided by the judge.
                                                                    Samuel Johnson

[College is] four years under the ethercone breathe deep gently now that's the way to be a good boy one two three four five six get A's in some courses but don't be a grind.
                                                                    John Dos Passos

If a thing is worth doing, it is worth doing badly.   G. K. Chesterton

6

Making a Plan

You've chosen a subject (or had one chosen for you), explored it, thought about the topics you discovered, gathered information about them. Now what? Are you ready to begin writing?

Well, yes. But first you need a plan. Perhaps nothing more than a loose sense of purpose, held in your mind and never written down—what jazz musicians call a head arrangement. Head arrangements can work very well—if you have the right kind of head and if you're thoroughly familiar with the subject.

But sometimes all of us (and most times most of us) require a more tangible plan. One kind is a statement of purpose; another is a preliminary, scratch outline.

The Statement of Purpose

It's nothing complicated—a paragraph or two broadly describing what you want to say, how you're going to organize it, what you want readers to understand, feel, believe. The paragraphs are written for yourself, to clarify your ideas and to give you a guide; you don't have to worry about anyone else's reading them. Even so, you may find on occasion that composing a statement of purpose is difficult, perhaps impossible. What that means is that you don't really know what your purpose is. Yet even failure is worth while if it makes you confront and answer the question: Just what am I aiming at in this paper?

Not facing that question before they begin to write is one of the chief causes people suffer from writing block. It's not so much that they *can't* think *of* what to say, as that they *haven't* thought *about* what they can say. Ideas do not come out of the blue; as we saw in the last chapter, they have to be sought. And when they are found, they don't arrange themselves. A writer has to think about the why and how of using them.

Many of us think better if we write down our ideas. That's all a statement of purpose is really, thinking out loud, except with a pencil. The thinking, however, is not so much about the subject itself as about the problems of focusing and communicating it.

Here's how a statement of purpose might look for a theme about attitudes toward sex, love, and marriage in the 1990s:

It seems to me that today people in their twenties feel differently about sex, love, and marriage than young people did in the 1960s. I'm not claiming the differences are universal, that every young adult today feels one way, while every young adult twenty years ago felt another. Just that the predominant tone has changed. I want to identify and describe these differences, focusing on the nineties, and to discuss why the changes came about. I see a problem of organization. Am I going to organize primarily around the differences themselves, first attitudes toward sex, then attitudes towards love and marriage? In this case, a discussion of causes would be subordinate. On the other hand, I could make the causes my main points of organization, beginning with a relatively detailed discussion of how attitudes today are different, but spending most of the paper in discussing how feminism, the hardening economy, and a tougher, more self-centered approach to life have combined to bring about the changes. I think I'll do it this second way. What I want readers to see is less of the facts about the new attitudes toward sex, love, and marriage, and more of the social and cultural causes generating the change.

The Scratch Outline

An outline is a way of dividing a subject into its major parts, of dividing these in turn into subparts, and so on, into finer and finer detail. There are formal outlines, which are usually turned in with a composition and even serve as compositions in their own right. And there are informal outlines, often called "working" or "scratch" outlines. The formal variety follows rules that prescribe the alternating use of numbers and letters and the way in which the analysis must proceed. But formal outlines and their rules will not concern us here.

Our interest is in the scratch outline, which serves only the writer's use and may be cast in any form that works. Begin by asking: What are the major sections of my composition? For example:

  I. Beginning
 II. How attitudes toward sex, love, and marriage in the 1990s differ from those in the 1960s
III. Why the differences occurred
IV. Closing

Now apply a similar question to each major section:

    I. Beginning
        A. Identify subject and establish focus—on the reasons for the change rather than on the change itself
        B. Qualify and limit: attitudes in question are the predominating ones, those which set the tone of a generation
    II. How attitudes toward sex, love, and marriage differ in the 1990s from those in the 1960s
        A. Sex—less permissive, less promiscuous
        B. Love—cooler, not so completely a preemptive good
        C. Marriage—more calculating, rational; avoid early marriage, first get career on track
   III. Why the differences occurred
        A. Feminism—more job opportunities for women and greater independence; also stronger sense of their own worth—all this weakens the allure of love and marriage
        B. Tighter economy—future has to be planned more carefully, less room for romantic illusions
        C. More self-centered view of life—partly a result of the two conditions above, but becomes a cause in its own right
   IV. Closing
        A. The attitudes of the nineties more realistic, less prone to disillusion
        B. But perhaps idealism has been sacrificed, or weakened, and the prevailing materialism is too ready to sell the world short

Thus the analysis could go on: the A's and B's broken down, examples introduced, comparisons offered, and so on. Generally, it is better to proceed with the analysis one step at a time, as in the example above. This keeps the whole subject better in mind and is more likely to preserve a reasonable balance. If you exhaustively analyze category I before moving on to II, then carry II down to fine detail before tackling III, you may lose sight of the overall structure of the composition.

How far you take a scratch outline depends on the length of your composition and obviously on your willingness to spend time in planning. But the more planning you do, the easier the actual writing will be. A good scratch outline suggests where possible paragraph breaks might come, and the ideas you have jotted down in the headings are the germs of topic statements and supporting sentences.

But however you proceed and however far you carry the scratch outline, remember that as a plan it is only tentative, subject to change. And the odds are that you *will* change it. No matter how much you think about a subject or how thoroughly you plan, the actuality of writing opens up unforeseen possibilities and reveals the weakness of points that seemed important. A scratch outline is a guide, but a guide you should never hesitate to change.

For Practice

▷ Imagine you are going to write an essay of eight or ten pages, using the topics you arrived at by exploring one of the quotations at the end of the preceding chapter. First, compose a statement of purpose for that essay in one or two paragraphs totaling about 250 words. Second, make a scratch outline for the theme, indicating the primary divisions and the major subdivisions within these.

CHAPTER 7

Drafts and Revisions

Drafting

A *draft* is an early version of a piece of writing. Most of us cannot compose anything well at the first try. We must write and rewrite. These initial efforts are called drafts, in distinction from the final version. As a rule, the more you draft, the better the result.

For drafting, the best advice is the same as for the free writing we discussed in Chapter 5: keep going and don't worry about small mistakes. A draft is not the end product; it is tentative and imperfect. Writing becomes impossible if you try to do it one polished sentence at a time. You get lost looking for perfection. Rough out your report or article, *then* develop and refine, keeping the total effect always in mind.

Accept imperfections. Don't linger over small problems. If you can't remember a spelling, get the word down and correct it later. If you can't think of exactly the term you want, put down what you can think of and leave a check in the margin to remind yourself to look for a more precise word. Your main purpose is to develop ideas and to work out a structure. Don't lose sight of major goals by pursuing minor ones—proper spelling, conventional punctuation, the exact word. These can be supplied later.

There is a limit, however, to the similarity between drafting and free writing. Free writing involves exploration and discovery; your pencil should move wherever your mind pushes it. A draft is more reined in. You know, more or less, what you want to do, and the draft is an early version of an organized composition. Therefore you are not as free as in the exploratory phase. If you get into blind alleys in a draft, you must back out and set off in a new direction. The mistake will not be unproductive if it tells you where you don't want to be.

Some people prefer to draft with a pen or pencil; others can work successfully on a typewriter or word processor. If you draft in longhand, skip every other line and leave adequate margins: you will need the space for revisions. If you type, double space. Use only one side of the paper, reserving the other side for extensive changes or additions. When you number the pages of your draft, it's a good idea to include a brief identifying title: "First draft, p. 1," "Second draft, p. 3."

In a composition of any length, consider stopping every so often at a convenient point. Read over what you've written, making corrections or improvements; then type what you've done. Seeing your ideas in print will usually be reassuring. If you don't have a typewriter or word processor, copy the section neatly in longhand; the effect will be much the same. Turn back to the draft; work out the next section; stop again and type. The alternation between drafting and typing will relieve the strain of constant writing and give you a chance to pause and contemplate what you have accomplished and what you ought to do next.

But this is advice, not dogma. People vary enormously in their writing habits; what works for one fails for another. The best rule is to find a time and a place for writing that enable you to work productively and to follow a procedure you find congenial. You may like to draft in green or purple ink, to listen to music as you write, to compose the entire draft of a ten-page essay and then retype the whole thing instead of doing it section by section. Do what works for you.

As a brief sample, here is a draft of the beginning of the composition we've been discussing for the last several chapters—how young people in the 1990s feel about sex, love, and marriage.

I have some friends in their late twenties. They live in Chicago, where he is starting out as a lawyer and she as an accountant. Both are presently junior members of large firms, but they are ambitious and hope eventually either to track upward in their companies or to get out on their own. They live together; they say they are in love, and they seem to be. But they are surprisingly cool about it and about the prospect of marriage. "Well," Dee says, "I have my career and Jack has his. It's good we're together, but who knows where we'll be in two years or how we'll feel?" Their coolness surprises me. I find it admirable and yet a bit repelling. I admire their good sense. Still, I think to myself, should young love be so cool, so rational, so pragmatic? Is such good sense at so youthful an age perhaps purchased at too great a price? My friends are not, I believe, unusual, not certainly among young, college-educated professionals. The lack of emotional intensity and commitment—about love, at least—seems the dominant tone of their generation. How is it different from the attitudes I grew up with, the attitudes of the sixties? And why is it different? These are the questions I want to consider.

A good deal of improvement can be made in that draft. First, though, it would help to say something about revision in general.

Revising

Both drafting and revising are creative, but they differ in emphasis. Drafting is more spontaneous and active; revision, more thoughtful and critical. As a writer of a draft you must keep going and not get hung up on small problems. As a reviser you change hats, becoming a demanding reader who expects perfection. When you write you see your words from inside; you know what you want to say and easily overlook lapses of clarity puzzling to readers. When you revise you put yourself in the reader's place. Of course you cannot get completely outside your own mind, but you can think about what readers know and do not know, what they believe and consider important. You can ask yourself if what is clear to you will be equally clear to them.

To revise effectively, force yourself to read slowly. Some people hold a straightedge so they read only one line at a time, one word at a time if possible. Others read their work aloud. This is more effective (though you cannot do it on all occasions). Reading aloud not only slows you down, it distances you from the words, contributing to that objectivity which successful revision requires. Moreover, it brings another sense to bear: you hear your prose as well as see it. Ears are often more trustworthy than eyes. They detect an awkwardness in sentence structure or a jarring repetition the eyes pass over. Even if you're not exactly sure what's wrong, you *hear* that something is, and you can tinker with the sentences until they sound better. It also helps to get someone else to listen to or to read your work and respond.

Keep a pencil in hand as you revise (some like a different color). Mark your paper freely. Strike out imprecise words, inserting more exact terms above them (here is the advantage of skipping lines). If you think of another idea or of a way of expanding a point already used, write a marginal note, phrasing it precisely enough so that when you come back to it in an hour or a day it will make sense. If a passage isn't clear, write "clarity?" in the margin. If there seems a gap between paragraphs or between sentences within a paragraph, draw an arrow from one to the other with a question mark. Above all, be ruthless in striking out what is not necessary. A large part of revision is chipping away unnecessary words.

As we study diction, sentences, and paragraph structure, you will become aware of what to look for when you revise, but we shall mention a few basics here. Most fundamental is clarity. If you suspect a sentence may puzzle a reader, figure out why and revise it. Almost as important is emphasis. Strengthen important points by expressing them in short or unusual sentences. Learn to position modifiers so that they interrupt a sentence and throw greater weight on important ideas. Look for unsupported generalizations. Even when it is clear, a generalization gains value from illustrative detail.

Sharpen your diction. Avoid awkward repetitions of the same word. Replace vague abstract terms with precise ones having richer, more provocative connotations. Watch for failures of tone: don't offend readers and don't strike poses.

Be alert for errors in grammar and usage and in spelling and typing. Make sure your punctuation is adequate and conventional, but no more frequent than clarity or emphasis requires. Guard against mannerisms of style. All of us have them: beginning too many sentences with "and" or "but"; interrupting the subject and verb; writing long, complicated sentences. None of these is wrong, but any word or sentence pattern becomes a mannerism when it is overworked. One "however" in a paragraph may work well; two attract a reader's notice; three will make him or her squirm.

As an example of revision let's look again at the opening of our imaginary essay.

Dull opening. Perhaps: "Dee and Jack are an attractive couple. . . ."	I have some friends in their late twenties. They live
Not important enough for a main clause	in Chicago, where he is starting out as a lawyer
	and she as an accountant. Both are presently junior
	members of large firms, but they are ~~ambitious and~~
Poor emphasis and wordy	committed to their careers, eager to move ahead ~~hope eventually either to track upward~~ in their
New paragraph	¶ companies or to get out on their own. They live to-
	gether; they say they are in love, and they seem to
	be. But they are surprisingly cool about it and
The point is that marriage is not a likely prospect.	possibility about the ~~prospect~~ of marriage. "Well," Dee says,
	"I have my career and Jack has his. It's good we're
	together, but who knows where we'll be in two
New sentence for emphasis New paragraph	. Or ¶I find years ~~or~~ how we'll feel?" Their coolness ~~surprises~~
Wordy "Repelling" is too strong.	unsettling ~~me. I find it~~ admirable and yet a bit ~~repelling~~. I ad-
	mire their good sense. Still, I think to myself,
	should young love be so cool, so rational, so prag-
	matic? Is such good sense at so youthful an age
New paragraph	¶Dee and Jack purchased at too great a price? ~~My friends~~ are not,
	I believe, unusual, not certainly among young,

Low-keyed
college-educated professionals. ~~The lack of emo-~~

Wordy and awkward
~~emotionalism seems the dominant tone of their song of love.~~
emotionalism seems the dominant tone of their song of love.
~~tional intensity and commitment—about love at~~

~~least seems the dominant tone of their generation.~~

Rework these rhetorical questions;
they seem heavy-handed and jar
the informal tone.

How is it different from the attitudes I grew up

with, the attitudes of the sixties? And why is it dif-

ferent? These are the questions I want to consider.

Here now is the revision:

Dee and Jack are an attractive couple in their late twenties—bright, well-educated, ambitious. He is starting out as a lawyer, she as an accountant. Junior members of large firms, they are committed to their careers and eager to move ahead.

They live together. They say they are in love, and they seem to be. But they are cool about it, and about the possibility of marriage. "Well," Dee says, "I have my career and Jack has his. It's good that we're together, but who knows where we'll be in two years? Or how we'll feel?"

I find their coolness admirable, and yet a bit unsettling. Should young love, I think to myself, be quite so cool, so rational, so pragmatic? Is good sense at so youthful an age purchased at too high a price?

Dee and Jack aren't unusual, not among college-educated young professionals. Low-keyed emotionalism seems the dominant tone of the contemporary song of love. It's all very different from the attitudes I shared in the sixties. It occurred to me to wonder why.

I don't think there is any single, simple reason. . . .

Probably you wouldn't write such extensive marginal notes to yourself, but those in the example suggest how you should be thinking. The revisions are toward precision, emphasis, and economy.

How many drafts and revisions you go through depends on your energy, ambition, and time. Most people who publish feel they stopped one draft too soon. Many teachers and editors are willing to accept corrections so long as they are not so numerous or messy that they interfere with reading. Some, on the other hand, do want clean copy—that is, pages with no corrections, additions, or deletions.

Final Copy

Whether or not you are allowed to revise it, your final copy should always be neat and legible. Keep margins of an inch or more. If you type, use standard typing paper and type on only one side. Double space and correct typos by erasure or tape, not by overstriking. Keep the keys clean and invest now and then in a new ribbon. If you write in longhand, use conventional, lined composition paper. Unless directed otherwise, skip every other line and write only on one side. Leave adequate margins for corrections and comments. Take time to write legibly. No one expects a beautiful copperplate hand, but it is fair to ask for readability.

PART II

The Essay

CHAPTER 8

Beginning

An essay is a relatively short composition. It does not claim scholarly thoroughness (that belongs to the *monograph*), but it does exhibit great variety. Essays can be about almost anything; they can be speculative or factual or emotional; they can be personal or objective, serious or humorous. The very looseness of the term is a convenience; it would be a mistake to define it precisely. Here *essay* really will simply mean a short prose piece. There *are* differences among articles and reports and essays. But they have much in common, and what we say about the essay—its beginning, closing, structure, and so on—applies to compositions generally.

Readers approach any piece of prose with a set of questions. What is this about? Will it interest me? What does the writer intend to do (or not do)? What kind of person is the writer?

To begin effectively you must answer these questions, one way or another. From the writer's point of view, beginning means announcing and limiting the subject, indicating a plan, catching the reader's attention, and establishing an appropriate tone and point of view.

Not all of these matters are equally important. Announcing and limiting the subject are essential. Laying out the plan of the paper and angling for the reader's interest, on the other hand, depend on your purpose and audience. Tone and point of view are inevitable: whenever you write you imply them. In the beginning, then, you must establish a tone and point of view conducive to your purpose.

The length of the beginning depends on the length and complexity of what it introduces. In a book the opening might take an entire chapter with dozens of paragraphs. In a short article a single sentence might be adequate. For most essays a single paragraph is enough. Whatever their length, all effective openings fulfill the same functions.

Announcing the Subject

In announcing a subject you have two choices: (1) whether to be explicit or implicit, and (2) whether to be immediate or to delay.

Explicit and Implicit Announcement

In explicit announcement you literally state in some fashion or other, "This is my subject." The philosopher Alfred North Whitehead begins *Religion in the Making* like this:

It is my purpose to consider the type of justification which is available for belief in the doctrines of religion.

The words "It is my purpose" make this an explicit announcement. It would have been implicit had Whitehead begun:

Belief in the doctrines of religion may be justified in various ways.

This sentence does not literally tell readers what the subject is, but the subject is clearly implied.

Because of its clarity, scholars and scientists writing for their colleagues often use explicit announcement. On less formal occasions it may seem heavy-handed. A school theme, for instance, ought not to begin "The purpose of this paper is to contrast college and high school." It is smoother to establish the subject by implication: "College and high school differ in several ways." Readers don't have to be hit over the head. Implicit announcements may appear as rhetorical questions, as in this essay about historians:

What is the historian?
The historian is he who tells a true story in writing.
Consider the members of that definition.
                                                                    Hilaire Belloc

Similarly the theme on college and high school might have opened:

In what ways do college and high school differ?

Opening questions, however, can sound mechanical. While better than no announcement at all, or the clumsiness of "The purpose of this paper is," rhetorical questions are not very original. Use them for announcement only when you can do so with originality or when all other alternatives are less attractive.

The same advice holds for opening with a dictionary definition, another way of announcing subjects implicitly. Nothing is inherently wrong in starting off with a quote from a reputable dictionary, but it is trite. Of course a clever or an unusual definition may make a good opening. John Dos Passos's definition of college as "four years under the ethercone" is certainly novel and provocative and might make a fine beginning.

When the purpose of an essay is to define a word or idea, it is legitimate to start from the dictionary. But these exceptions admitted, the dictionary quotation, like the rhetorical question, has been overworked as a way of implying the subject.

Immediate and Delayed Announcement

Your second choice involves whether to announce the subject immediately or to delay. This opening line of an essay called "Selected Snobberies" by the English novelist Aldous Huxley falls into the first category:

All men are snobs about something.

Letting readers in on the subject at once is a no-nonsense, businesslike procedure. But an immediate announcement may not hold much allure. If the subject is of great interest, or if the statement is startling or provocative (like Huxley's), it will catch a reader's eye. Generally, however, immediate announcement is longer on clarity than on interest.

So you may prefer to delay identifying the subject. Delay is usually achieved by beginning broadly and narrowing until you get down to the subject. The critic Susan Sontag, for instance, uses this beginning for an essay defining "Camp" (a deliberately pretentious style in popular art and entertainment):

Many things in the world have not been named; and many things, even if they have been named, have never been described. One of these is the sensibility—unmistakably modern, a variant of sophistication but hardly identical with it—that goes by the name of "Camp."

Less commonly the subject may be delayed by focusing outward, opening with a specific detail or example and broadening to arrive at the subject. Aldous Huxley opens an essay on "Tragedy and the Whole Truth" in this manner:

There were six of them, the best and the bravest of the hero's companions. Turning back from his post in the bows, Odysseus was in time to see them lifted, struggling, into the air, to hear their screams, the desperate repetition of his own name. The survivors could only look on, helplessly, while Scylla "at the mouth of her cave devoured them, still screaming, still stretching out their hands to me in the frightful struggle." And Odysseus adds that it was the most dreadful and lamentable sight he ever saw in all his "explorings of the passes of the sea." We can believe it;

Homer's brief description (the too-poetical simile is a later interpolation) convinces us.

Later, the danger passed, Odysseus and his men went ashore for the night, and, on the Sicilian beach, prepared their supper—prepared it, says Homer, "expertly." The Twelfth Book of the *Odyssey* concludes with these words: "When they had satisfied their thirst and hunger, they thought of their dear companions and wept, and in the midst of their tears sleep came gently upon them."

The truth, the whole truth and nothing but the truth—how rarely the older literatures ever told it! Bits of the truth, yes; every good book gives us bits of the truth, would not be a good book if it did not. But the whole truth, no. Of the great writers of the past incredibly few have given us that. Homer—the Homer of the *Odyssey*—is one of those few.

It is not until the third paragraph that Huxley closes in on his subject, of which the episode from the *Odyssey* is an example.

Delayed announcement has several advantages. It piques readers' curiosity. They know from the title that the opening sentences do not reveal the subject, and they are drawn in to see where they are headed. Curiosity has a limit, however; you can tease readers too long.

A broad beginning can also clarify a subject, perhaps supplying background or offering examples. Finally, delayed announcement can be entertaining in its own right. There is a pleasure like that of watching a high-wire performer in observing an accomplished writer close in on a subject.

More immediate announcement, on the other hand, is called for in situations where getting to the point is more important than angling for readers or entertaining them. How you announce your subject, then, as with so much in writing, depends on purpose—that is, on your reason for addressing your readers.

Limiting the Subject

In most cases a limiting sentence or clause must follow the announcement of the subject. Few essays (or books, for that matter) discuss *all* there is to say; they treat some aspects of a subject but not others. As with announcement, limitation may be explicit or implicit. The first—in which the writer says, in effect, "I shall say such and so"—is more common in formal, scholarly writing. The grammarian Karl W. Dykema begins an article entitled "Where Our Grammar Came From":

The title of this paper is too brief to be quite accurate. Perhaps with the following subtitle it does not promise too much: A partial account of the origin and development of the attitudes which commonly pass for grammatical in Western culture and particularly in English-speaking societies.

On informal occasions one should limit the subject less literally, implying the boundaries of the paper rather than literally stating them:

Publishers, I am told, are worried about their business, and I, as a writer, am therefore worried too. But I am not sure that the actual state of their affairs disturbs me

quite so much as some of the analyses of it and some of the proposals for reme-
dying what is admittedly an unsatisfactory situation.   Joseph Wood Krutch

Without literally saying so, Krutch makes it clear that he will confine his
interest in the problems publishers face to criticizing some of the attempts
that have been made to explain and solve those problems.

Besides being explicit or implicit, limitation may also be positive or negative (or both). The paragraphs by Dykema and Krutch tell us what the
writers *will* do; they limit the subject in a positive sense. In the following
case the English writer and statesman John Buchan tells what he will *not*
do (the paragraph opens the chapter "My America" of his book *Pilgrim's
Way*):

The title of this chapter exactly defines its contents. It presents the American scene
as it appears to one observer—a point of view which does not claim to be that
mysterious thing, objective truth. There will be no attempt to portray the "typical"
American, for I have never known one. I have met a multitude of individuals, but
I should not dare to take any one of them as representing his country—as being
that other mysterious thing, the average man. You can point to certain qualities
which are more widely distributed in America than elsewhere, but you will scarcely
find human beings who possess all these qualities. One good American will have
most of them; another, equally good and not less representative, may have few or
none. So I shall eschew generalities. If you cannot indict a nation, no more can
you label it like a museum piece.

Some limitation—explicit or implicit, positive or negative—is necessary
at the beginning of most essays. Term papers, long formal essays whose
purpose is to inform, technical and scholarly articles, all may have to en-
gage in extensive boundary fixing to avoid misleading or disappointing the
reader. Shorter themes, however, do not require much limitation. Readers
learn all they really need to know by an opening sentence like this:

College is different from high school in several ways—especially in teaching,
homework, and tests.

The final phrase conveys the limitations, following the announcement in
the first clause of the sentence. The subject is a contrast between college
and high school, the focus is on college, and the contents are limited to
three specific points of difference. That is limitation enough for a brief,
informal essay, and the writer can get on with the discussion without a
heavy statement like this:

I shall limit the contrast to teaching methods, homework, and tests.

There is no rule to test whether you have limited a subject sufficiently.
Just put yourself in the reader's place and ask if it is clear (whether by
direct statement or by implication) what the essay will do and what it will
not do.

Indicating the Plan of the Essay

Another function of the beginning, though not an invariable one, is to clarify how the essay will be organized. The writer has the plan in mind when composing the beginning paragraph (or revising it). The question is: Should the plan be revealed to the reader?

Writers often do consider it necessary. Harold Mattingly begins his book *Roman Imperial Civilization* with this paragraph:

> The object of this first chapter is to give a sketch of the Empire which may supply a background to all that follows: to explain what the position of Emperor from time to time was, how it was defined in law, how it was interpreted by the subjects; then, around the Emperor, to show the different parts of the State in relation to one another and to him. Later chapters will develop particular themes. We shall have to consider at the close how far the constitution of the Empire was satisfactory for its main purposes, how much truth there is in the contention that imperfections in the constitution were a main cause of Decline and Fall.

The paragraph indicates not only the plan of the first chapter and that of the whole book, but also how the opening chapter fits into the larger organization.

Even with subjects less complex and grand than the Roman Empire, writers may wish to tell us how they intend to develop their essays:

> I want to tell you about a woodsman, what he was like, what his work was, and what it meant. His name was Alfred D. Teare and he came originally from Nova Scotia, but all the time I knew him his home was in Berlin, New Hampshire. Probably the best surveyor of old lines in New England, he was—in his way—a genius.   Kenneth Andler

This straightforward paragraph not only announces and limits the subject but also reveals something about the organization of the essay. Readers are prepared for a three-part structure: Teare as a person, the nature of his work, and the significance of that work. Assuming that the writer knows his craft—as in this case he does—we know the order in which he mentions these aspects of his subject reflects the order in which he will treat them. The plan has been clarified implicitly and effectively.

Establishing your plan in the beginning has several virtues. It eases the reader's task. Knowing where they are headed, readers can follow the flow of ideas. An initial indication of the organization also simplifies later problems of transition. When a writer can assume that readers understand the general scheme of the essay, it is easier to move them from point to point.

As with limiting the subject, one cannot set down clear-cut rules about when to reveal the plan. Generally it is wise to indicate something about the organization of compositions that are relatively long and that fall into several well-defined parts. Shorter, simpler essays less often require that their plan be established in the opening paragraph.

When you must indicate your plan, do so as subtly as you can. The imaginary theme about high school and college that begins:

College is different from high school in several ways—especially in teaching methods, homework, and tests.

clearly implies the three parts of the essay and their order. In longer work you may occasionally feel it desirable to indicate organization explicitly. But be sure that your subject is substantial enough and your purpose serious enough to support such a beginning.

Interesting the Reader

Sometimes you can take readers' interest for granted. Scholars and scientists writing for learned journals, for instance, do not have to make much effort to catch their readers' attention. More commonly a writer's audience includes at least some people whose interest must be deliberately sought. Several strategies for doing this are available.

Stressing the Importance of the Subject

Treat the reader as a reasonable, intelligent person with a desire to be well informed and say, in effect: "Here is something you should know or think about." The American poet and critic John Peale Bishop begins an essay on Picasso with this sentence:

There is no painter who has so spontaneously and so profoundly reflected his age as Pablo Picasso.

Arousing Curiosity

This is usually a more effective strategy than stressing the importance of the subject. You may play upon curiosity by opening with a short factual statement that raises more questions than it answers. Astronomer Sir Arthur Eddington begins a chapter in his book *The Philosophy of Science* with this statement:

I believe there are 15,747,724,136,275,002,577,605,653,691,181,555,468,044, 717,914,527,116,709,366,231,425,076,185,631,031,296 protons in the universe and the same number of electrons.

It would be a curiously incurious reader who would not boggle at this and read on to learn how the writer arrived at so precise a figure.

A short step from such interest-arousing factual openings is the cryptic beginning, that is, a mysterious or not quite clear statement. Charles Lamb opens an essay with

I have no ear.

We soon learn that he means "no ear for music," but for a moment we are startled.

To be effective a cryptic opening must not simply be murky. It must combine clarity of statement with mystery of intent. We know *what* it says, but we are puzzled about *why*. The mystery has to be cleared up rather quickly if the reader's interest is to be retained. For most of us curiosity does not linger; without satisfaction it goes elsewhere.

Carrying mystification a little further, you may open with a rhetorical paradox—a statement that appears to contradict reality as we know it. Hilaire Belloc begins his essay "The Barbarians" this way:

It is a pity true history is not taught in the schools.

Readers who suppose true history is taught may be annoyed, but they are likely to go on.

Sometimes mystification takes the form of a *non sequitur*, that is, an apparently nonlogical sequence of ideas. An enterprising student began a theme:

I hate botany, which is why I went to New York.

The essay revealed a legitimate connection, but the seeming illogic fulfilled its purpose of drawing in the reader.

Amusing the Reader

Aside from arousing their curiosity, you may attract readers by amusing them. One strategy is to open with a witty remark, often involving an allusion to a historical or literary figure. Francis Bacon opens his essay "Of Truth" with this famous sentence:

What is truth? said jesting Pilate and would not stay for an answer.

A contemporary writer alludes both to Pontius Pilate and to Bacon by adapting that beginning for the essay "What, Then, Is Culture?":

"What is truth?" said jesting Pilate, and would not stay for an answer.
   "What is culture?" said an enlightened man to me not long since, and though he stayed for an answer, he did not get one.   Katherine Fullerton-Gerould

Another variety of the entertaining opening is the anecdote. Anecdotes have a double value, attracting us once by their intrinsic wittiness and then by the skill with which writers apply them to the subject. In the following opening Nancy Mitford describes the history of the French *salon*, a social gathering of well-known people who discuss politics, art, and so on:

"What became of that man I used to see sitting at the end of your table?" someone asked the famous eighteenth-century Paris hostess, Mme. Geoffrin.

"He was my husband. He is dead." It is the epitaph of all such husbands. The hostess of a salon (the useful word salonniere, unfortunately, is an Anglo-Saxon invention) must not be encumbered by family life, and her husband, if he exists, must know his place.

The salon was invented by the Marquise de Rambouillet at the beginning of the seventeenth century.

Mitford's story is amusing, in a cynical fashion. More important, it leads naturally into her subject. *Naturally*—that is important, for an opening anecdote fails if forced upon the subject from the outside.

Still another entertaining opening strategy is the clever and apt comparison. It may be an analogy, as in the following passage by Virginia Woolf, the first part of the opening paragraph of her essay "Reviewing":

In London there are certain shop windows that always attract a crowd. The attraction is not in the finished article but in the worn-out garments that are having patches inserted in them. The crowd is watching the women at work. There they sit in the shop window putting invisible stitches into moth-eaten trousers. And this familiar sight may serve as an illustration to the following paper. So our poets, playwrights, and novelists sit in the shop window, doing their work under the eyes of reviewers.

Notice, incidentally, the skill with which Woolf focuses down upon the subject.

A comparison calculated to arouse interest may be a simile or metaphor. G. K. Chesterton wittily begins an essay "On Monsters" with this metaphorical comparison:

I saw in an illustrated paper—which sparkles with scientific news—that a green-blooded fish had been found in the sea; indeed a creature that was completely green, down to this uncanny ichor in its veins, and very big and venomous at that. Somehow I could not get it out of my head, because the caption suggested a perfect refrain for a Ballade: A green-blooded fish has been found in the sea. It has so wide a critical and philosophical application. I have known so many green-blooded fish on the land, walking about the streets and sitting in the clubs, and especially the committees. So many green-blooded fish have written books and criticism of books, have taught in academies of learning and founded schools of philosophy that they have almost made themselves the typical biological product of the present age of evolution.

Chesterton uses "green-blooded fish" as a metaphor for all self-centered, dehumanized people, and the metaphor attracts us by its originality.

A Word About Titles

The title of an essay precedes the beginning and should clarify the subject and arouse interest. The title, however, does not take the place of a beginning paragraph. In fact it is good practice to make an essay self-sufficient so that subject, purpose, plan (if needed) are all perfectly clear without reference to a title.

As to titles themselves, they should ideally be both informative and eye-catching. It is difficult in practice to balance these qualities, and most titles come down on one side or the other; they are informative but not eye-catching, or unusual and attractive but not especially informative. In either case a title ought to be concise.

If you start your essay with a title in mind, be sure it fits the theme as it actually evolves. In the process of composition, essays have a way of taking unexpected twists and turns. For this reason it may be well not to decide on a final title until you see what you have actually written.

Conclusion

When composing beginnings, inexperienced writers are likely to err at either of two extremes: doing too little or doing too much. In doing too little they slight the opening, jumping too suddenly into the subject and piling ideas and information in front of the reader before he or she has time to settle back and see what all this is about.

In doing too much they make the beginning a precis of the essay and anticipate everything they will cover. The function of an opening is to introduce an essay, not to be a miniature version of it. To make it so is to act as inappropriately as the master of ceremonies at a banquet who introduces the main speaker by anticipating everything he or she is going to say.

The effective beginning stays between those extremes. It lets readers know what to expect, but it leaves them something to expect.

For Practice

▷ In about 100 words, compose a beginning paragraph either for the theme you outlined at the close of the preceding chapter or for one on another topic of interest. Make sure that readers understand your general subject, the limitations of your treatment, and your organization. Be implicit: do not write, "The subject will be . . .."; "The plan to be followed is . . . ." Try to interest your readers and to establish a point of view and a tone appropriate to your purpose.

▷ In conjunction with the exercise above, answer these questions, devoting several sentences or a brief paragraph to each:

A. What strategy did you use to interest your readers?
B. What tone were you seeking to establish—specifically, how did you feel about the subject, how did you wish readers to view you, and what kind of relationship did you hope to establish with them? Explain also how these aspects of tone led you to choose certain words in your beginning paragraph.

CHAPTER 9

Closing

Like the opening of an essay, the closing should be proportional to the length and complexity of the whole piece. Several paragraphs, or only one, or even a single sentence may be sufficient. But whatever its length, a closing must do certain things.

Termination

The most obvious function of a closing is to say, "The end." There are several ways of doing this.

Terminal Words

The simplest is to employ a word or phrase like *in conclusion, concluding, finally, lastly, in the last analysis, to close, in closing,* and so on. Adverbs showing a loose consequential relationship also work: *then, and so, thus.* Generally it is best to keep such terminal words unobtrusive. In writing, the best technique hides itself.

Circular Closing

This strategy works on the analogy of a circle, which ends where it began. The final paragraph repeats an important word or phrase prominent in the beginning, something the reader will remember. If the strategy is to work, the reader has to recognize the key term (but of course you cannot hang a sign on it—"Remember this"). You must stress it more subtly, perhaps by position or by using an unusual, memorable word. In an essay of any length it may be wise to repeat the phrase now and again, and sometimes writers emphasize the fact of completion by saying something like, "We return, then, to . . . ."

In a sketch of a famous aristocrat, Lady Hester Stanhope, the biographer Lytton Strachey opens with this paragraph:

The Pitt nose [Lady Stanhope belonged to the famous Pitt family] has a curious history. One can watch its transmigrations through three lives. The tremendous hook of Old Lord Chatham, under whose curves Empires came to birth, was succeeded by the bleak upward-pointing nose of William Pitt the younger—the rigid symbol of an indomitable *hauteur*. With Lady Hester Stanhope came the final stage. The nose, still with an upward tilt in it, had lost its masculinity; the hard bones of the uncle and grandfather had disappeared. Lady Hester's was a nose of wild ambitions, of pride grown fantastical, a nose that scorned the earth, shooting off, one fancies, towards some eternally eccentric heaven. It was a nose, in fact, altogether in the air.

And here are the final three sentences of Strachey's sketch:

The end came in June, 1839. Her servants immediately possessed themselves of every moveable object in the house. But Lady Hester cared no longer: she was lying back in her bed—inexplicable, grand, preposterous, with her nose in the air.

Not only does Strachey's phrase latch the end of his essay to its beginning, it also conveys his attitude toward Lady Hester Stanhope. The expression that completes the circle necessarily looms large in the reader's mind, and it must be genuinely important.

Rhythmic Variation

Prose rhythm is complex. Here it is enough to understand that, however it works, rhythm is inevitable and important. Because it is, you can use it to signal the closing by varying the movement of the final sentence or sentences.

Usually the variation is to slow the sentence and make its rhythm more regular. A famous example is the end of Lewis Carroll's *Alice in Wonderland:*

Lastly, she pictured to herself how this same little sister of hers would, in the after-time, be herself a grown woman; and how she would keep, through all her riper years, the simple and loving heart of her childhood; and how she would gather about her other little children, and make *their* eyes bright and eager with many a strange tale, perhaps even with her dream of Wonderland of long ago; and how she would feel with all their simple sorrows, and find a pleasure in all their simple joys, remembering her own child life, and the happy summer days.

The passage is slowed by interrupting constructions (for example, "in the aftertime") and regularized by repeating similar constructions ("and how," for instance) to create an almost poetic rhythm (the X marks unstressed syllables and the / denotes stressed):

x x / x / x /
and the happy summer days.

Occasionally writers take the other tack and close with a short, quick sentence rather than a long, slow, regular one. Such an ending is most effective played against a longer statement, as in this passage, which concludes Joan Didion's essay "On Morality":

Because when we start deceiving ourselves into thinking not that we want something or need something, not that it is a pragmatic necessity for us to have it, but that it is a *moral imperative* that we have it, then is when we join the fashionable madmen, and then is when the thin whine of hysteria is heard in the land, and then is when we are in bad trouble. And I think we are already there.

Failing to use a brief sentence as a way of ending sometimes wastes a potentially good closing:

At last the hard-working housewife is ready to watch her favorite television program, but before fifteen minutes are up she is sound asleep in her chair and before she realizes it the 6:30 alarm is going off and it is time to start another day.

It is better like this:

Before she realizes it the 6:30 alarm is going off. Another day.

Natural Point of Closing

A final way of signaling the end is simply to stop at a natural point, one built into the subject. For example, in a biographical sketch of someone who is dead the obvious place to end is with the death scene, as in the passage quoted earlier by Lytton Strachey about Lady Hester Stanhope. Another instance is this paragraph, the end of Llewelyn Powys's essay "Michel de Montaigne":

On 13 September, 1592, Michel de Montaigne, having distributed certain legacies to his servants, summoned his parish priest to his bedside, and there in his curious room with the swallows already gathering on the leaden gutters outside, he heard Mass said for the last time in the company of certain of his neighbors. With due solemnity the blessed sacrament was elevated, and at the very moment that this good heretical Catholic and Catholic heretic (unmindful for once of his nine learned virgins) was raising his arms in seemly devotion toward the sacred which in its essence—*que sçais-je*—might, or might not, contain a subtle and crafty secret, he fell back dead.

Here the effectiveness of closing with the death scene is reinforced by the careful construction of the last sentence, which does not complete its main thought until the very final word. "Dead" falls into place like the last piece of a puzzle.

Natural closings are not restricted to death-bed descriptions. Writing about your daily routine, for instance, you might well end with some variation of the phrase the diarist Samuel Pepys made famous: "And so to bed." Even when a subject does not have a built-in closing, a comparison or figure of speech can provide one.

These, then, are some of the ways of making clear that you are through. The various techniques do not exclude one another; they are often combined. Nor are these the only devices of closing. Inventive writers tailor their endings to subject and purpose. The poet Dylan Thomas wittily concludes his essay "How To Begin a Story" by doing what inexperienced writers should *not* do—simply stopping in mid-sentence:

I see there is little, or no, time to continue my instructional essay on "How To Begin a Story." "How to End a Story" is, of course, a different matter. . . . *One way of ending a story is. . . .*

And Virginia Woolf closes an essay called "Reading" with this sentence:

Some offering we must make; some act we must dedicate, if only to move across the room and turn the rose in the jar, which, by the way, has dropped its petals.

It is difficult to say why this works. The rhythm is important. But so is the image. The flower that has dropped its petals is perhaps a metaphor of ending. And the seeming irrelevancy of the final clause also signals finality, like the gracious closing of a conversation. In any case, the passage ends the essay neatly and unmistakably. That is the important thing.

Summation and Conclusion

Termination is always a function of the closing paragraph or sentence. Sometimes, depending on subject and purpose, you may need to make a summary or to draw a conclusion, in the sense of a final inference or judgment.

Summaries are more likely in long, complicated papers. Usually they are signaled by a phrase like *in summary, to sum up, summing up, in short, in fine, to recapitulate.* The label may be more subtle: "We have seen, *then*, that . . . ," and subtlety is usually a virtue in such matters.

Logical conclusions or judgments may be necessary even in short essays. Certain subjects make them obligatory. Here the journalist Samuel Hopkins Adams concludes an article on the controversial Warren Harding (the twenty-ninth president, who served from 1921 to 1923):

The anomaly of Warren Gamaliel Harding's career is that without wanting, knowing, or trying to do anything at all unusual, he became the figurehead for the most flagrantly corrupt regime in our history. It was less his fault than that of the country at large. Maneuvered by the politicians, the American people selected to represent them one whom they considered an average man. But the job they assigned him is not an average job. When he proved incapable of meeting its requirements, they blamed him and not themselves.

That is the tragedy of Harding.

On occasion it may not be the best strategy, or even be possible, to round off an essay with a neat final judgment. The novelist Joseph Conrad once remarked that the business of the storyteller is to ask questions, not to answer them. That truth applies sometimes to the essayist, who may wish to suggest a judgment rather than to formulate one. The strategy is called an *implicative closing*. The writer stops short, allowing the reader to infer the conclusion. In effect the final sentences open a door instead of closing one. Here, for instance, is the ending of an essay about a teenage hangout:

The old lady who lives across the street from the place says that the most striking thing is the momentary silences which, now and again, break up the loud, loud laughter.

CHAPTER 10

Organizing the Middle

Just as an essay must begin and end well, so it must be clearly organized in between. An important part of a writer's job is assisting readers in following the organization. It can be done in two ways, which are often used together. One is by *signposts*—words, phrases, sentences (occasionally even a short paragraph) which tells readers what you have done, are doing, will do next, or even will not do at all. The other way is by *interparagraph transitions,* that is, words and phrases that tie the beginning of a new paragraph to what precedes it.

Signposts

The most common signpost is an initial sentence that indicates both the topic and the general plan of treating it. For instance, the scientist J. B. S. Haldane organizes a five-paragraph section of a long essay like this:

Science impinges upon ethics in at least five different ways. In the first place . . .
  Secondly . . .
  Thirdly . . .
  Fourthly . . .
  Fifthly . . .

Sequence may be signaled by actual numbers or letters—usually enclosed in parentheses—rather than by words like *first, second, in the first place,* and so on. The poet W. B. Yeats explains why he believes in magic:

I believe in the practice and philosophy of what we have agreed to call magic, in what I must call the evocation of spirits, though I do not know what they are, in the power of creating magical illusions, in the visions of truth in the depths of the mind when the eyes are closed; and I believe in three doctrines, which have, as I think, been handed down from early times, and been the foundation of nearly all magical practices. These doctrines are—

1. That the borders of our mind are ever shifting, and that many minds can flow into one another, and create or reveal a single mind, a single energy.

2. That the borders of our memories are as shifting, and that our memories are a part of one great memory, the memory of Nature herself.

3. That this great mind and great memory can be evoked by symbols.

Numbers, however, and number words like *first, second, third,* must be handled cautiously. Overused, they confuse readers, losing them in a labyrinth of (1)s and (2)s and (a)s and (b)s.

Rather than using numbers, it is better, if possible, to set up an analysis by employing key terms. These identify the major points and can be repeated at the beginning of the appropriate paragraph or section. For example, the television critic Edith Efron, discussing soap operas, writes:

Almost all dramatic tension and moral conflict emerge from three basic sources: mating, marriage and babies.

She begins the next paragraph by picking up the key word "mating":

The mating process is the cornerstone of the tri-value system.

And the following paragraph she opens by using the loose synonym "domesticity" to link "marriage and babies":

If domesticity is a marital "good," aversion to it is a serious evil.

Signposts demand consistency. Once you begin using them you must carry through. Some writers make the mistake of starting off with something like this:

There were three reasons why the pact was not satisfactory. First . . . .

But then they fail to introduce the next two reasons with the obligatory *second* or *third* (or *secondly, finally*). The lack of signals may confuse readers who fail to recognize when the writer passes from one reason to another.

Aside from setting up a group of paragraphs, signposts may also anticipate future sections of an essay or make clear what will not be treated. Few subjects divide neatly into watertight compartments. As you develop one point, you touch upon another that you do not plan to discuss fully until later or perhaps not to discuss at all. When this happens you may wish to give a warning.

Signposts may also point backward, reminding readers of something treated earlier which bears upon the current topic. Thus a writer may say "(See page 8)," or "As we saw in Chapter 7 . . . ."

The signposts we have looked at are *intrinsic*—that is, they are actually a part of the writer's text. There are also *extrinsic* signposts, ones that stand outside the actual discussion yet clue readers to its organization. An outline or a table of contents is such an extrinsic signal. So are chapter titles, subtitles of sections, running heads at the top of each page.

Typography and design convey other extrinsic indications of organization: the indentation of paragraph beginnings and of quotations, the extra spacing between lines to signal a new major section, and occasionally the numerals (usually Roman) centered above the division of an essay. Philosophical and scientific writers sometimes use a more elaborate system, beginning each paragraph with a two-part number, the first digit to designate the chapter, the second the paragraph.

Interparagraph Transitions

Transitions link a paragraph to what has immediately preceded it. They occur at or near the beginning of the new paragraph because it represents a turn of thought, needing to be linked to what has gone before. Transitions act like railroad switches, smoothing and easing the turn from one track to another.

The Repetitive Transition

The simplest type of transition repeats a key word. Writing about the Louisiana politician Huey Long, Hodding Carter ends one paragraph and begins the next with the following link (the italics are added in this and in all following examples, unless noted otherwise):

Behind Huey were the people, and the people wanted these things.
    And with *the people behind him, Huey* expanded ominously.

A repeated word makes a strong and simple connection. It works well when the key term leading into the new paragraph occurs naturally at the end of the preceding one. But it is awkward and artificial when the term is forced into the final sentence merely to set up the transition.

The Question-and-Answer Transition

A second way of linking paragraphs is to ask and answer a rhetorical question. Usually the question is placed at the end of the preceding paragraph and the answer at the beginning of the following one. Nancy Mitford, commenting upon the apparently compulsive need of tourists to travel, concludes one paragraph and opens the next like this:

Why do they do it?
The answer is that the modern dwelling is comfortable, convenient, and clean, but it is not a home.

Less often the question appears at the opening of the new paragraph, as in this discussion of the ultimate defeat of the crusades:

With want of enthusiasm, want of new recruits, want, indeed, of stout purpose, the remaining Christian principalities gradually crumbled. Antioch fell in 1268, the Hospitaler fortress of Krak des Chevaliers in 1271. In 1291, with the capture of the last great stronghold, Acre, the Moslems had regained all their possessions, and the great crusades ended, in failure.
    Why? What went wrong? There was a failure of morale clearly. . . .
                                                                    Morris Bishop

The question-and-answer transition makes a very strong tie, but, as with the rhetorical question generally, it is too obvious a strategy to be called upon very often.

The Summarizing Transition

This link begins with a phrase or clause that sums up the preceding paragraph and then moves to the main clause, which introduces the new topic. (Unless idiom prohibits it, the elements of the transition should always be in that order: summary of old topic, statement of new one.)
    If- and *while*-clauses frequently carry such transitions:

If I went through anguish in botany and economics—for different reasons—gym-
nasium was even worse.   James Thurber

But while Bernard Shaw pleasantly surprised innumerable cranks and revolutionists
by finding quite rational arguments for them, he surprised them unpleasantly also
by discovering something else.   G. K. Chesterton

Long summarizing transitions tend to be formal in tone. On informal occasions it may be better to avoid a full *if-* or *while*-clause and state the summary more briefly. Here, for example, a writer moves from the topic of college teaching methods to that of personal responsibility:

Because of *these differences in teaching methods,* college throws more responsibility upon the student.

A summarizing transition may take even briefer form, using pronouns like *this, that, these, those,* or *such* to sum up the preceding topic. The historian J. Fred Rippy moves from the severe geographical conditions of South America to a discussion of its resources:

These are grave handicaps. But Latin America has many resources in compensa-
tion.

Although the "these" in that example is perfectly clear, such pronouns can be ambiguous when used as the subjects of sentences, especially when they refer to the whole of a long, complex idea. If you do use such a pronoun in this way, be sure that readers understand what it refers to. Should there be a doubt, make the pronoun an adjective modifying a word or phrase that fairly sums up the preceding point: for example, *"These handicaps* are grave."

Logical Transitions

Finally, you may link paragraphs by words showing logical relationships: *therefore, however, but, consequently, thus, and so, even so, on the other hand, for instance, nonetheless,* and many, many more. In the following passage the historian and political scientist Richard Hofstadter is contrasting "intelligence" and "intellect." In the first paragraph he defines "intelligence." By placing the transitional phrase *on the other hand* near the beginning of the second paragraph, he signals the other half of the contrast:

. . . intelligence is an excellence of mind that is employed within a fairly narrow, immediate, and predictable range. . . . Intelligence works within the framework of limited but clearly stated goals.

   Intellect, *on the other hand,* is the critical, creative, and contemplative side of mind.

Here is another example—a discussion of *Hamlet*—in which *moreover* indicates that the new paragraph will develop an extension of the preceding idea:

If I may quote again from Mr. Tillyard, the play's very lack of a rigorous type of causal logic seems to be a part of its point.

   Moreover, the matter goes deeper than this. Hamlet's world is preeminently in the interrogative mode.   Maynard Mack

Logical connectives seldom provide the only link between paragraphs. Actually, they work in conjunction with word repetitions, summaries, pronouns. In fact, all the various transitional strategies we have looked at commonly occur in some combination. But whatever its form, an interparagraph transition should be clear and unobtrusive, shifting readers easily from one topic to the next.

For Practice

▷ Read closely an essay or article you like and study how the writer links paragraphs.
▷ Go through something you have written and underline the linkages between paragraphs. If you find places where the connections seem weak, improve them.

CHAPTER 11

Point of View, Persona, and Tone

Point of View

Thus far we have looked at how to begin and end essays and how to help readers follow the flow of thought. It remains to consider several other aspects of a composition, more abstract but no less important. These are point of view, persona, and tone.

Point of view relates to how you present a subject. Two approaches are possible. In a *personal* point of view you play the role of writer openly, using "I," "me," "my." An *impersonal* point of view, on the other hand, requires that you avoid all explicit reference to yourself. The difference is not that in a personal point of view the subject is the writer, while in an impersonal one it is something else. Every subject involves, though it is not necessarily *about*, the writer. The difference is a question of strategy.

On many occasions one point of view or the other is preferable. Some topics so intimately involve the writer that they require a first-person presentation. It would sound silly to describe your summer vacation impersonally. Don't be afraid to use "I" if it fits your subject and purpose.

On other occasions a personal point of view is *not* appropriate. A scientist, writing professionally, usually tries to keep his or her personality below the surface, and properly so: scientific subjects are best treated objectively.

Of course many topics can be presented from either point of view, though the two approaches will result in different essays. In such cases you must consider occasion and reader and the degree of formality you want. An impersonal point of view seems more formal, a personal one less so.

Whichever you select, establish it in the opening paragraph. You needn't say, "My point of view will be personal [or impersonal]." Simply use "I" if you intend to write personally, or avoid it if you do not. (Such substitutes for "I" as "this observer," "your reporter," or "the writer" are wordy and awkward and best avoided.)

Maintain point of view consistently. Don't jump back and forth between a personal and an impersonal presentation. At the same time, you can make small adjustments. For example, you may expand "I" to "we" when you wish to imply "I the writer and you the reader." Whether writing personally or impersonally you may address readers as individuals by employing "you," or shift to "one," "anyone," "people," and so on, when you are referring to no one specifically.

But such shifts in point of view should be compatible with the emphasis you desire, and they should be slight. Radical changes, nine times in ten, are awkward. It is good practice, then, (1) to select a point of view appropriate to your subject, (2) to establish that point of view in the opening paragraph, and (3) to maintain it consistently.

Persona

Persona derives from the Latin word for an actor's mask (in the Greek and Roman theaters actors wore cork masks carved to represent the type of character they were playing). As a term in composition, *persona* means the writer's presence in the writing.

The derivation from "mask" may be misleading. It does not imply a false face, a disguise, behind which the real individual hides. A writer's *persona* is always "real." It is *there,* in the prose. The words you choose, the sentence patterns into which you arrange them, even the kinds of paragraphs you write and how you organize your essay, suggest a personality, which is, for that particular piece of writing, you.

But, you may object, a persona is not really the person who writes. (*Person,* interestingly enough, comes from the same Latin word.) Of course, that is true, and it is true that the same writer may assume different personas on different occasions. Still, the only contact readers generally have with a writer is through his or her words. For readers the persona implicit in those words is the real, existential fact about the writer.

The question to ask about any persona is not, Is this really the writer? The questions are, Is it really how the writer wants to appear? And, Is it how he or she can best appear? To put the matter another way: Is the persona authentic and appropriate?

Authenticity means that the personality readers sense in your words is the personality you want them to perceive. To say that a persona is authentic does not necessarily mean that it is really you. We are all many different people, showing one face to friends, another to strangers, still another to the boss. Here authenticity simply means that how you appear in what you write is how you wish to appear.

But authenticity is not enough. A persona must also be appropriate, efficacious in the sense that it achieves your ends. At the very least it ought not to get in the way.

Persona is most immediately and directly revealed when a writer discusses himself or herself. For instance, a clear personality emerges in the following passage from Benjamin Franklin's *Autobiography*. Franklin is explaining that when he educated himself as a youth he learned to drop his habit of "abrupt contradiction, and positive argumentation" and to become more diffident in putting forward his opinions. (He is, of course, talking about the same thing we are—persona.)

[I retained] the habit of expressing myself in terms of modest diffidence, never using when I advance any thing that may possibly be disputed, the words, *certainly, undoubtedly,* or any others that give the air of positiveness to an opinion; but rather I say, *I conceive,* or *I apprehend* a thing to be so or so, *It appears to me,* or *I should think it so for such & such reasons,* or *I imagine it to be so,* or *it is so if I am not mistaken.* This habit I believe has been of great advantage to me, when I have had occasion to inculcate my opinions & persuade men into measures that I have been from time to time engag'd in promoting. And as the chief ends of conversation are to *inform,* or to be *informed,* to *please* or to *persuade,* I wish well meaning sensible men would not lessen their power of doing good by a positive assuming manner that seldom fails to disgust, tends to create opposition, and to defeat every one of those purposes for which speech was given us, to wit, giving or receiving information, or pleasure: for if you would *inform,* a positive dogmatical manner in advancing your sentiments, may provoke contradiction & prevent a candid attention. If you wish information & improvement from the knowledge of others and yet at the same time express your self as firmly fix'd in your present opinions, modest sensible men, who do not love disputation, will probably leave you undisturb'd in the possession of your error; and by such a manner you can seldom hope to recommend yourself in *pleasing* your hearers, or to persuade those whose concurrence you desire.

Franklin strikes us as a discerning and candid man, sensitive to how he affects people, but sensitive in an unabashedly egocentric way. His advice about not coming on too strong—still worth heeding—is based not so much on concern for others as on a clear-eyed awareness that modesty is the way to get on in the world. Yet the very openness and ease with which Franklin urges that advice washes away its taint of self-serving manipulation.

We sense a different personality in these paragraphs from Bertrand Russell's *Autobiography:*

Three passions, simple but overwhelmingly strong, have governed my life: the longing for love, the search for knowledge, and unbearable pity for the suffering of mankind. These passions, like great winds, have blown me hither and thither, in a wayward course, over a deep ocean of anguish, reaching to the very verge of despair.

I have sought love, first, because it brings ecstasy—ecstasy so great that I would often have sacrificed all the rest of life for a few hours of this joy. I have sought it, next, because it relieves loneliness—that terrible loneliness in which one shivering consciousness looks over the rim of the world into the cold unfathomable lifeless abyss. I have sought it, finally, because in the union of love I have seen, in a mystic miniature, the prefiguring vision of the heaven that saints and poets have imagined. This is what I sought, and though it might seem too good for human life, this is what—at least—I have found.

With equal passion I have sought knowledge. I have wished to understand the hearts of men. I have wished to know why the stars shine. And I have tried to apprehend the Pythagorean power by which number holds sway above the flux. A little of this, but not much, I have achieved.

Love and knowledge, so far as they were possible, led upward toward the heavens. But always pity brought me back to earth. Echoes of cries of pain reverberate in my heart. Children in famine, victims tortured by oppressors, helpless old people a hated burden to their sons, and the whole world of loneliness, poverty, and pain make a mockery of what human life should be. I long to alleviate the evil, but I cannot, and I too suffer.

This has been my life. I have found it worth living, and would gladly live it again if the chance were offered me.

Russell is more emotional than Franklin. His attitude toward knowledge and toward other people is less self-serving and more passionate. He is driven to knowledge not because it serves his ambition but because of a compulsive desire to know (though Franklin too could show a disinterested quest for knowledge). Russell sees other people not as helps or hindrances to his career, but as fellow humans, for whose suffering he can feel compassion and sorrow.

Yet there is more to Russell's persona than the obvious emotionalism. His feelings are constrained within a rational framework. The organization of his paragraphs is tightly analytical, and the whole passage can easily be reduced to an outline. Here is someone who not only feels intensely but whose intellect imposes order upon emotions, giving them a sharper focus. We sense a powerful, complex mind, in which emotion and reason are not at war but are reinforcing allies. Russell's passionate response to life gains intensity because it is shaped by reason.

Persona, as you can see, is a function of the *total* composition. It emerges not only from the meanings of words but also from the more abstract, less obviously expressive patterns of sentences and paragraphs and from overall organization.

While most obvious in autobiographies, persona is not confined to such writing. It exists in all compositions. Even when a writer uses an impersonal point of view, avoiding "I," "me," "my," we sense a personality. In the following passage a historian is discussing dress and personal cleanliness in the Middle Ages:

Hemp was much used as a substitute for flax in making linen; the thought of hemp curdles the blood.

In the thirteenth-century romance *L'Escoufle* Sir Giles, beside the fire, removes all his clothes to scratch himself. (Fleas, no doubt.)   Morris Bishop

Such comments reveal writers as personalities, with their own ways of looking at the world—in Bishop's case with a pleasantly cynical humor.

Even in relatively faceless writing there exists a persona. Here is Charles Darwin describing the mouth of a duck:

The beak of the shoveller-duck (*Spatula clypeata*) is a more beautiful and complex structure than the mouth of a whale. The upper mandible is furnished on each side (in the specimen examined by me) with a row or comb formed of 188 thin, elastic lamellae, obliquely bevelled so as to be pointed, and placed transversely to the longer axis of the mouth.

Darwin's is an observant, precise mind. He refrains from saying more than facts allow: notice the qualification "(in the specimen examined by me)." Although he does allow emotion occasionally to show (a "beautiful . . . structure"), Darwin's tone is essentially sober, objective, painstaking, which, for his purpose, is exactly what it should be.

Tone

If persona is the complex personality implicit in the writing, tone is a web of feelings stretched throughout an essay, feelings from which our sense of the persona emerges. Tone has three main strands: the writer's attitude toward subject, reader, and self.

Each of these determinants of tone is important, and each has many variations. Writers may be angry about a subject or amused by it or discuss it dispassionately. They may treat readers as intellectual inferiors to be lectured (usually a poor tactic) or as friends with whom they are talking. Themselves they may regard very seriously or with an ironic or an amused detachment (to suggest only three of numerous possibilities). Given all these variables, the possibilities of tone are almost endless.

Tone, like persona, is unavoidable. You imply it in the words you select and in how you arrange them. It behooves you, then, to create an appropriate tone and to avoid those—pomposity, say, or flippancy—which will put readers off. Here are a few examples of how skillful writers make tone work for them.

Tone Toward Subject

Toward most subjects many attitudes are possible. Often tone is simple objectivity, as in these two paragraphs:

Physical science is that department of knowledge which relates to the order of nature, or, in other words, to the regular succession of events.

The name of physical science, however, is often applied in a more or less restricted manner to those branches of science in which the phenomena considered are of the simplest and most abstract kind, excluding the consideration of the more complex phenomena, such as those observed in living beings.

James Clerk Maxwell

Maxwell's purpose is to define physical science, not to express his feelings about it. His language, accordingly, is denotative and his tone objective and unemotional.

The writer of the following paragraph, on the other hand, is angry:

The Exorcist is a menace, the most shocking major movie I have ever seen. Never before have I witnessed such a flagrant combination of perverse sex, brutal violence, and abused religion. In addition, the film degrades the medical profession and psychiatry. At the showing I went to, the unruly audience giggled, talked, and yelled throughout. As well they might. Although the picture is not X-rated, it is so pornographic that it makes *Last Tango in Paris* seem like a Strauss waltz.

Ralph R. Greenson, M.D.

And in this example an angry tone is expressed more subtly, beneath a surface of irony. The writer is describing the efforts of nineteenth-century laborers to improve their working conditions:

[A]s early as June 8, 1847 the Chartists had pushed through a factory law restricting working time for women and juveniles to eleven hours, and from May 1, 1848 to ten hours. This was not at all to the liking of the manufacturers, who were worried about their young people's morals and exposure to vice; instead of being immured for a whole twelve hours in the cozy, clean, moral atmosphere of the factories, they were now to be loosed an hour earlier into the hard, cold, frivolous outer world.

Fritz J. Raddatz

Tone Toward Reader

You may think of your readers in widely different ways. Some writers tend to be assertive and dogmatic, treating readers as a passive herd to be instructed. The playwright and social critic George Bernard Shaw attacks the evils of capitalism in such a manner:

Just as Parliament and the Courts are captured by the rich, so is the Church. The average parson does not teach honesty and equality in the village school: he teaches deference to the merely rich, and calls that loyalty and religion.

At the other extreme a writer may establish a more intimate face-to-face tone, as though talking to a friend. In the following case Ingrid Bengis is discussing the problem of being the "other woman" in a married man's life, of having to share him with his wife:

One or the other of you is going to spend the night with him, the weekend with him, Christmas with him. (I've tried all three of us spending it together. Doesn't work.) One or the other of you is going to go on trips with him.

Bengis' informal, conversational tone depends on several things. For one, she addresses her readers directly, acknowledging their presence and bringing them and herself into a more intimate, and seemingly more equal, relationship. For another, she cultivates a colloquial style, one suggesting the voice of a friend: the contractions ("I've," "Doesn't") and the terse fragment ("Doesn't work").

A friendly informal tone need not be restricted to commonplace subjects. In much contemporary exposition, even of a scholarly sort, writers often relax the older convention of maintaining a formal distance between themselves and their audience. Here, for instance, is a well-known scholar writing about Shakespeare:

> Great plays, as we know, do present us with something that can be called a world, a microcosm—a world like our own in being made of people, actions, situations, thoughts, feelings, and much more, but unlike our own in being perfectly, or almost perfectly, significant and coherent.
> Maynard Mack

While certainly not as colloquial as Ingrid Bengis, Mack acknowledges his readers ("As we know") and subtly flatters their intelligence and sophistication.

Writers working for the illusion of a talking voice sometimes use italics to suggest the loudness and pitch by which we draw attention to important words. The historian Barbara Tuchman does this effectively in the following passage (she is arguing that freedom of speech does not require that we accept any and all pornography):

> The cause of pornography is *not* the same as the cause of free speech. There *is* a difference. Ralph Ginsburg is *not* Theodore Dreiser and this is *not* the 1920s.

Used sparingly, in that way, italics help to suggest a voice with which readers can connect. But note the caution: *sparingly.* Italics used for emphasis can easily become a mannerism, and then an annoyance.

Tone Toward Self

Toward himself or herself a writer can adopt an equally great variety of tones. Objective, impersonal exposition involves a negative presentation of the writer, so to speak. By avoiding personal references or idiosyncratic comments, he or she becomes a transparency through which we observe facts or ideas. A British writer discussing the Battle of Anzio in Italy during World War II begins like this:

> The full story of Anzio, which was originally conceived as a minor landing behind enemy lines but evolved through many ups and downs into a separate Italian front of major importance, needs a history to itself. Within the scope of the present work it is possible only to summarize the main events and their significance in so far as they affected the main front at Cassino.
> Fred Majdalany

On the other hand, writers may be more self-conscious and deliberately play a role. In exposition it is often a good tactic to present yourself a bit deferentially, as Benjamin Franklin suggests in the passage quoted earlier. An occasional "it seems to me" or "I think" or "to my mind" goes a long way toward avoiding a tone of cocksureness and restoring at least a semblance of two-way traffic on that unavoidably one-way street from writer to reader. Thus a scholar writing about Chaucer's love poetry escapes dogmatism by a qualifying phrase:

His early love complaints are less conventional than most and have the unmistakable ring, or so it seems to me, of serious attempts at persuasion.   John Gardner

A writer's exploitation of a self-image may go considerably beyond an occasional "I think." Humorous writers, for example, often present themselves as ridiculous.

Every so often, when business slackens up in the bowling alley and the other pin boys are hunched over their game of bezique, I like to exchange my sweatshirt for a crisp white surgical tunic, polish up my optical mirror, and examine the corset advertisements in the New York *Herald Tribune* rotogravure section and the various women's magazines. It must be made clear at the outset that my motives are the purest and my curiosity that of the scientific research worker rather than the sex maniac.   S. J. Perelman

Such role-playing is not quite the same as a persona. A writer's persona is reflected in all aspects of a composition, not simply in a self-caricature designed to amuse us or in the guise of a deferential friend hoping to charm us. Beyond any momentary character the writer may be playing is the creator of that role. It is that creator, that total intelligence and sensibility, which constitutes the persona.

For Practice

▷ Selecting a passage from a magazine or book, write a description of its point of view, persona, and tone. Be specific, anchoring your assessments in particular words and phrases.

PART III

The Expository Paragraph

CHAPTER 12

Basic Structure

Expository paragraphs deal with facts, ideas, beliefs. They explain, analyze, define, compare, illustrate. They answer questions like What? Why? How? What was the cause? The effect? Like what? Unlike what? They are the kinds of paragraph we write in reports or term papers or tests.

The term *paragraph* has no simple definition. Occasionally a single sentence or even a word may serve as an emphatic paragraph. Conventionally in composition, however, a paragraph is a group of sentences developing a common idea, called the *topic*.

An expository paragraph is essentially an enlargement of a subject/predicate pattern like "Dogs bark." But the subject is more complicated and needs to be expressed in a clause or sentence, called the *topic statement*, which is usually placed at or near the beginning. The predicate—that is, what is asserted about the topic—requires several sentences. These constitute the body of the paragraph, developing or supporting the topic in any of several ways, ways we shall study in subsequent chapters.

No one can say how long a paragraph should be. Subject, purpose, audience, editorial fashion, and individual preference, all affect the length and complexity of paragraphs. As a rough rule of thumb, however, you might think of expository paragraphs in terms of 120 or 150 words. If most of your paragraphs fall below 100 words—50 or 60, say—the chances are they need more development. If your paragraphs run consistently to 200 or 300 words, they are probably too long and need to be shortened or divided. Numerous brief paragraphs are liable to be disjointed and underdeveloped. Great long ones fatigue readers. But remember—we are talking about a very broad average. An occasional short paragraph of 15 to 20 words may work very well; so may an occasional long one of 300.

The Topic Sentence

A good topic sentence is concise and emphatic. It is no longer than the idea requires, and it stresses the important word or phrase. Here, for instance, is the topic statement which opens a paragraph about the collapse of the stock market in 1929:

The Big Bull Market was dead.   Frederick Lewis Allen

Notice several things. (1) Allen's sentence is brief. Not all topics can be explained in six words, but whether they take six or sixty, they should be phrased in no more words than are absolutely necessary. (2) The sentence is clear and strong: you understand exactly what Allen means. (3) It places the key word—"dead"—at the end, where it gets heavy stress and leads naturally into what will follow. Of course, if a topic sentence ends on a key term, it must do so naturally, without violating any rules of word order or idiom. (4) The sentence stands first in the paragraph. This is where topic statements generally belong: at or near the beginning.

To attract attention topic sentences sometimes appear in the form of rhetorical questions:

What then is the modern view of Joan's voices and messages from God?
George Bernard Shaw

What did Lincoln's Emancipation Proclamation accomplish?   J. G. Randall

Rhetorical questions are easy ways of generating paragraphs. Perhaps too easy; so use them with restraint. Once is probably enough in a short piece of writing.

Another eye-catching form of topic statement is the fragment, the grammatically incomplete sentence, as in the second paragraph of this passage (italics added):

Approaching the lake from the south, spread out, high up in a great V, was a flock of Canada geese. They did not land but continued on their way, trailed by the brass notes of their honking.
Spring. How perfect its fanfare. No trumpets or drums could ever have so triumphantly announced the presence of royalty. I stood marveling in their wake until, cold, I returned to the firs to see what else I could summon up.   Ruth Rudner

But fragments, too, are effective only if they are used with restraint. Most of the time the best topic statement is a strong, clear, grammatically complete, declarative sentence.

Sentences as the Analytic Elements
of a Paragraph

The sentences of a good expository paragraph reflect a clear, rational analysis of the topic. Here is a brief example, this one by Bertrand Russell. (The sentences have been numbered for convenience.)

[1] The intellectual life of the nineteenth century was more complex than that of any previous age. [2] This was due to several causes. [3] First: the area concerned was larger than ever before; America and Russia made important contributions, and Europe became more aware than formerly of Indian philosophies, both ancient and modern. [4] Second: science, which had been a chief source of novelty since the seventeenth century, made new conquests, especially in geology, biology, and organic chemistry. [5] Third: machine production profoundly altered the social structure, and gave men a new conception of their powers in relation to the physical environment. [6] Fourth: a profound revolt, both philosophical and political, against traditional systems of thought, in politics and in economics, gave rise to attacks upon many beliefs and institutions that had hitherto been regarded as unassailable. [7] This revolt had two very different forms, one romantic, the other rationalistic. [8] (I am using these words in a liberal sense.) [9] The romantic revolt passes from Byron, Schopenhauer, and Nietzsche to Mussolini and Hitler; the rationalistic revolt begins with the French philosophers of the Revolution, passes on, somewhat softened, to the philosophical radicals in England, then acquires a deeper form in Marx and issues in Soviet Russia.

Russell's nine sentences correspond to his steps in analyzing his topic:

Sentence	Idea
1	*Topic:* increasing intellectual complexity
2	*Plan:* list several causes
3	*First cause:* larger area
4	*Second cause:* science
5	*Third cause:* machine production
6	*Fourth cause:* intellectual revolt
7	two forms
8	qualification
9	specification of the two forms

Examining whether the sentences of a paragraph correspond with its ideas is a good test of the coherence of the paragraph. The correspondence need not be as exact as in Russell's paragraph (and usually will not be). But if you cannot outline a generally clear relationship, the paragraph is probably confused and confusing.

The fact that a paragraph like Russell's reveals a coherent logical structure does not imply that the writer worked from an outline. One can proceed in this way, but in writing of any length an outline is tedious and time-consuming. Experienced writers adjust sentences to thought intuitively, without constantly thinking about when to begin a new sentence. Those with less experience must remain more conscious of the problem. Working up paragraphs from outlines provides good practice. But whether it is consciously thought out or intuitive, a well-made paragraph uses sentences to analyze the subject.

For Practice

▷ Selecting one of the general subjects listed below, compose ten topic sentences, each on a different aspect of the subject, with an eye to developing a paragraph of about 150 words. Aim at clarity, emphasis, concision. Experiment with placing key words at the end of the sentence and with one or two rhetorical questions and fragments.

The economic future as you see it
National or local politics
Popular entertainment
Sports
Sexual relationships

▷ Make an outline like that for Russell's paragraph, showing how the sentences of the following paragraph relate to its ideas. The analysis might begin like this:

Sentence	Idea
1	*Topic:* a paradox about grammar
2	*Specification:* first part of the paradox—people regard grammar as dull

▷ [1] A curious paradox exists in regard to grammar. [2] On the one hand it is felt to be the dullest and driest of academic subjects, fit only for those in whose veins the red blood of life has long since turned to ink. [3] On the other, it is a subject upon which people who would scorn to be professional grammarians hold very dogmatic opinions, which they will defend with considerable emotion. [4] Much of this prejudice stems from the usual sources of prejudice—ignorance and confusion. [5] Even highly educated people seldom have a clear idea of what grammarians do, and there is an unfortunate confusion about the meaning of the term "grammar" itself.

W. Nelson Francis

CHAPTER 13

Paragraph Unity

Paragraph unity involves two related but distinct concepts: coherence and flow. *Coherence* means that the ideas fit together. *Flow* means that the sentences link up so that readers are not conscious of gaps. Flow is a matter of style and exists in specific words and grammatical patterns tying one sentence to another. Coherence belongs to the substructure of the paragraph, to relationships of thought, feeling, and perception. Both are necessary if a paragraph is to be truly unified.

Coherence

To be coherent a paragraph must satisfy two criteria: First, *relevance*—every idea must relate to the topic. Second, *effective order*—ideas must be arranged in a way that clarifies their logic or their importance. There is, in addition, a negative criterion—*inclusiveness,* that nothing vital must be omitted.

Relevance

A topic sentence makes a promise that the paragraph must fulfill. Do not wander from the topic. No matter how attractive an idea may seem, let it go if you cannot fit it into the topic you have staked out or cannot revise the topic to include it. Here is an example of a paragraph marred by irrelevance:

[1] College is very different from high school. [2] The professors talk a great deal more and give longer homework assignments. [3] This interferes with your social

life. [4] It may even cost you your girlfriend. [5] Girls don't like to be told that you have to stay home and study when they want to go to a show or go dancing. [6] So they find some other boy who doesn't have to study all the time. [7] Another way college is different is the examinations. . . .

The paragraph begins well. The first sentence establishes the topic and the second supports it. Then the writer begins to slide away. Sentences 3 and 4 might be allowed if they were subordinated. But 5 and 6 lose contact. True, some people do not like to take second place to homework, but that is not pertinent here. In sentence 7 the writer tacitly acknowledges that he has wandered, throwing out a long transitional lifeline to haul us back to the topic. Rid of irrelevance, the paragraph might read:

College is very different from high school. The professors talk a great deal more and give longer homework assignments, which interfere with your social life. College examinations, too, are different. . . .

Order of Thought

Relevance alone is not enough to establish coherence. All the ideas in a paragraph can relate to the topic yet be poorly arranged.

Arrangement often inheres in the subject itself. A paragraph about baking a cake or preparing to water ski is committed to following the steps of the process it describes. Telling a story, you must follow a certain sequence of events. And in some subjects there is a logical structure implicit in the subject that determines order of thought, as in this example about the value of opposition in politics:

The opposition is indispensable. A good statesman, like any other sensible human being, always learns more from his opponents than from his fervent supporters. For his supporters will push him to disaster unless his opponents show him where the dangers are. So if he is wise he will often pray to be delivered from his friends, because they will ruin him. But, though it hurts, he ought also to pray never to be left without opponents; for they keep him on the path of reason and good sense.   Walter Lippmann

There is a necessary order of thought here: first the assertion, next a reason supporting it, and then a conclusion, introduced by "so."

There are times, however, when the order of thought is less a function of the subject itself than of the writer's view of it. For instance, if you were writing about the three things that most surprised you the first time you visited, say, New York City, you might not find any logical or temporal relationship between those things.

One solution in such cases is to arrange ideas in order of relative importance, either climactically, placing the most important last, or anti-climactically, putting it first. If you cannot discern any shadings of importance, consider which order best connects with what has gone before or with what will come next. Should you find no basis whatever for arranging the ideas within a paragraph, then, of course, any order is legitimate. But this is not likely to happen often. Most of the time a proper or at least a most effective way of sequencing ideas does exist.

Paragraph Flow

Flow, those visible links which bind the sentences of a paragraph, can be established in two basic ways. (They are compatible; a paragraph may employ both.) The first is to establish a master plan at the beginning of the paragraph and to introduce each new idea by a word or phrase that marks its place in the plan. The second concentrates on linking sentences successively as the paragraph develops, making sure that each statement connects with the one or ones preceding it.

Setting Up a Master Plan

The opening sentence makes clear, not only the topic, but also how it will be analyzed and developed:

There are three kinds of book owners. The first has all the standard sets and best-sellers—unread, untouched. (This deluded individual owns woodpulp and ink, not books.) The second has a great many books—a few of them read through, most of them dipped into, but all of them as clean and shiny as the day they were bought. (This person would probably like to make books his own, but is restrained by a false respect for their physical appearance.) The third has a few books or many—every one of them dog-eared and dilapidated, shaken and loosened by continual use, marked and scribbled in from front to back. (This man owns books.)

Mortimer Adler

Adler early on indicates his plan ("three kinds") and introduces each aspect of the topic with the appropriate term: "First," "second," "third." Sometimes, instead of words, numbers or letters introduce the parts of a paragraph:

For the majority of situations in which a dictionary is consulted for meaning, words may be roughly divided into three groups: (1) Hard words which circumstances make immediately important: "The doctor prescribed synthesized *cortisone.*" "*Recidivism* is a serious criminal problem in some urban communities." "*Existentialism* is a subjective philosophy." (2) Words frequently seen, usually understood loosely, but suddenly and recurrently unstable (for the individual): *synthesize, urban* and *subjective* in the preceding sentences. (3) Common familiar words which unexpectedly need to be differentiated (*break* vs. *tear, shrub* vs. *bush*) or specifically clarified, such as *fable, adventure, shake, door, remainder, evil.* Most people get by without having to clarify these common words in the third group until they become an issue. Without an issue definitions of these common words are frequently jumped on because the word looks easy to the uninitiated, although in practice they are usually more difficult than hard words to define.   Philip B. Gove

Numbering the parts of a paragraph—whether with words or with figures—is simple and clear. But it suits only topics which can be easily broken into parts. Moreover, it can seem mechanical and, overused, prove confusing. In a short essay one paragraph using this method of flow is enough.

The obviousness of "first," "second," "third" can be avoided by introducing key terms right in the topic sentence to label the particular parts of the subject, and repeating those terms as each aspect is brought forward in the body of the paragraph (italics are added):

We are controlled here by our confusion, far more than we know, and the American dream has therefore become something much more closely resembling a nightmare, on the *private, domestic,* and *international* levels. *Privately,* we cannot stand our lives and dare not examine them; *domestically,* we take no responsibility for (and no pride in) what goes on in our country; and, *internationally,* for many millions of people we are an unmitigated disaster.   James Baldwin

One way of creating flow, then, is to announce your plan and explicitly fit each unit into that plan. It is not a method confined to single paragraphs. You can use it to organize a portion of a long paragraph (which is what Baldwin does), or expand it to organize a short theme, in which case the units would be individual paragraphs rather than sentences. But it is, as we said, a mechanical mode of organization to be employed with restraint.

Linking Successive Sentences

The second way of maintaining flow is to connect sentences as you go. Less obvious than "first," "second," "third," this means of achieving flow seems more natural. And it can accommodate more complex relationships among ideas; it is not confined to topics that can be broken into a numbered series.

Sentences can be linked in several ways.

▷ *Repeating Key Words*
Verbal repetition is the most obvious link. Sometimes the identical word is repeated—as in the short paragraph which follows on Saint Patrick—sometimes variant forms of the same word, and sometimes synonymous terms:

We know that among the marks of holiness is the working of miracles. Ireland is the greatest miracle any saint ever worked. It is a miracle and a nexus of miracles. Among other miracles it is a nation raised from the dead.   Hilaire Belloc

The repeated words may occur in a variety of positions. Of these the most useful are the beginnings of successive sentences, the endings of such sentences, and the close of one sentence and the opening of the one immediately following (the italics are added in the following examples):

No man of note was ever further separated from life and fact than Lindbergh. *No man* could be more reluctant to admit it.   John Lardner

Charles R. Forbes *went to jail.* Albert B. Fall *went to jail.* Alien Property Custodian Thomas W. Miller *went to jail.*   Samuel Hopkins Adams

Such plants to operate successfully had *to run at capacity. To run at capacity* they needed outlets for their whole output.   Thurman Arnold

A special case of synonymous repetition involves pronouns and demonstratives such as *one, another, some, the former, the latter, the first, the second, the third,* and so on. These words link sentences by substituting for an earlier word or phrase. *This* and *that* (along with their plurals *these* and *those*) are especially useful in this way and may be employed either as pronouns or as adjectives (italics are added):

The blind in particular seem to become indifferent to climatic extremes; and there must be in everyone's cognizance two or three immovable sightless mendicants defying rain and chill. . . .
    This insensitiveness to January blasts and February drenchings may be one of the compensations that the blind enjoy. Whatever else happens to them they never, perhaps, catch cold. And *that* is more than something.   E. V. Lucas

There is a danger, however, in using *this* or *that* as subjects. A connection clear to the writer does not always jump at the reader. The risk increases when the antecedent of the *this* or *that* is not a single word but a group of words, even a complex idea stretched over several sentences. It is sometimes better to use these words not as nouns but as adjectives modifying a more precise subject-word which clearly sums up the preceding point, as Lucas does with "*this* insensitiveness." As an adjective the *this* still hooks the new sentence to what has preceded it, but with less risk of confusion.

▷ *Conjunctive Adverbs*
Sentences can also be linked by conjunctive (also called transitional) adverbs, which indicate relationships between ideas. The relationship may be one of time *(presently, meanwhile, afterwards)*; of space *(above, below, in front)*; or of logic *(therefore, however, as a result).*
    In the following example the critic F. L. Lucas creates flow by transitional words (here italicized) in a passage answering the claim that metaphor has no place in prose:

The truth seems that metaphor too is older than any literature—an immemorial human impulse perhaps as much utilitarian as literary. *For* there appears little ground for assigning poetic motives to the first man who called the hole in a needle its "eye," or the projections on a saw its "teeth." *In fine,* metaphor is an inveterate human tendency, as ancient perhaps as the days of the mammoth, yet vigorous still in the days of the helicopter. Why *then* should it be banned from prose?

"For . . . . In fine . . . then" establish the logical framework of the argument:

Assertion	Sentence 1
Reason	"For," sentence 2
Assertion restated	"In fine," sentence 3
Conclusion	"then," sentence 4

Transitional adverbs are best placed at or near the beginning of the sentence. Readers are like people groping down a dark passage, and an important part of the writer's task is to show them the way. Connective words are signal lights telling readers what to expect. *However* flashes, "Contradiction ahead"; *in fact* warns, "Here comes a strong restatement of something just said"; and *therefore*, "A conclusion or a consequence is approaching."

Acquiring a working set of conjunctive adverbs is not difficult. English is rich in them. Just to show some sort of contradiction or opposition, for example, we have *but, however, still, yet, nonetheless, nevertheless, though, instead, on the other hand, on the contrary, notwithstanding, even so,* and the list is not complete. While they show generally the same basic relationship, these words are not exact equivalents. They convey nuances of idea and tone. *Nevertheless,* for instance, is a more formal word than *though.* Because of such slight but important differences in meaning and tone, good writers have ready at hand a number of transitional adverbs. If you can call only upon *but* or *however* you cannot communicate what is implied by *yet* or *still* or *though.*

And and *but* present a special case. Most often they act as conjunctive adverbs, joining words, phrases, or clauses within a sentence. But they can also function adverbially. Sometimes one hears the warning, "Never begin a sentence with *and* or *but.*" The fact is that good writers do begin with these words (the italics are added):

Is not indeed every man a student, and do not all things exist for the student's behoof? *And,* finally, is not the true scholar the only true master?
Ralph Waldo Emerson

I come finally to the chief defiler of undergraduate writing. *And* I regret to say that we professors are certainly the culprits. *And* what we are doing we do in all innocence and with the most laudable of motives.   Willard Thorp

Natural philosophy had in the Middle Ages become a closed chapter of human endeavour. . . .
But although the days of Greek science had ended, its results had not been lost.
Kurt Mendelssohn

As sentence openers *and* and *but* are very useful. *But* is less formal than *however,* while *and* is less formal and ponderous than *furthermore* or *moreover* or *additionally.* Don't be afraid of initial *and*s and *but*s. But use them moderately.

▷ *Syntactic Patterning*

Syntactic patterning simply means repeating the same basic structure in successive or near successive sentences. It often holds together the parts of a comparison or contrast:

In bankless Iowa City eggs sell for ten cents a dozen. In Chicago the breadlines stretch endlessly along the dirty brick walls in windy streets.   Wallace Stegner

That New York was much more dry [non-alcoholic] on Sunday during the summer is true. That it was as dry as [Theodore] Roosevelt believed it—"I have, for once, absolutely enforced the law in New York"—is improbable. That it was dry enough to excite the citizenry to new heights of indignation is clear.   Henry F. Pringle

Syntactic patterning may be more extensive, working throughout most of a paragraph:

It is common knowledge that millions of underprivileged families want adequate food and housing. What is less commonly remarked is that after they have adequate food and housing they will want to be served at a fine restaurant and to have a weekend cottage by the sea. People want tickets to the Philharmonic and vacation trips abroad. They want fine china and silver dinner sets and handsome clothes. The illiterate want to learn how to read. Then they want education, and then more education, and then they want their sons and daughters to become doctors and lawyers. It is frightening to see so many millions of people wanting so much. It is almost like being present at the Oklahoma land rush, except that millions are involved instead of hundreds, and instead of land, the prize is everything that life has to offer.   Samuel C. Florman

While reusing the same sentence pattern often involves repeating some words, the similar grammatical structure is in itself a strong connective device. However, you cannot impose such syntactic patterning on just any group of sentences. It works only when the underlying thought is repetitious, as in the example above, where the sentences list a series of rising expectations common to Americans. In such cases the similarity of pattern does what ideally all sentence structure should do: the form reinforces the sense.

For Practice

▷ List all the transitional devices that link the sentences in the following paragraph:

Above the beginner's level, the important fact is that writing cannot be taught exclusively in a course called English Composition. Writing can only be taught by the united efforts of the entire teaching staff. This holds good of any school, college, or university. Joint effort is needed, not merely to "enforce the rules"; it is needed to insure accuracy in every subject. How can an answer in physics or a translation from the French or an historical statement be called correct if the phrasing is loose or the key word wrong? Students argue that the reader of the paper knows perfectly well what is meant. Probably so, but a written exercise is designed to be read; it is not supposed to be a challenge to clairvoyance. My Italian-born tailor periodically sends me a postcard which runs: "Your clothes is ready and should come down for a fitting." I understand him, but the art I honor him for is cutting cloth, not precision of utterance. Now a student in college must be inspired to achieve in all subjects the utmost accuracy of perception combined with the utmost artistry of expression. The two merge and develop the sense of good workmanship, or preference for quality and truth, which is the chief mark of the genuinely educated man.   Jacques Barzun

▷ The paragraph below lacks unity. The problem may be inadequate links between sentences, or it may go deeper, involving incoherence of thought. Rewrite the paragraph, staying as close as possible to the original wording but changing what needs to be changed to give the paragraph coherence and flow:

There are several kinds of test. Quizzes deal with only a small amount of material, usually that covered in the preceding week or two. Pop quizzes are often given without any announcement. Students often miss them and have to arrange make-ups. Examinations are longer and cover more ground. The mid-term comes in about the sixth or seventh week and in some courses is the only grade the teacher has for the mid-semester mark. It is important. The final comes at the end of the course and is a large part of your grade. Students work hard preparing for finals.

14

Paragraph Development:
(1) Illustration and Restatement

In this and the following several chapters we study how expository paragraphs develop. We focus on one technique of development at a time, beginning with the simplest ones, illustration and restatement. Of course, writers often combine techniques. But walking comes before running, and for the moment we concentrate on relatively uncomplicated paragraphs.

Methods of paragraph development fall into three loose groups: (1) those that stay strictly within the topic, offering examples of it or merely repeating it in varying ways; (2) techniques involving another subject—whether secondary or of equal importance—introduced for comparison or contrast or analogy; and (3) techniques that explore the ramifications of the topic more fully—defining it or looking into its causes or effects.

Illustration

Citing examples is an easy way to support a generalization:

Some of those writers who most admired technology—Whitman, Henry Adams, and H. G. Wells, for example—also feared it greatly.   Samuel C. Florman

But an effect can become a cause, reinforcing the original cause and producing the same effect in an intensified form, and so indefinitely. A man may take to drink because he feels himself a failure, and then fail all the more completely because he drinks.   George Orwell

Illustrations show that you are not talking through your hat. Thus Florman gives us names, grounding his assertion in facts and enabling us to check that assertion against our own knowledge. Illustrations have a second virtue: they anchor an abstraction in particulars, translating difficult ideas into everyday terms. This is what Orwell does.

Brief examples like those by Florman and Orwell do not make paragraphs, of course. But examples can be extended to provide the substance of an entire paragraph. Sometimes the paragraph consists of a single example worked out in detail:

Some of the most abstract terms in the language are really faded metaphors. On examination it turns out that an earlier meaning, now forgotten, is often lively in the extreme. Hence an obvious means of invigorating our jejune vocabulary is to fall back on those lively older meanings. True enough, the average speaker does not know that they ever existed. He is not *reminded* that "express" once meant, literally and physically, "to press out." But he can learn it instantaneously from a context. It may be that only the archaic literal sense is intended, or it may be that both the physical and the metaphorical are to be grasped simultaneously. In any event, the impact of the divergent use on an attentive reader forces him to a new experience of the word, without sacrificing comprehension. An example of the use of "express" in this revivified fashion will be found in Emily Dickinson:

Essential Oils—are wrung—
The Attar from the Rose
Be not expressed by Suns—alone—
It is the gift of Screws—

                                                                                        Margaret Schlauch

On the other hand a paragraph may consist of a number of brief examples, as in this passage about the change in modern modes of eating and drinking:

As far as the home is concerned, the biggest change in what P. G. Wodehouse called "browsing and sluicing" is probably not the decline in huge, formal meals, or shorter menus, but the odd form our food is in nowadays when we buy it. Coffee comes as a powder. Fish arrives as a frozen rectangular block. Soup, stiff with preservatives, comes in a tin or as a powder. Potatoes no longer wear their jackets but arrive pale and naked in an impenetrable plastic bag. Embryonic mashed potato comes in little dry lumps, like cattle-feed pellets. Bread, untouched by human baker, arrives wrapped and sliced in a soft lump, the "crust" seemingly sprayed on. Beer, urged upward by gas, emerges from a steel dustbin.   Frank Muir

Whether you use one example or several, be sure your reader will take them for what they are. Often it is advisable explicitly to introduce an illustration by some such phrase as *for example, for instance, as a case in point* or, a bit more subtly, *say, thus, consider.* Vary these expressions; do not introduce every illustration with *for example.* Nor is it necessary always to place the phrase in the opening position. A *for instance* or *for example* is equally effective set between subject and verb, where it is still near the beginning but seems less mechanical.

When the illustrative function of a detail is obvious, you can safely dispense with an introductory phrase. Orwell does not write, "For example, a man may take to drink . . ."; nor does Muir label his instances of the oddity of modern food. They depend on the reader's common sense. No infallible rule tells you when a *for example* is superfluous and when its absence will confuse a reader. You must try to imagine yourself in the reader's place. If an illustration seems even a bit bewildering without an introductory word or phrase, put one in.

Introduced or not, examples are most effective when they are specific. In Muir's paragraph the abstract expression "the odd form our food is in" is given heft and shape by "frozen rectangular block," "pale and naked in an impenetrable plastic bag," "little dry lumps, like cattle-feed pellets."

For Practice

▷ Study the paragraph below. Identify the topic sentence. Where do the examples begin? Are they explicitly introduced? Do you think them clear and effective, adequately supporting the topic? Why or why not?

Primitive peoples often build much of their religious and cultural behavior on this belief in the natural relationship of word and thing. For example, they believe that to know the name of an object, person, or deity is to gain a certain control over it: in "Ali Baba and the Forty Thieves," the words "Open Sesame!" cause the stone doors of the cave to move aside. Conversely, certain powers in the universe are thought to dislike the use of their names by mortals. Words are therefore tabooed, or euphemisms and descriptive phrases are invented such as *the little people* instead of *fairies*. The Greeks came to call those vengeful mythological creatures whose "real name" was *Erinyes* (or Furies) the *Eumenides* (or "good-tempered ones").
                                                                          W. Nelson Francis

The Restatement Paragraph

At its simplest, restatement involves nothing more than repeating the main idea. It is common as a way of emphasizing something important:

1964 threatens to be the most explosive year America has witnessed. The most explosive year.
                                                                          Malcolm X

Sufficiently extended, restatement will provide the substance of an entire paragraph, as in this passage about why American men are unlikely to cry (the paragraph expresses attitudes of our culture, not the writer's own beliefs):

American men don't cry, because it is considered unmasculine to do so. Only sissies cry. Crying is a "weakness" characteristic of the female, and no American male wants to be identified with anything in the least weak or feminine. Crying, in our culture, is identified with childishness, with weakness and dependence. No one likes a crybaby, and we disapprove of crying even in children, discouraging it in them as early as possible. In a land so devoted to the pursuit of happiness as ours, crying really is rather un-American. Adults must learn not to cry in situations in which it is permissible for a child to cry. Women being the "weaker" and "dependent" sex, it is only natural that they should cry in certain emotional situations. In women, crying is excusable. But in men, crying is a mark of weakness. So goes the American credo with regard to crying.   Ashley Montagu

Repeating what you have just said is both an easy and a difficult way of developing a paragraph. Easy because you do not have to search for examples or comparisons or causes. Difficult because you must repeat a basic idea without being monotonous. Because of this difficulty, restatement passages are usually brief.

The risk of monotony is increased by the similarity in sentence structure common in restatement. Sentences that say the same thing are often cast in the same mold. A good example of such repeated structure appears in this passage about the prevalence of piracy in the seventeenth century:

It is difficult for one accustomed to the law and order of the present day to understand the dangers which threatened the Jacobean traveller. The seas swarmed with pirates; so that few merchantmen dared to put to sea without arms; while very few came home without some tale of an encounter. There were pirates in the Atlantic, to intercept the ships coming home from the Newfoundland fisheries. There were pirates in the West Indies, roving for Spanish treasure-ships. There were pirates in the Orkneys, preying upon the Iceland trades. There were pirates near Ireland, especially in the south and west, ranging over the Channel, and round these coasts. But there were, perhaps, more pirates in the Mediterranean than in all the other waters put together. In the Mediterranean they had the most part of the trade of Europe for their quarry; while the coasts of Africa, and the islands of the [Greek] Archipelago, provided obscure harbours (with compliant Governors) for the recruiting of companies after a cruise.   John Masefield

Aside from knowing when to stop, success in handling restatement depends on sufficiently varying the diction and sentence form. Masefield, for example, keeps the same pattern for four successive sentences: "There were pirates in" + a verbal phrase. But each sentence differs in its specific content (and hence in diction). At the same time the similarity of structure reinforces the point that piracy existed everywhere. Masefield also uses the repeated sentence structure to build toward his main topic—piracy in the Mediterranean. In a fifth "there were" sentence he signals the climactic significance of the Mediterranean by varying the pattern: opening with "But," placing "perhaps" in an interrupting position, and changing completely the second half of the sentence.

Negative-Positive Restatement

Negative-positive restatement begins by saying what is *not* the case, then asserts what is. (Sometimes the order is reversed.)

I am not thinking of philosophy as courses in philosophy or even as a subject exclusive of other subjects. I am thinking of it in its old Greek sense, the sense in which Socrates thought of it, as the love and search for wisdom, the habit of pursuing an argument where it leads, the delight in understanding for its own sake, the passionate pursuit of dispassionate reasonableness, the will to see things steadily and to see them whole.   Brand Blanshard

Specification

Another special type of restatement is specification, which moves from the general to the particular. Brief specifications are often found within single sentences as a means of giving substance to an abstraction (italics added):

Bound to the production of staples—*tobacco, cotton, rice, sugar*—the soil suffered from erosion and neglect.   Oscar Handlin

A more extended instance occurs in this paragraph about politics in Louisiana. The paragraph develops by specifying all that is included in the phrase "the same political pattern":

Throughout the years the same political pattern prevailed. The city dominated the state: New Orleans, the nation's mecca of the fleshpots, smiling in not altogether Latin indifference at its moral deformities, and, like a cankered prostitute, covering those deformities with paint and lace and capitalizing upon them with a lewd beckoning to the stranger. Beyond New Orleans, in the south, French Louisiana, devoutly Catholic, easy-going, following complacently its backward-glancing patriarchs, suspicious of the Protestants to the north. And in central and northern Louisiana, the small farmers, principally Anglo-Saxon; bitter, fundamentalist Protestants, hating the city and all its evil works, leaderless in their disquiet and only vaguely aware that much of what they lacked was in some way coupled with the like-as-like office seekers whom they alternately voted into and out of public life.
                                                                         Hodding Carter

While specification resembles illustration, it differs in an important way. An illustration is one of several possible cases. Specification covers all the cases. In the sentence above by Professor Handlin, "tobacco, cotton, rice, sugar" are not simply examples of the staple crops of southern agriculture; they *are* the staple crops. Similarly Hodding Carter, beginning with the abstract phrase "political pattern," specifies that pattern in its entirety, rather than citing one or two parts by way of example.

For Practice

▷ Compose a brief (about 120 words) restatement paragraph on a topic of your own choice. Construct your sentences to resemble one another, though with enough variety to avoid monotony.

▷ Specification, as in the paragraph by Hodding Carter (page 83), begins with a broad statement of the topic and then repeats it in detail. Work up such a paragraph on a topic chosen from one of these broad subjects:

large cities   politics
television   vacations
supermarkets   restaurants

15

Paragraph Development: (2) Comparison, Contrast, and Analogy

The methods of development we study in this chapter involve two subjects (occasionally more than two). *Analogy* is a special kind of comparison in which a subject of secondary importance and often of a quite different nature is introduced to clarify or justify some aspect of the main subject. *Comparison* treats two subjects of the same nature, as does *contrast;* but the former shows how the subjects are alike, while the latter focuses on how they differ. But despite this difference, comparison and contrast work in the same way, and we consider them together, putting off analogy until the end of the chapter.

Comparison and Contrast

Focusing

Because they involve at least two subjects and offer several possibilities of emphasis, comparison and contrast pose problems of focus. For one thing, you must decide whether to deal only with similarities or only with dissimilarities, or to cover both. The topic sentence must make your intention clear to readers:

The difference between a sign and a symbol is, in brief. . . .   Susanne K. Langer

It is a temptation to make a comparison between the nineteen twenties and the nineteen sixties, but the similarities are fewer than the differences.   Russell Lynes

Bears and dogs are alike in one intriguing way.   Evelyn Jones

   A second decision of focusing concerns the subjects. Will you concentrate on one subject or treat both equally? If you are comparing (or contrasting), say, New York and Los Angeles, you have three possibilities of
focus: New York, Los Angeles, or both. Make clear which it will be. But
don't be heavy-handed; a topic sentence like "I shall focus here upon New
York" is mechanical and obvious. Instead, construct the topic sentence so
that the key idea functions as the subject word and thus naturally indicates
your focus. If your chief concern is, say, New York:

In many ways New York is like Los Angeles.

If it is both places:

In many ways New York and Los Angeles are alike.

   In the following paragraph notice how the historian J. G. Randall keeps
his focus constantly before us. (He is comparing the failure of Reconstruc-
tion after the Civil War and the refusal of the U.S. Senate to accept President Wilson's League of Nations policy after World War I. The italics have
been added.)

In the case of *both Lincoln and Wilson* the soldiers did their part and so did the
Executive, but *in each case* partisanship and narrow-mindedness wrecked the program. *Under Lincoln and Johnson, as under Wilson,* there was failure of high-minded
unity behind the plan of peace that bore promise of success. *In each case,* instead
of needful co-operation, there was stupid deadlock between President and Congress. There was *in each case* a fateful congressional election whose effect was felt
far down in later years: 1918 may be matched against the "critical year" 1866. *In
each case* the President's plan failed in the sense that it failed to be adopted; the
opposite plan *in each case* failed miserably by being adopted.

Organizing a Comparison or Contrast

When you compare or contrast any two subjects, which we can call A and
B, you do so with regard to specific points, which we'll call 1, 2, 3. Now
you may proceed in two ways, organizing around A and B or around 1,
2, 3. Thus in contrasting New York and Los Angeles you might devote
the first half of the paragraph (or an entire paragraph) to New York and
the second half (or a new paragraph) to Los Angeles. In each section you
would cover the same particular points and in the same order—say, climate, cultural facilities, and night life. Conversely, you might prefer to
make climate, cultural facilities, and night life the primary centers of your
organization, devoting a paragraph or portion of a paragraph to each and
discussing how the two cities differ.
   Neither way of proceeding is necessarily better. Organizing around A
and B stresses each subject in its totality. Organizing around 1, 2, and 3
emphasizes particular likenesses or differences. It all depends on what you

want to do. In the following case the writer elected to organize around A and B—here Western civilization and Eastern:

Americans and Western Europeans, in their sensitivity to lingering problems around them, tend to make science and progress their scapegoats. There is a belief that progress has precipitated widespread unhappiness, anxieties and other social and emotional problems. Science is viewed as a cold mechanical discipline having nothing to do with human warmth and the human spirit.

But to many of us from the nonscientific East, science does not have such repugnant associations. We are not afraid of it, nor are we disappointed by it. We know all too painfully that our social and emotional problems festered long before the age of technology. To us, science is warm and reassuring. It promises hope. It is helping us at long last gain some control over our persecutory environments, alleviating age-old problems—not only physical but also, and especially, problems of the spirit.   F. M. Esfandiary

In the next example, on the other hand, a historian contrasting Catholics and Protestants in the sixteenth century organizes not around the broad categories of Roman and Reformer, but rather around the specific differences that set them at war:

The Catholic believed in the authority of the Church; the Reformer, in the authority of reason. Where the Church had spoken, the Catholic obeyed. His duty was to accept without question the laws which councils had decreed, which popes and bishops administered, and so far as in him lay to enforce in others the same submission to an outward rule which he regarded as divine. All shades of Protestants on the other hand agreed that authority might err; that Christ had left no visible representative, whom individually they were bound to obey; that religion was the operation of the Spirit on the mind and conscience; that the Bible was God's word, which each Christian was to read, and which with God's help and his natural intelligence he could not fail to understand. The Catholic left his Bible to the learned. The Protestant translated the Bible, and brought it to the door of every Christian family. The Catholic prayed in Latin, and whether he understood his words or repeated them as a form the effect was the same; for it was magical. The Protestant prayed with his mind as an act of faith in a language intelligible to him, or he could not pray at all. The Catholic bowed in awe before his wonder-working image, adored his relics, and gave his life into the guidance of his spiritual director. The Protestant tore open the machinery of the miracles, flung the bones and ragged garments into the fire, and treated priests as men like himself. The Catholic was intolerant upon principle; persecution was the corollary of his creed. The intolerance of the Protestant was in spite of his creed. In denying the right of the Church to define his own belief, he had forfeited the privilege of punishing the errors of those who chose to differ from him.   James Anthony Froude

Building the Comparison or Contrast

Closely related to the question of organization is a final problem: in what compositional units will the comparison be built—that is, out of paragraphs, portions of paragraphs, sentences, halves of sentences? Probably the simplest plan is to spend a paragraph, or several sentences within a paragraph, on one of the two subjects and a unit of roughly equal length on the other. This is what F. M. Esfandiary does in discussing the differences between Eastern and Western attitudes toward science.

But you may also construct a comparison or contrast in pairs of sentences:

The original Protestants had brought new passion into the ideal of the state as a religious society and they had set about to discipline this society more strictly than ever upon the pattern of the Bible. The later Protestants reversed a fundamental purpose and became the allies of individualism and the secular state.

Herbert Butterfield

Or both parts of the comparison may be held within a single sentence, the total effect being built up from a series of such sentences:

At first glance the traditions of journalism and scholarship seem completely unlike: journalism so bustling, feverish, content with daily oblivion; the academic world so sheltered, deliberate, and hopeful of enduring products. It is true that both are concerned with ascertainment and diffusion of truth. In journalism, however, the emphasis falls on a rapid diffusion of fact and idea; in academic work it falls on a prolonged, laborious ascertainment.   Allen Nevins

How you build a comparison or contrast is related, of course, to how you organize it. Using two paragraphs (or two portions of a single paragraph) is better when you are organizing around A and B—that is, treating each subject in its entirety. Proceeding by balanced sentences or halves of sentences is better if you wish to focus on specific points of similarity or difference.

Writing a comparison or contrast requires finally that you think carefully about what you want to accomplish and how you can best focus, organize, and work up the material. The problem is further complicated by the fact that none of the choices we have discussed is absolute. A paragraph is not restricted to comparing *or* contrasting: it can do both. It does not have to maintain only one focus: a skillful writer can shift. And extended comparisons and contrasts can, and do, very their methods of building.

For Practice

▷ Study the following paragraph and consider these questions: (a) Is the writer comparing, contrasting, or doing both? (b) Which of the two subjects receives the focus? (c) How is the comparison or contrast organized and how is it built?

Let's compare the U.S. to India, for example. We have 203 million people, whereas she has 540 million on much less land. But look at the impact of people on the land.

The average Indian eats his daily few cups of rice (or perhaps wheat, whose production on American farms contributed to our one percent per year drain in quality of our active farmland), draws his bucket of water from the communal well and sleeps in a mud hut. In his daily rounds to gather cow dung to burn to cook his rice and warm his feet, his footsteps, along with those of millions of his countrymen, help bring about a slow deterioration of the ability of the land to support people. His contribution to the destruction of the land is minimal.

An American, on the other hand, can be expected to destroy a piece of land on which he builds a home, garage and driveway. He will contribute his share to the 142 million tons of smoke and fumes, seven million junked cars, 20 million tons of paper, 48 billion cans, and 26 billion bottles the overburdened environment must absorb each year. To run his air conditioner he will stripmine a Kentucky hillside, push the dirt and slate down into the stream, and burn coal in a power generator, whose smokestack contributes to a plume of smoke massive enough to cause cloud seeding and premature precipitation from Gulf winds which should be irrigating the wheat farms of Minnesota.   Wayne H. Davis

▷ Work up a contrast in one or two paragraphs on one of the following subjects. Confine yourself to three or four points of difference and organize around the two subjects—that is, discuss all the points with regard to A before going on to B:

1. Any two cities you know well
2. People of two different nationalities
3. A sports car and the family sedan
4. Young people and the middle-aged
5. Two sports

▷ Now compose another paragraph (or paragraphs) on the same subject but this time organize around the three or four points of difference.
▷ Finally, still working with the same topics, write a third paragraph beginning like this:

Yet despite these differences ___A___ and ___B___ are alike in several ways.

Analogy

Analogy is a special kind of comparison in which a second subject is introduced to explain or justify something about the main topic. Here the American writer Flannery O'Connor addresses a class in creative writing:

I understand that this is a course called "How the Writer Writes," and that each week you are exposed to a different writer who holds forth on the subject. The only parallel I can think of to this is having the zoo come to you, one animal at a time; and I suspect that what you hear one week from the giraffe is contradicted next week by the baboon.

O'Connor's main subject is the course on writing. Her analogy is visiting the zoo, or rather having the zoo visit you. By means of the analogy she presents herself with comic self-deprecation and, more seriously, suggests something about the limitations of teaching creative writing.

Analogies differ from straightforward comparisons in several ways. First, they are always focused on one topic, the analogical subject being secondary, serving to clarify or emphasize or persuade. Second, the analogical subject usually is of a different nature from the main subject, so different that most of us would not think the two at all similar. Comparison typically involves things of similar sort—a Ford and Chevrolet, for example, or New Orleans and San Francisco, high school and college. Analogies, on the other hand, often find unexpected similarities in unlike things, such as a course in writing and a visit from the zoo.

Analogy as Clarification

In exposition the most common function of an analogy is to translate an abstract or difficult idea into more concrete or familiar terms. That is certainly one of the aims of O'Connor's analogy, as it is of this longer example, in which an astronomer explains the philosophy of science:

Let us suppose that an ichthyologist is exploring the life of the ocean. He casts a net into the water and brings up a fishy assortment. Surveying his catch, he proceeds in the usual manner of a scientist to systematize what it reveals. He arrives at two generalizations:

1. No sea-creature is less than two inches long.
2. All sea-creatures have gills.

These are both true of his catch, and he assumes tentatively that they will remain true however often he repeats it.

In applying this analogy, the catch stands for the body of knowledge which constitutes physical science, and the net for the sensory and intellectual equipment which we use in obtaining it. The casting of the net corresponds to observation; for knowledge which has not been or could not be obtained by observation is not admitted into physical science.

An onlooker may object that the first generalization is wrong. "There are plenty of sea-creatures under two inches long, only your net is not adapted to catch them." The ichthyologist dismisses this objection contemptuously. "Anything uncatchable by my net is *ipso facto* outside the scope of ichthyological knowledge, and is not part of the kingdom of fishes which has been defined as the theme of ichthyological knowledge. In short, what my net can't catch isn't fish." Or—to translate the analogy—"If you are not simply guessing, you are claiming a knowledge of the physical universe discovered in some other way than by the methods of physical science, and admittedly unverifiable by such methods. You are a metaphysician. Bah!"   Sir Arthur Eddington

Analogy as Persuasion

As well as clarifying the unfamiliar, analogies often have considerable persuasive force. Before we look at an example, though, we need to distinguish between *logical* and *rhetorical* analogies. In logic, analogies are a special form of proof; we are *not* concerned with them here.

Our interest is exclusively in rhetorical analogies, and rhetorical analogies *never* constitute logical proof. At best they are what has been called "a weak form of reasoning." They merely suggest that because A resembles B in certain respects, it also resembles it in others. But since the resemblance between A and B is never total and exact, what is true of one cannot necessarily be applied to the other.

For example, some political thinkers have used the "similarity" of a state to a ship to justify an authoritarian society. They argue that a ship can survive storms only when authority is completely in the hands of the captain, who rightfully demands unquestioning obedience. So, they conclude, a state can survive only if its citizens submit unhesitatingly to an absolute ruler. But, of course, ships and states are *not* identical. What may be needed for safety at sea cannot be assumed to apply to good government on land. Such analogies which claim to "prove" unwarranted conclusions are called "false" or "unfair."

But even though they are not a form of logical proof, rhetorical analogies can be very persuasive. Consider this one used by Abraham Lincoln in a speech opposing the spread of slavery to territories outside the South:

If I saw a venomous snake crawling in the road, any man would say I might seize the nearest stick and kill it; but if I found that snake in bed with my children, that would be another question. I might hurt the children more than the snake, and it might bite them. Much more, if I found it in bed with my neighbor's children, and I had bound myself by a solemn compact not to meddle with his children under any circumstances, it would become me to let that particular mode of getting rid of the gentleman alone. But if there was a bed newly made up, to which the children were to be taken, and it was proposed to take a batch of young snakes and put them there with them, I take it no man would say there was any question how I ought to decide. That is just the case. The new territories are the newly made bed to which our children are to go, and it lies with the nation to say whether they shall have snakes mixed up with them or not. It does not seem as if there could be much hesitation what our policy should be.

Lincoln's argument simply assumes that slavery—the "snake"—is wrong and does not prove it. But most of his audience would not have needed proof. The essential point is that slavery should not be allowed to spread beyond the South, and the analogy is a striking, forceful explanation of why not.

For Practice

▷ Identify the analogies in the following paragraph. What purpose does each serve? Do you think they are effective?

I am an explorer, then, and I am also a stalker, or the instrument of the hunt itself. Certain Indians used to carve long grooves along the wooden shafts of their arrows. They called the grooves "lightning marks," because they resembled the curved fissures lightning slices down the trunks of trees. The function of lightning marks is this: if the arrow fails to kill the game, blood from a deep wound will channel along the lightning mark, streak down the arrow shaft, and spatter to the ground, laying a trail dripped on broadleaves, on stones, that the barefoot and trembling archer can follow into whatever deep or rare wilderness it leads. I am the arrow shaft, carved along my length by unexpected lights and gashes from the very sky, and this book is the straying trail of blood.   Annie Dillard

▷ Analogies are personal things that must grow out of one's experience and values. Here, however, are a few possibilities:

Reading a difficult book and climbing a mountain
A library and a cemetery
A person's (or a nation's) conception of reality and the wearing of glasses

Try to develop an analogy in a single paragraph. The usual procedure is to begin with the main topic (placed first in these examples), or you may prefer to start off with the analogy, moving from there into your main topic.

16

Paragraph Development: (3) Cause and Effect

Cause

One cannot write for very long without having to explain why something happened or why it is true or false. There are numerous strategies for developing causes or reasons.[1] The simplest is to ask the question "Why?" and then to supply the answer:

If, then, the language of the original colonists was merely the English of England, why does ours differ somewhat from theirs today? Three reasons can be offered.

First, the people of Great Britain in the seventeenth century spoke different local dialects. What we now consider to be standard English for England developed from the language of London and the near-by counties. But the settlers of America came not only from that region but also from many others. New England was settled largely from the eastern counties. Pennsylvania received a heavy immigration from the north of Ireland. English as it came to be spoken in New England and much of Pennsylvania thus naturally was not the same English that developed as the standard in England. For instance in what we consider typical British English of today, the final r has been lost. It is, however, partially preserved in General American, possibly because the Scotch-Irish of the eighteenth century preserved that sound, as they still do in Ireland.

A second cause for the difference between the two countries lies in mere isolation. Language is always changing. When two groups of people speaking the same language are separated and remain in comparative isolation, change continues in the language of both groups, but naturally it does not continue in the same direc-

---

1. *Cause* and *reason* are not strict synonyms: the former is more general and includes the latter. But we'll use them interchangeably.

tion and at the same rate with both of them. The languages thus tend to become different.

Third, the language in the United States has been subjected to various influences that have not affected the language in Great Britain—the environment, the languages of other early colonists and of later immigrants.   George R. Stewart

Development by reasons may be more subtle. Instead of using a question-answer strategy and explicitly announcing reasons, a writer may leave the causal relationships implicit. The connection exists in the substructure of ideas but is not spelled out. In the following paragraph, for instance, only the "for" in the opening sentence makes the idea of causality explicit:

The cult of beauty in women, which we smile at as though it were one of the culture's harmless follies, is, in fact, an insanity, for it is posited on a false view of reality. Women are not more beautiful than men. The obligation to be beautiful is an artificial burden, imposed by men on women, that keeps both sexes clinging to childhood, the woman forced to remain a charming, dependent child, the man driven by his unconscious desire to be—like an infant—loved and taken care of simply for his beautiful self. Woman's mask of beauty is the face of a child, a revelation of the tragic sexual immaturity of both sexes in our culture.

Una Stannard

Ordering Reasons within the Paragraph

Sometimes you will work with only a single reason, repeating or expanding it in various ways: this is what Una Stannard does in the preceding paragraph. Other topics involve several reasons, as in the passage by Professor Stewart. In that case you must arrange them in a significant order. If the causes are serial—that is, if A is caused by B, B by C, and C by D—the organization is predetermined: A—B—C—D.

But several reasons all contributing to the same consequence may be parallel, that is, having no causal connection within themselves and related only in all contributing to the same result. (Again, the passage by Professor Stewart is an example.) With parallel reasons you have more choice of arrangement. If they have an order in time, you will probably follow that. If they do not, you will probably have to rank the reasons in order of importance, usually, though not invariably, leading up to the most important:

I doubt if the English temperament is wholly favourable to the development of the essayist. In the first place, an Anglo-Saxon likes doing things better than thinking about them; and in his memories, he is apt to recall how a thing was done rather than why it was done. In the next place, we are naturally rather prudent and secretive; we say that a man must not wear his heart upon his sleeve, and that is just what the essayist must do. We have a horror of giving ourselves away, and we like to keep ourselves to ourselves. "The Englishman's home is his castle," says another proverb. But the essayist must not have a castle, or if he does, both the grounds and the living-rooms must be open to the inspection of the public.   A. C. Benson

Reversing the order of Benson's two reasons would not impair the logic of his paragraph. However, it would disrupt the climactic structure. While Benson nowhere says that he considers the second reason more important, he gives it more than twice the space and repeats it three times.

Effects

Effects or consequences[2] are handled much the same as reasons. But now the topic idea is regarded as causing the consequences discussed in the remainder of the paragraph. The paragraph may treat only a single effect, as in this passage about the moon affecting the tides:

If the moon were suddenly struck out of existence, we should be immediately appraised of the fact by a wail from every seaport in the kingdom. From London and from Liverpool we should hear the same story—the rise and fall of the tide had almost ceased. The ships in dock could not get out; the ships outside could not get in; and the maritime commerce of the world would be thrown into dire confusion.   Robert Ball

Multiple Effects

Often, however, a topic entails several effects, not just one, as in the following case (the writer is concerned with what the automobile has done to our society):

Thirdly, I worry about the private automobile. It is a dirty, noisy, wasteful, and lonely means of travel. It pollutes the air, ruins the safety and sociability of the street, and exercises upon the individual a discipline which takes away far more freedom than it gives him. It causes an enormous amount of land to be unnecessarily abstracted from nature and from plant life and to become devoid of any natural function. It explodes cities, grievously impairs the whole institution of neighborliness, fragmentizes and destroys communities. It has already spelled the end of our cities as real cultural and social communities, and has made impossible the construction of any others in their place. Together with the airplane, it has crowded out other, more civilized and more convenient means of transport, leaving older people, infirm people, poor people and children in a worse situation than they were a hundred years ago. It continues to lend a terrible element of fragility to our civilization, placing us in a situation where our life would break down completely if anything ever interfered with the oil supply.   George F. Kennan

Kennan does not label the logic of his paragraph, not even by brief connectives like *therefore* or *and so*. But the sentence structure keeps the logic clear. Sentence after sentence begins with subject-verb, which suggests the cause-effect relationship: "It [the private automobile] is . . . It pollutes . . . It causes . . . It explodes . . . It has . . ." The repetition of this

---

2. These terms, too, will be used synonymously.

pattern supports and clarifies the logic—an example of how sentence structure contributes to paragraph unity.

Cause and Effect

Thus far we have seen paragraphs that develop reasons to support the topic and those that develop effects, Often, however, cause and effect are more intimately related. Many things are simultaneously causes and effects, as when the result you expect an action to have is the reason you do it. In Kennan's paragraph above the dire consequences of the automobile are why he worries about it. The journalist Pete Hamill expresses much the same point in the following paragraph, explaining that what the car has done to our society makes it "one of our jailers":

In fact, the automobile, which was hailed has a liberator of human beings early in this century, has become one of our jailers. The city air, harbor-cool and fresh at dawn, is a sewer by 10. The 40-hour week, for which so many good union people died, is now a joke; on an average day, a large number of people now spend three to four hours simply traveling to those eight-hour-a-day jobs, stalled on roads, idling at bridges or in tunnels. Parking fees are $5 to $10 a day. The ruined city streets cost hundreds more for gashed tires, missing hubcaps and rattled engines.

Frequently cause and effect compose a chain. A gives rise to B, B to C, and so on. Thus B would be both the effect of A and the cause of C. This paragraph about the effect of television in the 1950s on boxing (what the writer calls "the Sweet Science") develops such a series of causes and effects:

The immediate crisis [of boxing] in the United States, forestalling the one high living standards might bring on, has been caused by the popularization of a ridiculous gadget called television. This is utilized in the sale of beer and razor blades. The clients of the television companies, by putting on a free boxing show almost every night of the week, have knocked out of business the hundreds of small-city and neighborhood boxing clubs where youngsters had a chance to learn their trade and journeymen to mature their skill. Consequently the number of good new prospects diminishes with every year, and the peddlers' public is already being asked to believe that a boy with perhaps ten or fifteen fights behind him is a topnotch performer. Neither advertising agencies nor brewers, and least of all the networks, give a hoot if they push the Sweet Science back into a period of genre painting. When it is in coma they will find some other way to peddle their peanuts.

A. J. Liebling

Liebling treats both reasons and consequences. The initial cause is the use of television to sell products, the ultimate effect is the deterioration of prizefighting. But linking these are several conditions, each the effect of a preceding cause and the cause of a subsequent effect:

Initial cause: The hucksterism of television
        ↓
Effect: Too many prizefights
        ↓
Effect: Disappearance of the small fight club
        ↓
Effect: Inadequate training of young boxers
        ↓
Final effect: Deterioration of professional boxing

All this is clearly conveyed with only a single transitional adverb ("consequently"), used to signal the chief result.

For Practice

▷ Analyze the cause-effect pattern in the following paragraph by making a rough diagram like that following the passage by A. J. Liebling.

It has been a cruel decade for the magazine business. Rising production costs, postal increases and soaring paper prices have made it much more difficult to turn a profit. Television has proved a tough competitor for advertising and audience, and many of the mass circulation giants, among them *Life, Look,* and *The Saturday Evening Post,* have floundered or failed in the contest.   Nancy Henry

▷ Compose a single paragraph developing three or four reasons to support one of the following topics:

The enormous increase in the cost of housing
The contemporary mania for exercise
The expansion of professional sports in the last twenty-five years
Racial (or sexual or religious) bias
Why you like solitary activities—for example, hiking, jogging, bicycling, sailing—
or why you do not

Consider carefully the order of the reasons and be sure they are clearly linked. Feel free to use an illustration, a restatement, a comparison or contrast, but give the bulk of the paragraph to reasons.

▷ Now, using the same topic, compose a paragraph discussing three or four effects.

17

Paragraph Development: (4) Definition, Analysis, and Qualification

In its most basic sense *to define* means "to set limits or boundaries." But in practice defining is rarely simple. Consider, for example, trying to set the limits of so vast an abstraction as "democracy." The problem of defining is further complicated by the fact that there are different kinds of definitions, serving different purposes, and using different means.

Nominal and Real Definitions

There is an elementary distinction in philosophy between the definition of a word and that of the entity (object, concept, emotion, whatever) which the word signifies. Definitions of words are called *nominal* (a dictionary definition is an example). Those of entities are called *real*. (This does *not* imply that nominal definitions are somehow false.) In practice the distinction between nominal and real definitions often does not matter very much. But sometimes it does. You should always be clear in your own mind whether you are primarily concerned with the word or the entity, and you must make it equally clear to the reader. If you are defining a word, underline it (equivalent to italic type). In the following paragraph, for instance, the writer wishes to make clear how the word *history* is commonly used:

By its most common definition, the word *history* now means "the past of mankind." Compare the German word for *history—Geschichte*, which is derived from *geschehen*, meaning to happen. *Geschichte* is *that which has happened.* This meaning of the word *history* is often encountered in such overworked phrases as "all history teaches" or the "lessons of history." Louis Gottschalk

Professor Gottschalk's is a nominal definition. The essayist G. K. Chesterton, on the other hand, in defining marriage is concerned with the institution and not the word—that is, he is making a *real* definition:

Marriage is not a mere chain upon love as the anarchists say; nor is it a mere crown upon love as the sentimentalists say. Marriage is a fact, an actual human relation like that of motherhood, which has certain human habits and loyalties, except in a few monstrous cases where it is turned to a torture by special insanity and sin. A marriage is neither an ecstasy nor a slavery; it is a commonwealth; it is a separate working and fighting thing like a nation.

Consensual, Stipulative, and Legislative Definitions

Rather than kinds of definitions, the distinction here is more a matter of purpose. The purpose of a *consensual* definition is simply to tell us how people commonly use a word or what they understand a thing to be. It is what you find when you open your dictionary. A *stipulative* definition is a special meaning given to a word or entity for a particular purpose. It differs from the usual (consensual) definition, but is perfectly legitimate so long as the writer clearly explains what he or she means and uses the term consistently in its special sense. A *legislative* definition also differs from the conventional sense; it is put forward as what the word *ought* to mean. It differs from a stipulative definition in that the writer is not saying, "For convenience I shall use X to mean such and so." Instead, the writer is asserting, "I shall use X to mean such and so, and this is its proper sense and everyone else should use it in this way too."

Techniques of Defining

Definitions are developed in various ways. For convenience we consider these techniques one at a time. However, they do not exclude one another, and in practice they are often combined.

Defining by Genus–Species

This is one of the most common means of definition. The entity or word being defined (called the *definiendum*) is first set into its genus (class) and then distinguished from other members of that class:

History is the recital of facts given as true, in contradistinction to the fable, which is the recital of facts given as false.   Voltaire

Voltaire begins by setting "history" (the thing, not the word) into the genus "recital of facts." Then he differentiates it from the other member of that class, "fable."

The bulk of a genus-species definition usually goes to differentiation. This may be done explicitly, as in Voltaire's case; that is, you actually mention the other member(s) of the class and explain how the definiendum differs from them. Or it may be done implicitly, where you do not actually name the other member(s) of the class but simply describe the definiendum so completely that it is, by implication, differentiated from them. Obviously a class of any size makes complete explicit differentiation impractical. If you were defining, say, football, it would take many, many pages to distinguish it from every other team sport.

However you differentiate the thing you are defining, you must be clear about which of its attributes are essential and which are not. For example, the fact that football is played in stadiums (usually outdoors) before large crowds is not essential to its definition: baseball and soccer are also team sports played under similar conditions. On the other hand, the rules of football, the dimensions and the markings of the field, these facts are unique. Such essential attributes are what distinguish a definiendum. But this does not mean that you should ignore incidental attributes altogether. If you were explaining football to a foreign friend, it would be important that he or she understand something about where and when it is played.

The following explanation of what a map is illustrates a genus-species definition:

A map is a conventional picture of an area of land, sea, or sky. Perhaps the maps most widely used are the road maps given away by the oil companies. They show the cultural features such as states, towns, parks, and roads, especially paved roads. They show also natural features, such as rivers and lakes, and sometimes mountains. As simple maps, most automobile drivers have on various occasions used sketches drawn by service station men, or by friends, to show the best automobile route from one town to another.

The distinction usually made between "maps" and "charts" is that a chart is a representation of an area consisting chiefly of water; a map represents an area that is predominantly land. It is easy to see how this distinction arose in the days when there was no navigation over land, but a truer distinction is that charts are specially designed for use in navigation, whether at sea or in the air.

Maps have been used since the earliest civilizations, and explorers find that they are used in rather simple civilizations at the present time by people who are accustomed to traveling. For example, Arctic explorers have obtained considerable help from maps of the coast lines showing settlements, drawn by Eskimo people. Occasionally maps show not only the roads, but pictures of other features. One of the earliest such maps dates from about 1400 B.C. It shows not only roads, but also lakes with fish, and a canal with crocodiles and a bridge over the canal. This is somewhat similar to the modern maps of a state which show for each large town some feature of interest or the chief products of that town.   C. C. Wylie

Wylie first places "map" in its genus ("a conventional picture of an area of land, sea, or sky") and illustrates it ("road maps"). Next he distinguishes "map" from the other member of its class ("chart"). Finally, in the third paragraph, he gives us information about maps which, although not essential to the definition, is interesting and enlightening.

In working out a genus-species definition, then, the essential questions to ask yourself are these:

To what class does it belong?
What unique qualities distinguish it from other members of that class?
What other qualities—even though not unique—are important if readers are fully to understand the word or thing?

Defining by Synonyms

A synonymous definition is simply explaining something in different words, usually simpler words. Synonyms are useful when you must use a term readers cannot reasonably be expected to know:

Huge "pungs" (ox- or horse-drawn sledges), the connecting links between ocean commerce and New England farms, are drawn up in Dock Square three deep. . . .   Samuel Eliot Morison

The questions Mr. Murrow brought up will rise to plague us again because the answers given are not, as lawyers say, "responsive"—they are not the permanent right answers, although they will do for the day.   Gilbert Seldes

Synonyms are also helpful if you must use an everyday word in a special sense (what earlier we called a "stipulative definition"):

Love takes off the masks that we fear we cannot live without and know we cannot live within. I use the word "love" here not merely in the personal sense but as a state of being, or a state of grace—not in the infantile American sense of being made happy but in the tough and universal sense of quest and daring and growth.   James Baldwin

There is no sure guide to when you need to define a word. Certainly a definition is called for when you use a technical term in a passage intended for nontechnical readers. Lawyers do not have to be told the legal sense of *responsive*, but the rest of us do. And a definition is needed when you use a common word in a special or personal sense, as Baldwin does with *love*. On the other hand, you waste time and insult readers by defining commonplace words used conventionally.

Defining by Illustration

Examples are valuable when you define, especially in dealing with abstractions. *Heroism*, for instance, is most easily explained by illustrating heroic (and perhaps nonheroic) actions. In the following paragraph an anthropologist is explaining to Americans what "self-respect" means to the Japanese. She contrasts the Japanese conception of the quality with the American.

The heart of her definition, however, lies in the examples of how the Japanese behave to maintain self-respect:

In any language the contexts in which people speak of losing or gaining self-respect throw a flood of light on their view of life. In Japan "respecting yourself" is always to show yourself the careful player. It does not mean, as it does in English usage, consciously conforming to a worthy standard of conduct—not truckling to another, not lying, not giving false testimony. In Japan self-respect (jicho) is literally "a self that is weighty," and its opposite is "a self that is light and floating." When a man says "You must respect yourself," it means, "You must be shrewd in estimating all the factors involved in the situation and do nothing that will arouse criticism or lessen your chances of success." "Respecting yourself" often implies exactly the opposite behavior from that which it means in the United States. An employee says, "I must respect myself (jicho)," and it means, not that he must stand on his rights, but that he must say nothing to his employers that will get him into trouble. "You must respect yourself" had this same meaning, too, in political usage. It meant that a "person of weight" could not respect himself if he indulged in anything so rash as "dangerous thoughts." It had no implication, as it would in the United States, that even if thoughts are dangerous a man's self-respect requires that he think according to his own lights and his own conscience.   Ruth Benedict

Defining by Metaphor and Simile

Metaphors and similes, which draw a kind of comparison, sometimes help to clarify the meaning of a word or concept. In a famous passage, the seventeenth-century Anglican clergyman Jeremy Taylor defined prayer using a series of metaphors, which culminated in the image of a lark:

Prayer is the peace of our spirit, the stillness of our thoughts, the evenness of recollection, the seat of meditation, the rest of our cares, and the calm of our tempest; prayer is the issue of a quiet mind, of untroubled thoughts, it is the daughter of charity and the sister of meekness; and he that prays to God with an angry, that is, with a troubled and discomposed spirit, is like him that retires into a battle to meditate, and sets up his closet in the outquarters of an army, and chooses a frontier-garrison to be wise in. Anger is a perfect alienation of the mind from prayer, and therefore is contrary to that attention which presents our prayers in a right line to God. For so have I seen a lark rising from his bed of grass, and soaring upwards, singing as he rises, and hopes to get to heaven, and climb above the clouds; but the poor bird was beaten back with the loud sighings of an eastern wind, and his motion made irregular and unconstant, descending more at every breath of the tempest than it could recover by the libration and frequent weighing of his wings: till the little creature was forced to sit down and pant, and stay till the storm was over; and then it made a prosperous flight, and did rise and sing, as if it had learned music and motion from an angel as he passed sometimes through the air about his ministries here below.

Defining by Negatives

Negative definition tells us what something is not. Thus in the passage below miserliness is defined in terms of its antithesis, thrift:

Thrift by derivation means thriving; and the miser is the man who does not thrive. The whole meaning of thrift is making the most of everything; and the miser does not make anything of anything. He is the man in whom the process, from the seed to the crop, stops at the intermediate mechanical stage of the money. He does not grow things to feed men; not even to feed one man; not even to feed himself. The miser is the man who starves himself, and everybody else, in order to worship wealth in its dead form, as distinct from its living form.   G. K. Chesterton

Paired or Field Definition

Occasionally the sense of one word or concept is intimately tied to that of a second (or of several) so that the terms can be defined only be reference to one another. Such words comprise a field of meaning; for example, think of the titles designating commissioned rank in the United States Army: *captain* cannot be understood without reference to *first lieutenant* and *major*—the ranks on either side—and these in turn imply *second lieutenant* and *lieutenant colonel* and so on through the entire series of grades. In this paragraph a scholar defines the two kinds of source material available to historians:

Written and oral sources are divided into two kinds: primary and secondary. A *primary source* is the testimony of an eyewitness, or of a witness by any other of the senses, or of a mechanical device like the dictaphone—that is, of one who or that which was present at the events of which he or it tells (hereafter called simply *eyewitness*). A *secondary source* is the testimony of anyone who is not an eyewitness—that is, of one who was not present at the events of which he tells. A primary source must thus have been produced by a contemporary of the events it narrates. It does not, however, need to be original in the legal sense of the word original— that is, the very document (usually the first written draft) whose contents are the subject of discussion—for quite often a later copy or a printed edition will do just as well; and in the case of the Greek and Roman classics seldom are any but later copies available.   Louis Gottschalk

Defining by Etymology and Semantic History

Another way of getting at the meaning of a word is through its root meaning (the etymology) and the changes that meaning has undergone (the semantic history). In the following paragraph the concept of a university is defined by returning to an older name for the institution and exploring the implications of the term:

If I were asked to describe as briefly and popularly as I could, what a University was, I should draw my answer from its ancient designation of a *Studium Generale* or "School of Universal Learning." This description implies the assemblage of strangers from all parts in one spot;—*from all parts;* else, how will you find professors and students for every department of knowledge? and *in one spot;* else, how can there be any school at all? Accordingly, in its simple and rudimental form, it is a school of knowledge of every kind, consisting of teachers and learners from every quarter. Many things are requisite to complete and satisfy the idea embodied in this description; but such as this a university seems to be in its essence, a place for the communication and circulation of thought, by means of personal intercourse, through a wide extent of country.   John Henry Newman

While relatively easy, using etymolgies and older meanings has limitations. You must use dictionaries cautiously. The etymology of a word is not necessarily its "proper" sense. Word meanings change and it cannot be argued that the contemporary sense of a word is somehow wrong because it has strayed from the original. Nor do dictionary definitions tell the whole story. No matter how sensitive and thorough, they have to exclude many subtleties of meaning.

Analysis or Classification

In a broad sense all expository paragraphs are analytical. To write about any subject you must analyze it into particulars (whether reasons or comparisons, illustrations or consequences) and then organize these into a coherent whole. More narrowly, however, *analysis* refers to the specific technique of developing a topic by distinguishing its components and discussing each in turn. G. K. Chesterton, for example, analyzes the category "people" in this way:

Roughly speaking, there are three kinds of people in this world. The first kind of people are People; they are the largest and probably the most valuable class. We owe to this class the chairs we sit down on, the clothes we wear, the houses we live in; and, indeed (when we come to think of it), we probably belong to this class ourselves. The second class may be called for convenience the Poets; they are often a nuisance to their families, but, generally speaking, a blessing to mankind. The third class is that of the Professors or Intellectuals, sometimes described as the thoughtful people; and these are a blight and a desolation both to their families and also to mankind. Of course, the classification sometimes overlaps, like all classification. Some good people are almost poets and some bad poets are almost professors. But the division follows lines of real psychological cleavage. I do not offer it lightly. It has been the fruit of more than eighteen minutes of earnest reflection and research.

Chesterton develops his point by asking, in effect, "What kinds of people are there?" This strategy of paragraph building is also called classification. (Chesterton uses the terms *classification* and *class* several times.) Speaking strictly, analysis and classification are not identical. The first begins with the general and works into particulars; the second starts with the particulars and sorts them into categories. But, practically speaking, the difference is not very significant. Both are concerned with a class and a number of specifics, and the problem is to make clear that a class encompasses particulars. Thus in Chesterton's humorous analysis the broad category "people" is composed of the particular groups "People," "Poets," and "Professors."

Sorting out concrete topics, whether people or varieties of apples, is the easiest kind of analysis. But the technique also works with abstractions— the organization of a club, for instance, or the economic classes of a complex society. In the following example the writer explains how the watches were arranged on a nineteenth-century sailing vessel. (The term *watch* has a double meaning: the two divisions of the crew, who alternated in working the ship, and the periods of the twenty-four-hour day when the groups were on duty.)

The crew are divided into two divisions, as equally as may be, called the watches. Of these, the chief mate commands the larboard, and the second mate the starboard. They divide the time between them, being on and off duty, or as it is called, on deck and below, every other four hours. The three night watches are called the first, the middle, and the morning watch. If, for instance, the chief mate with the larboard watch have the first night watch from eight to twelve, at that hour the starboard watch and the second mate take the deck, while the larboard watch and the first mate go below until four in the morning, when they come on deck again and remain until eight. As the larboard watch will have been on deck eight hours out of the twelve, while the starboard watch will have been up only four hours, the former have what is called a "forenoon watch below," that is, from eight A.M. till twelve A.M. In a man-of-war, and in some merchantmen, this alternation of watches is kept up throughout the twenty-four hours, which is called having "watch and watch"; but our ship, like most merchantmen, had "all hands" from twelve o'clock till dark, except in very bad weather, when we were allowed "watch and watch."
                                                                      Richard Henry Dana

Analysis of a Process

A process is a sequence of operations directed toward a specific end. Knitting a sweater, for example, is a process, from buying the pattern and wool to the final blocking and shaping. So is the election of a political candidate or registering for college.

In most cases the steps are clearly defined. The writer's task is first to understand the process, analyzing its stages in his or her own mind; and second to explain those stages clearly. Here is an example, more abstract than knitting a sweater, describing the methodology of science:

[T]here is a fairly clear pattern of the operation of the scientific method. First, regularities are recognized as such and recorded. Then, a formulation is sought which, preferably in the simplest and most general way, contains these regularities. This then has the status of a law of nature. The newly formulated law may, and usually will, predict further regularities which were previously unknown. Finally, the objective is a combination of two or more of these laws into a still more general formulation. For instance, the great significance of Einstein's theory of special relativity is due to the fact that it provides a combination of the electromagnetic laws with those of mechanics.
                                                                      Kurt Mendelssohn

For Practice

▷ Choosing any two of the following topics, compose two separate paragraphs of analysis. Begin with a topic sentence like Chesterton's (page 104) and unify the paragraph with appropriate connecting words.

Types of husbands (or wives)
Kinds of dancing
Varieties of detective fiction
Different kinds of hammers (or other tool)
Automobile salesmen

▷ Write a set of directions for some simple activity (hitting a golf ball, say, repotting a plant, or any such process). The problem—and it is not easy—is to analyze the process into its steps and to explain these clearly.

Qualification

It is often necessary to admit that what you are asserting is not absolutely true or always applicable. Doing so is called *qualification*. Qualification always risks blurring your focus. Suppose, for example, that a writer is urging a criticism of college football. He or she begins:

College football is a semiprofessional sport.

This is clear and emphatic. But it isn't exactly true: the issue is not that simple.

Now suppose that, recognizing this complexity, the writer adds a second sentence:

College football is a semiprofessional sport. Some universities do play a purely amateur game.

The new sentence makes the writer less vulnerable to the charge of over-simplification, but the protection has been purchased at the expense of possibly confusing readers, who are no longer sure what to expect. Will the paragraph be about universities which subsidize football, or about those which do not?

As this example suggests, qualification involves at least the appearance of contradiction. The trick is to qualify without confusing readers as to the main point. It is not difficult to do, once you understand a few basic principles.

▷ *Whenever possible, subordinate the qualification.*

College football is a semiprofessional sport, although some universities do play a purely amateur game.

This makes better sense. By expressing the qualification in the adverbial *although*-clause, the writer now reduces its importance. The thought, however, still progresses awkwardly. Placing the qualification last leaves it uppermost in the reader's mind. This brings us to a second principle.

▷ *When you can, place the qualification first and wind up on the main point.*

Although some universities do play a purely amateur game, college football is a semiprofessional sport.

▷ *Use qualifying words and phrases.*

Although a few universities do play a purely amateur game, big-time college football is, in general, a semiprofessional sport.

The addition of such expressions as "a few," "big-time," and "in general" further limits the writer's assertion. So phrased, the sentence has sufficient qualification to forestall easy challenge from those who disagree with it. Yet it remains clearly focused.

▷ *When a qualification must be expressed in a separate sentence, begin it with a word stressing its obviousness and follow it by repeating the major idea.*

Big-time college football is a semiprofessional sport. Of course a few universities do play a purely amateur game. But these are only a few; on the whole, the game is subsidized.

It is not always possible to include a qualification in the same sentence that carries the main point. In that event, introducing the qualification with an admission of its truth tends to disarm it. "Of course" (or "certainly," "obviously," "admittedly," "it is true that"), you write, "such and such is the case." The initial adverb tells the reader that you are well aware of the exception, which, the adverb implies, doesn't matter very much. With the qualification completed, you then reassert your main point, beginning it with a strong signal of contradiction ("but," "however," "yet," "still," "even so").

At times a qualification requires several sentences or even an entire paragraph. For example, George R. Stewart, arguing that the American colonists constituted an essentially homogeneous culture, writes:

With few exceptions the colonists of European stock were of northwestern European origins, and there can have been, racially, only negligible differences among them. Even in their cultural backgrounds they differed little. They were heirs of the European Middle Ages, of the Renaissance, and of the Reformation. They were Christians by tradition, and nearly all were Protestants.

Naturally the groups differed somewhat, one from another, and displayed some clannishness. They were conscious of their differences, often more conscious of differences than of resemblances. Thus a Pennsylvania governor of 1718 was already voicing the cry that the American conservative has echoed ever since. "We are being overwhelmed by the immigrants!" he said in effect. "Will our country not become German instead of English?"

Nevertheless, from the perspective of two centuries and from the point of view of the modern world with its critical problems of nationality and race, the differences existing among the various colonial groups fade into insignificance. We sense, comparatively speaking, a unified population. In the political realm, indeed, there were divergences that might lead even to tarrings and featherings, but racially and socially and religiously the superficial differences were less important than the basic unity.

Professor Stewart's second paragraph qualifies the point he makes in the first and returns to in the third. Notice that he begins paragraph two with "Naturally," removing the sting from the concession, and that he opens paragraph three with an emphatic "Nevertheless." (The final sentence of that paragraph, incidentally, contains a brief qualification of its own. Can you identify it?)

For Practice

▷ Identify the qualifications in these passages and decide whether they are effective:

To my mind King James's Bible has been a very harmful influence on English prose. I am not so stupid as to deny its great beauty. It is majestical. But the Bible is an oriental book. Its alien imagery has nothing to do with us. Those hyperboles, those luscious metaphors, are foreign to our genius.   Somerset Maugham

"When the belly is full," runs the Arab proverb, "it says to the head, 'Sing, fellow!' " That is not always so; the belly may get overfull. Such a proverb clearly comes from a race familiar with bellies painfully empty. Yet it remains true, I think, that when the body is in radiant health, it becomes extremely difficult for it not to infect the mind with its own sense of well-being.   F. L. Lucas

▷ Four pairs of sentences follow. Revise each pair twice combining them into a single sentence to make an effective qualification. In the first revision of each pair use idea (1) as the main point and (2) as the qualification; in the second, reverse the relationship. Try to keep to the wording, but you may change the order of the clauses and add qualifying words:

A. (1) Baseball is the great American game.
   (2) Its supremacy is being challenged by other sports.
B. (1) The Romans are regarded as culturally inferior to the Greeks.
   (2) The Romans created a great and long-lasting empire.
C. (1) Exercise is necessary to health.
   (2) Too much exercise, or the wrong kind, can hurt you.

PART IV

The Sentence

CHAPTER **18**

The Sentence: A Definition

Good sentences are the sinew of style. They give to prose its forward thrust, its flexibility, its strong and subtle rhythms. The cardinal virtues of such sentences are clarity, emphasis, concision, and variety. How to achieve these qualities will be our major concern in this part. First, however, we must understand, in a brief and rudimentary way, what a sentence is.

It is not easy to say. In fact, it is probably impossible to define a sentence to everyone's satisfaction. On the simplest level it may be described as a word or group of words standing by itself, that is, beginning with a capital letter and ending with a period, question mark, or exclamation point. (In speech the separateness of a sentence is marked by intonation and pauses.)

And yet an effective sentence involves more than starting with a capital and stopping with a period. The word or words must make sense, expressing an idea or perception or feeling clear enough to stand alone. For example, consider these two sentences:

The package arrived. Finally.

The first consists of a subject and verb. The second is only a single word, an adverb detached from a verb *(arrived)*. The idea might have been expressed in one sentence:

The package finally arrived.
The package arrived, finally.
Finally, the package arrived.

But we can imagine a situation in which a speaker or writer, wanting to stress exasperation, feels that *finally* should be a sentence by itself.

As that example indicates, there are sentences which contain subjects and verbs and sentences which do not. The first kind *(The package arrived)* is "grammatically complete" and is the conventional form sentences take in composition. The second type of sentence *(Finally* in our example) does not contain a subject and verb and is called a *fragment*. Fragments are more common in speech than in writing, but even in formal composition they have their place, which we'll consider in a subsequent chapter.

The Grammatical Sentence

The grammatically complete sentence is independent, contains a subject and a predicate, and is properly constructed. That definition may sound a bit formidable, but it really isn't. Let's briefly consider each of those three criteria.

Grammatical Independence

Grammatical independence simply means that the words constituting the sentence are not acting as a noun or modifier or verb in connection with any other word or words. For example, *Harry was late* is independent. *Because Harry was late* is not. *Because* turns the words into an adverb (more exactly, an adverbial clause). The construction should modify another verb or clause as in *The men were delayed in starting because Harry was late.*[1]

To take one more case. *They failed to agree* is a grammatical sentence. *That they failed to agree* is not. It is a noun clause and could function as the subject of a verb:

That they failed to agree was unfortunate.

Or as the object of one:

We know *that they failed to agree.*

Subject and Predicate

The heart of a grammatical sentence is the subject and predicate. In a narrow sense the subject is the word or words identifying who or what the sentence is about, and the predicate is the verb, expressing something about the subject. In a broader sense, the subject includes the subject word(s)

---

1. The fact that *Because Harry was late* is not independent does not mean it cannot serve as a sentence. In the right context it could effectively stand alone. But it would be a fragment.

plus all modifiers, and the predicate includes the verb together with its objects and modifiers. For instance in *The man who lives next door decided last week to sell his house,* the narrow, or grammatical, subject is *man,* and the narrow, or grammatical, verb is *decided.* The broad, or notional, subject is *The man who lives next door,* and the broad, or notional, predicate is *decided last week to sell his house.*

The verb in a grammatical sentence must be finite, that is, limited with reference to time or person or number. English has several nonfinite verb forms called participles and infinitives (*being,* for example, and *to be*). These can refer to any interval of time and can be used with any person or with either number. But by convention these nonfinite forms cannot by themselves make a sentence. Thus *Harry was late* is a grammatical sentence, but *Harry being late* isn't because it contains only the participle *being* instead of a finite form such as *was.*

Proper Construction

Even though a group of words is grammatically independent and contains a subject and a finite verb, it will not qualify as a grammatical sentence unless it is put together according to the rules. "Rules" here does not mean regulations arbitrarily laid down by experts. It means how we, all of us, use English. Thus *Harry late was* is not a good sentence. We simply do not arrange these words in that order.

Here's one other example of a nonsentence resulting from bad construction:

Harry was late, and although he was sorry.

And can only combine elements that are grammatically equal—two or more subjects of the same verb, for instance. In this case *and* joins two unequal constructions—the independent clause *Harry was late* and the dependent (adverbial) clause *although he was sorry.* The construction can be turned into a legitimate grammatical sentence in either of two ways:

Harry was late, although he was sorry.
Harry was late, and he was sorry.

The Building Blocks

The basic slots of a grammatical sentence—that is, the subject, verb, object, and modifier—may be filled by many kinds of words, phrases, and dependent clauses, the building blocks of sentences.

Phrases and dependent clauses are both functional word groups—two or more words acting collectively in a grammatical function, as a subject, for instance, or direct object or adverb, and so on. Functional word groups are enormously important. They enable us to treat ideas too complex to be expressed in single words as though they were, grammatically, only one word. Take these two sentences:

I know *Susan*.

I know *that you won't like that movie.*

Susan is the direct object of *know*. So is *that you won't like that movie.* For purposes of grammar the six-word clause functions like the one-word proper noun. Being able to use the full range of functional word groups available in English is essential to writing well. Here is a quick summary.

Phrases

A phrase is a functional word group that does not contain a subject-finite verb combination, although some phrases do use nonfinite verb forms. We can distinguish five kinds of phrases: verb, prepositional, participial, gerundive, and infinitive.

A verb phrase is a main verb plus any auxiliaries:

They *have been calling* all day.

A prepositional phrase consists of a preposition (*in, of, to,* and so on) plus an object, plus (often though not invariably) modifiers of the object:

Three people were sitting *on the beautiful green lawn.*

The chief function of prepositional phrases is to modify, either as adjectives or as adverbs. A participial phrase is constructed around a participle, usually in the present (*running,* for example) or past *(run)* participle form. It acts as an adjective:

The man *running down the street* seemed suspicious.

Here the participial phrase modifies *man.* A gerundive phrase also uses the present participle but in a construction that functions as a noun. In the following example the gerundive phrase is the subject of the verb phrase *can be:*

Running for political office can be very expensive.

An infinitive phrase, finally, is built around one of the infinitives (usually the active present—for example, *to run*). Infinitive phrases may act either as nouns or as modifiers. In this sentence the phrase is the direct object of the verb, a nounal function:

They want *me to go to medical school.*

Here it is an adjective modifying *time:*

We had plenty of time *to get there and back.*

Clauses

A clause is a functional word group that does contain a subject and a finite verb. There are two basic clauses—independent and dependent. An independent clause can stand alone as a sentence. In fact a simple sentence like *We saw you coming* is an independent clause. But usually the term is reserved for such a construction when it occurs as part of a larger sentence. The sentence below, for instance, consists of two independent clauses:

We saw you coming, and we were glad.

A dependent clause cannot stand alone as a grammatically complete sentence. It serves as part of a sentence—a subject, object, adjective, or adverb. If we were to place *when* before the opening clause in the example above, we would turn it into a dependent (adverbial) clause modifying the second clause (which remains independent):

When we saw you coming we were glad.

Dependent clauses may also act as nouns, either as subjects (as in the first of the following sentences) or as objects (as in the second):

Why he went at all is a mystery to me.
We knew *that she would be pleased.*

And as adjectives:

The point *that you're trying to make* just isn't very clear.

Absolutes

An absolute is something more than a functional word group but less than a sentence. It is connected by idea but not through grammar to the rest of the statement in which it occurs:

She flew down the stairs, *her children tumbling after her.*

This absolute tells us something about the circumstances attending the lady's rush downstairs, but it doesn't modify anything in the main clause, nor is it an object or a subject. It simply is not a grammatical part of that clause. (The term *absolute* derives from a Latin word meaning "free, unrestricted.")

The Basic Types of Grammatical Sentences

Depending on the number and type of clauses they contain, grammatical sentences fall into three patterns: the simple, the compound, and the complex. In addition, there are compound-complex sentences, though they are not truly basic.

The Simple Sentence

Simple sentences consist of one subject-verb nexus (*Nexus* means a grammatical connection between words, as in *The children laughed.*) Usually a simple sentence has only one subject and one verb, but it may have—and many do—several of each and remain simple, providing that the various subjects and verbs comprise a single connection, as in the sentence *The children and their parents laughed and were glad,* in which the single nexus may be indicated like this:

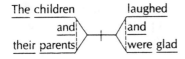

The Compound Sentence

A compound sentence consists of at least two independent subject-verb nexus:

The children laughed, and their parents were glad.

Compound sentences often have three independent clauses or even four or five. In theory there is no limit. In practice, however, most compound sentences contain only two clauses. Stringing out a number is likely to make an awkward, rambling sentence.

The two (or more) independent clauses comprising a compound sentence may be united in two ways. One is coordination, connecting clauses by a coordinating conjunction—*and, but, for, or, nor, either . . . or, neither . . . nor, not only . . . but also, both . . . and:*

The sea was dark and rough, *and* the wind was strong from the east.

The second method of joining clauses is parataxis, which is simply butting them together without a conjunction (conventionally they are punctuated by a semicolon):

The sea was dark and rough; the wind was strong from the east.

As we shall see later (Chapter 19) these two ways of connecting independent clauses are not necessarily interchangeable. In most cases one will be better than the other.

The Complex Sentence

A complex sentence contains one independent clause and at least one dependent clause. Here are several examples:

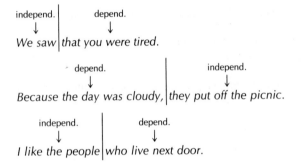

In a complex sentence the independent clause is called the main clause, and the dependent clause—which always functions as a noun or adverb or adjective—is called the subordinate. Of course a complex sentence may contain a number of subordinate clauses, but it can only have one main clause. This type of sentence is very important in composition, and we shall study it more closely in Chapter 19.

The Compound-Complex Sentence

A compound-complex sentence must have at least two independent clauses and at least one dependent:

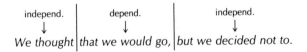

Summary

1. A sentence is a group of words (and sometimes a single word) that makes sense standing alone.
2. Some sentences are grammatically complete; others—called fragments—are not.
3. Grammatical sentences must satisfy three criteria: they must (a) be grammatically independent, (b) have a subject and a finite verb, and (c) be properly constructed.

4. The parts of a sentence are subject, verb, object, and modifier.
5. These parts may be filled by single words or by functional word groups.
6. Functional word groups act grammatically as though they were one word. They include phrases and dependent clauses.
7. A phrase does not contain a subject-finite verb combination, though it may have a subject and a nonfinite verb form, either a participle or an infinitive.
8. There are several kinds of phrases—verb phrases, prepositional, participial, gerundive, and infinitive.
9. Clauses may be independent or dependent. Only dependent clauses act as functional word groups.
10. Dependent clauses are classified according to their grammatical role as noun, adverbial, or adjectival clauses.
11. An absolute is more than a functional word group but less than a sentence. It is related in idea but not in grammar to the rest of the sentence in which it occurs.
12. Grammatical sentences come in three basic types—simple, compound, and complex—plus a combination of the last two, the compound-complex sentence.

19

Sentence Styles

In the last chapter we defined three grammatical sentences—simple, compound, and complex—plus the fragment, which, though not grammatically complete, may still stand as a sentence. From these types derive seven sentence styles: the segregating sentence, the freight-train sentence, the cumulative, parallel, balanced, subordinating, and—once again—the fragment. We shall review them in this chapter.

We need to be clear at the outset about two points. First, none of these styles is inherently better or worse than the others. Each is suited to some effects, ill-adapted to others. Second, the styles are not mutually exclusive. In fact, a skillful writer calls upon all of them.

The Segregating Style

At its purest the segregating sentence is grammatically simple, expressing a single idea.[1] A segregating style consists of a series of such sentences. In practice the style is rarely confined to technically simple, one-idea statements. That would be monotonous. Instead, a segregating style consists of relatively short, uncomplicated sentences, even though some of them may not be simple in the grammatical sense. Here, for example, a critic is describing how a particular novelist works:

---

1. "Idea" is a slippery word. Here it means simply one subject plus one predication about that subject: *The night was dark* expresses a single idea. Most sentences consist of several: *The night was dark, and it was lonely.* Or, with the two predications more closely connected: *The night was dark and lonely.*

He writes, at most, 750 words a day. He writes and rewrites. He polishes and repolishes. He works in solitude. He works with agony. He works with sweat. And that is the only way to work at all.
Beverly Nichols

As this passage shows, a segregating style can be very effective. Short sentences are strong and repetitive, qualities exactly suited to Nichols's purpose. He wants to stress that writing often is—usually is—monotonous work. Such "fit" between sentence style and purpose is important to good writing. The same general point may be put in any of various ways, but no two of the ways will be the same, and only one will be exactly what you want to say.

Segregating sentences are especially useful in descriptive and narrative writing. They analyze a complicated perception or action into its parts and arrange these in a significant order. In the following passage W. Somerset Maugham describes a Chinese criminal being led to his place of execution (in colonial times the British vice-consul had to be present when the victim of the crime was English):

The judge gave an order and the vice-consul rose and walked to the gateway, where their chairs awaited them. Here stood the criminal with his guard. Notwithstanding his tied hands he smoked a cigarette. A squad of little soldiers had been sheltering themselves under the overhanging roof, and on the appearance of the judge the officer in charge made them form up. The judge and the vice-consul settled themselves in their chairs. The officer gave an order and the squad stepped out. A couple of yards behind them walked the criminal. Then came the judge in his chair and the vice-consul.

This is a fine example of a segregating style. The sentences are short and uncomplicated (even though three of them are not simple, and none treats only a single idea). They break the scene into a series of tableaux, each rendered without comment. The effect is to distance us from the action. yet the technique is not that of a callous observer, but of an artist willing to let the event speak for itself. Like all effective styles, Maugham's deepens meaning, shocking us into seeing that in the society he is describing life and death do not matter very much.

The segregating style, then, can be effective in description and narration. It is less useful in exposition, where you must combine ideas in subtle gradations of logic and importance. These subtleties cannot be conveyed by a series of short, independent statements, which treat all ideas as equally important.

Individually used, however, segregating sentences are valuable in exposition, especially set beside longer statements, where they will seem strong and clear:

Before election day he [Huey Long] predicted he would win if rain didn't keep the mud farmers away from the polls. It rained.
Hodding Carter

The first premise of the college elective system is that the subjects are of approximately equal importance. Well, they are not.   Brand Blanshard

Short sentences like these are emphatic and create variety. (More examples will be seen in Chapters 21 and 23, where we discuss emphasis and variety.) Every writer should be able to handle the short sentence to stress particular ideas and, when the occasion warrants, to compose brief passages in a segregating style. On the whole, however, the style is too limited for general use in exposition. In unskilled hands it soon begins to sound like a third-grade reader: *Dick has a dog. The dog's name is Spot. Spot is a friendly dog.*

For Practice

▷ In a brief paragraph of about 100 words describe a football game or a party. Use a segregating style to analyze the scene or action.

The Freight-Train Style

Several kinds of sentences do what the segregating style does not do—that is, combine ideas. The simplest of these is the freight-train style, so called because it couples short, independent clauses to make longer sequential statements. It is a development of the compound sentence (see page 116) and has an old and honored history:

And the rain descended and the floods came, and the winds blew, and beat upon the house; and it fell: and great was the fall of it.   Matthew, 7:27

The freight-train sentence has several virtues. It is useful when you wish to link a series of events, ideas, impressions, feelings, or perceptions as immediately as possible, without judging their relative value or imposing a logical structure upon them. Children often experience reality in this immediate, accepting way, and authors writing for children or trying to suggest a childlike vision may employ the style:

And I'll look out for you, and you'll sing out as soon as you see me. And we'll go down the street arm in arm, and into all the shops, and then I'll choose my house, and you'll choose your house, and we'll live there like princes and good fellows.   Kenneth Grahame

Even in writing that expresses more adult attitudes, the same desire to convey mental experience directly may lead a writer to select the freight-train style. In the following passage from Ernest Hemingway's novel *A Farewell to Arms* the hero forgets the dull routine of army life by fantasizing a romantic adventure with the heroine:

Maybe she would pretend that I was her boy that was killed and we would go in the front door [of a small hotel] and the porter would take off his cap and I would stop at the concierge's desk and ask for the key and she would stand by the elevator and then we would get in the elevator and it would go up very slowly clicking at all the floors and then our floor and the boy would open the door and stand there and she would step out and I would step out and we would walk down the hall and I would put the key in the door and open it and go in and then take down the telephone and ask them to send a bottle of capri bianca in a silver bucket full of ice and you would hear the ice against the pail coming down the corridor and the boy would knock and I would say leave it outside the door please.

Both Grahame and Hemingway use the freight-train sentence to describe an experience taking place within the mind. The style suggests the continuous flow of dreaming, for we fantasize in a stream of loosely connected feelings and ideas and images, not in neatly packaged sentences of intricately related clauses and phrases tied together by *if, but, yet, therefore, consequently, on the other hand.* Indeed, we sometimes fantasize not in words at all but in imagined perceptions, as Hemingway implies ("and you would hear the ice against the pail"). Hemingway also goes further than Grahame in imitating the mental state of fantasy: his one sentence is much longer and its flow unimpeded by punctuation. This technique is a variety of what is called "stream of consciousness," a way of writing that suggests a mind feeling, dreaming, thinking in a loose associational manner.

Multiple Coordination and Parataxis

The Grahame, Hemingway, and biblical examples all use multiple coordination, linking clauses by coordinating conjunctions—in these cases, as in most, by using the word *and.* Instead of being coordinated, however, independent clauses can be butted together without conjunctions, in which case they are conventionally punctuated by semicolons, though sometimes commas are clear enough. This is called parataxis.

Although either multiple coordination or parataxis is possible in a freight-train sentence, they are not exact equivalents. Broadly speaking, the first is called for when the ideas or feelings or perceptions are changing—and when the writer desires a quick and fluid movement from clause to clause. These conditions are true of the three examples we have just seen, as they are of the following relatively short sentence by Hemingway:

It was a hot day and the sky was bright and the road was white and dusty.

There is movement here, involving both the scene and the sense by which we perceive it: we feel the heat, see the sky, lower our eyes to gaze down the road. The sentence style directs our senses much as a camera directs them in a film, guiding us from one perception to another, yet creating a continuous experience. The freight-train style, then, can analyze experience much like a series of segregating sentences. But it brings the parts more closely together, and when it uses multiple coordination, it achieves a high degree of fluidity.

On the other hand, fluidity is not always desirable. Ideas or perceptions may be repetitive, with little change and nothing to flow together. Then parataxis is preferable to multiple coordination. In the following example Virginia Woolf, summarizing a diary of an eighteenth-century Englishman visiting France, uses a freight-train style to mock his insularity:

This is what he writes about, and, of course, about the habits of the natives. The habits of the natives are disgusting; the women hawk on the floor, the forks are dirty; the trees are poor; the Pont Neuf is not a patch on London Bridge; the cows are skinny; morals are licentious; polish is good; cabbages cost so much; bread is made of coarse flour.

Each detail is another instance of the same underlying insensitivity. By hooking her clauses with semicolons (in one case with a comma) Woolf stresses the dull, unyielding vision of the diarist.

Along with its advantages, the freight-train sentence has limitations. Like the segregating style, it does not handle ideas very subtly. The freight-train sentence implies that the thoughts it links together with grammatical equality are equally significant. But usually ideas are not of the same order of importance; some are major, others secondary. Moreover, this type of construction cannot show very precise logical relationships of cause and effect, condition, concession, and so on. It joins ideas only with such general conjunctions as *and, but, or, nor* or even less exactly with semicolons and commas.

The Triadic Sentence

A second deficiency of the freight-train sentence is that it lacks a clear shape. Being open-ended, it has no necessary stopping place; one could go on and on adding clauses. As a way of providing it with a clearer structural principle, the freight-train sentence is sometimes composed in three units and is called a triad:[2]

Her showmanship was superb; her timing sensational; her dramatic instinct uncanny. Robert Coughlan

Business executives, economists, and the public alike knew little of the industrial system they were operating; they were unable to diagnose the malady; they were unaware of the great forces operating beneath the surface. Thurman Arnold

2. These sentences are also called *tricolons*. Loosely, *colon* designated in ancient Greek rhetoric an independent clause that was part of a longer sentence. A *tricolon* is a sentence of three such clauses.

Often, as in these examples, the three clauses are paratactic rather than coordinated because the triadic sentence tends to be repetitive. But it can use conjunctions when shifts in subject occur:

Then the first star came out and the great day was over and in the vestibule I saw my grandmother saluted by her sons who wished her a happy holiday.

Ludwig Lewisohn

In Lewisohn's sentence the final clause is substantially longer than the two that precede it. Movement to a longer, more complicated final construction is a refinement of the triadic sentence:

The canisters were almost out of reach; I made a motion to aid her; she turned upon me as a miser might turn if anyone attempted to assist him in counting his money.

Emily Brontë

Occasionally the shift may work in the opposite direction, from long to short:

Calvin Coolidge believed that the least government was the best government; he aspired to become the least President the country ever had; he attained his desire.

Irving Stone

The Cumulative Sentence

Most commonly a cumulative sentence consists of an initial independent clause followed by a number of subordinate constructions which accumulate details about the person, place, event, or idea. Though the elements that come after the main clause are technically subordinate, they carry the main load of the sentence and are fully as important.

Cumulative sentences appear most often in description. The writer begins with a general picture, like an artist's charcoal sketch, then fills in the details:

A creek ran through the meadow, winding and turning, clear water running between steep banks of black earth, with shallow places where you build a dam.

Mark Schorer

7000 Romaine St. looks itself like a faded movie exterior, a pastel building with chipped art moderne detailing, the windows now either boarded up or paned with chicken-wire glass and, at the entrance, among the dusty oleander, a rubber mat that reads WELCOME.

Joan Didion

Cumulative sentences are also useful in character sketches:

She [Anne Morrow Lindbergh] was then twenty-one, a year out of Smith College, a dark, shy, quiet girl with a fine mind and a small but pure and valuable gift for putting her thoughts and fancies, about the earth, sky, and sea, on paper.

John Lardner

Though less often used in narration, the cumulative sentence can also handle a series of events, as in this account of an English military expedition into France in 1359:

The unwieldy provision carts, draught horses, and heavily armed knights kept the advance down to nine miles a day, the huge horde moving in three parallel columns, cutting broad highways of litter and devastation through an already abandoned countryside, many of the adventurers now traveling on foot, having sold their horses for bread or having slaughtered them for meat.   John Gardner

Like the freight-train style, the cumulative has the problem of being open-ended, without a natural stopping place. But the deficiency may be made good by artful construction. In the following example the writer, describing a photograph of his parents, opens with the clause "When they sat for a photograph together," follows this with accumulated details, and ends by assessing the meaning of the picture:

When they sat for a photograph together—two neat slim bodies, the girl unsmiling and her eyes astare, elbows and knees tight, hands clenched in her lap, immaculate to the throat in lacy white, and the young man with grin and straw hat both aslant, jaunty on the bench arm, one leg crossed, natty in his suit and tie complete with stickpin, his arm around her with fingers outspread possessively upon her shoulder—it was a portrait not only of contrasts, but of a nation's lower middle class coming out of its cocoon.   William Gibson

What happens in that sentence is that the accumulation is gathered between dashes and intrudes into the middle of the main sentence ("When they sat for a photograph together . . . it was a portrait not only of contrasts, but of a nation's lower middle class coming out of its cocoon"). That sentence becomes a frame enclosing the details, a pattern nicely suited to what the sentence is about.

Finally, there is another variety of the cumulative sentence, in which the order is reversed: the accumulated details precede the main clause instead of following it. In the following example a novelist, discussing her art, begins by listing the essentials of a story.

Conflicts and rivalries and their resolutions, pride and its fate, estrangement and reconciliation, revenge or forgiveness, quests and searches rewarded or unrewarded; abidingness versus change, love and its proof—these are among the constants, the themes of the story.   Elizabeth Bowen

Notice how Bowen uses *these* to sum up all the preceding nouns and to act as the subject of the sentence. (*These, this, that, those,* and *such* are other pronouns which may be used in this way.)

For Practice

▷ Describe one of your typical days, first in five or six segregating sentences, then in two freight-train sentences, and finally in one long cumulative sentence. Keep to the same details and order in each rendering.

The Parallel Style

Parallelism means that two or more words or constructions stand in an identical grammatical relationship to the same thing. In *Jack and Jill went up the hill* the subjects, *Jack* and *Jill,* are parallel because both relate to the verb *went.* In the following sentence, the italicized clauses are parallel, both modifying the verb *will come:*

We will come *when we are ready* and *when we choose.*

Parallelism occurs in all types of sentences as a way of organizing minor constructions. When major ideas are involved, we speak of a parallel style, as in this sentence, where three parallel objects follow the preposition "in":

In *its energy, its lyrics, its advocacy of frustrated joys,* rock is one long symphony of protest.   *Time* magazine

And here, three infinitive phrases modifying the word "campaign":

The Department of Justice began a vigorous campaign *to break up the corporate empires, to restore the free and open market,* and *to plant the feet of industry firmly on the road to competition.*   Thurman Arnold

Parallel constructions are subject to a strict rule of style: *they must be in the same grammatical form.* Consider this opening of a sentence by the eighteenth-century political writer Edmund Burke:

To complain of the age we live in, to murmur at the present possessors of power, to lament the past, to conceive extravagant hopes of the future, are the common dispositions of the greatest part of mankind. . . .

According to the rule the four subjects of the verb *are* must be in the same grammatical form, and Burke has made them all infinitives. They could have been gerunds *(complaining, murmuring, lamenting, conceiving)* or nouns *(complaints, murmurs, laments, conceptions).* But in any case the point is that they must all be the same. To combine different forms would violate the rule—for example, mixing an infinitive with a gerund *(To complain of the age we live in, murmuring against the present possessors of power).* Such awkward mixtures are called *shifted constructions* and are regarded as a serious breach of style, sloppy and often ambiguous.

Extended parallelism is not a hallmark of modern writing, as it was in the eighteenth century, when the parallel style was predominant in formal prose. On the other hand it is foolish and unseeing to dismiss parallel sentences as out of date. They are still useful and by no means uncommon:

We must somehow take a wider view, look at the whole landscape, really see it, and describe what's going on out there.   Annie Dillard

The professor shuffled into the room, dumped his notes onto the desk, and began his usual dull lecture.   College Student

Advantages of Parallelism

Parallel sentences have several advantages. First, they are impressive and pleasing to hear, elaborate yet rhythmic and ordered, following a master plan with a place for everything and everything in its place.

Second, parallelism is economical, using one element of a sentence to serve three or four others. Piling up several verbs after a single subject is probably the most common parallel pattern, as in the two examples just above. Paralleling verbs is particularly effective when describing a process or event. The sequence of the verbs analyzes the event and establishes its progress, and the concentration on verbs, without the recurrent intervention of the subject, focuses the sentence on action. Here is an example, a description of prairie dogs, written by the American historian Francis Parkman:

As the danger drew near they would wheel about, toss their heads in the air, and dive in a twinkling into their burrows.

And another, an account of an invasion of Italy in 1494 by Charles VIII of France:

Charles borrowed his way through Savoy, disappeared into the Alps, and emerged, early in September, at Asti, where his ally met him and escorted him to the suburbs.   Ralph Roeder

A third advantage of parallelism is its capacity to enrich meaning by emphasizing or revealing subtle connections between words. For instance, in the example by Roeder the parallelism hints at the harebrained nature of Charles's expedition. Similarly Bernard Shaw, writing about Joan of Arc, insinuates a sardonic view of humanity below the surface of this prosaic summary of Joan's life:

Joan of Arc, a village girl from the Vosges, was born about 1412, burnt for heresy, witchcraft, and sorcery in 1431; rehabilitated after a fashion in 1456; designated venerable in 1904; declared Blessed in 1908; and finally canonized in 1920.

Of course, Shaw's irony is carried essentially by the words themselves, but the rapid parallel progression of the verbs enables us to see more easily the wicked folly of which human beings are capable, destroying a woman whom later they would deem saintly.

The meaning reinforced by a parallel style does not have to be ironic. It can have any emotional or intellectual coloring. In the first of the following examples we can hear a sly amusement; in the second, anger; and in the third, eloquence:

She laid two fingers on my shoulder, cast another look into my face under her candle, turned the key in the lock, gently thrust me beyond the door, shut it; and left me to my own devices.   Walter de la Mare

He [George III] has plundered our seas, ravaged our coasts, burnt our towns, and destroyed the lives of our people.   Thomas Jefferson

Let every nation know, whether it wishes us well or ill, that we shall pay any price, bear any burden, meet any hardship, support any friend, oppose any foe to assure the survival and success of liberty.   John F. Kennedy

Limitations of Parallelism

The parallel style handles ideas better than do the segregating or freight-train sentences. However, it suits only ideas that are logically parallel: several effects of the same cause, for instance, or three or four conditions of a single effect. When writers try to force parallelism onto ideas that are not logically parallel, they obscure rather than clarify meaning.

A second disadvantage of the parallel style is that it seems a bit formal for modern taste. And a third is that parallelism can be wordy rather than economical if writers allow the style to dominate them, padding out ideas to make a parallel sentence, instead of making a parallel sentence to organize ideas.

Yet despite these limitations parallelism remains an important resource of sentence style, one which many people neglect. It is a most effective way of ordering perceptions or ideas or feelings, of shaping a sentence, and of attaining economy and emphasis.

For Practice

▷ Following the pattern of the sentence by Edmund Burke (page 126), construct parallel sentences on these topics (or any others that you may prefer):

Duties of a policeman or other official
Complaints about a job
Mistakes you make in writing

The Balanced Sentence

A balanced sentence consists of two parts roughly equivalent in both length and significance and divided by a pause:

In a few moments everything grew black, and the rain poured down like a cataract.   Francis Parkman

Balanced elements may repeat the same idea, show cause and effect, precedence and subsequence, or any of other various relationships. Often balanced sentences develop a contrast; when the contrast is sharply pointed it is called an *antithesis*.

While balance can involve any kind of clause or phrase, it is most common with independent clauses, as in the example above, or in these:

Visit either you like; they're both mad.   Lewis Carroll

Children played about her; and she sang as she worked.   Rupert Brooke

These examples are compound sentences. Not all compound sentences, however, are balanced, nor are all balanced sentences compound. Balance requires simply that a sentence divides into roughly equal halves on either side of a central pause. This may occur even in a sentence that is not technically compound:

They read hardly at all, preferring to listen.   George Gissing

Gissing's sentence is grammatically simple, the first half being the main clause and the second a participial phrase. Even so, it is balanced since the halves are about the same length (each has six syllables) and equally important.[1]

The examples thus far looked at exhibit elementary balance between two units (————/————). That pattern, however, may be varied in many ways. Sometimes one half is split again (————/— ——) or (— ——/ ————); sometimes the half is split into three (————/— —— ——) or (— —— ——/————). Both halves may be broken into two (— ——/ —— ——), and so on. Here are a few examples:

For being logical they strictly separate poetry from prose; and as in prose they are strictly prosaic, so in poetry, they are purely poetical.
(————/— ——)   G. K. Chesterton

But called by whatever name, it is a most fruitful region; kind to the native, interesting to the visitor.
(— ——/— ——)   Thomas Carlyle

I stood like one thunderstruck, or as if I had seen an apparition: I listened, I looked round me, but I could hear nothing, nor see anything.
(— ——/— —— —— ——)   Daniel Defoe

---

1. Not everyone would agree to call such sentences balanced, arguing that balanced constructions must be of the same grammatical order and therefore that a balanced sentence requires that its halves be independent clauses. However, to the degree that we hear a sentence as consisting of two parts more or less equal in length and importance, it is balanced. The balance is more exact when the parts are independent clauses cut to the same pattern.

Parallelism and Balance

The difference between parallelism and balance is that in the former the elements involved must stand in an identical grammatical relationship to the same word or construction. Balanced words or constructions, however, do not have to be parallel (though they can be). Thus in the sentence above by Defoe the six clauses are separate and independent, not related to anything.

But parallelism and balance often go hand in hand, and nothing prevents the same constructions from being both parallel and balanced, if they are performing an identical grammatical function, are in the same form, and roughly equal in length. Here are two examples:

As for me, I frankly cleave to the Greeks and not to the Indians, and I aspire to be a rational animal rather than a pure spirit.   George Santayana

The sentence balances two coordinated clauses of similar structure and length. Within the first clause, the prepositional phrases "to the Greeks and not to the Indians" are parallel and antithetical. In the second clause "a rational animal rather than a pure spirit" is a parallel construction, and balance (in this case antithesis) is provided by playing "rational animal" against "pure spirit."

Most people, of course, made no distinction between a Communist—who believed in nothing but government—and such philosophical anarchists as Vanzetti—who believed in no government at all.   Phil Strong

"A communist" and "such philosophical anarchists as Vanzetti" are parallel objects of "between," though the second is too much longer than the first to constitute a balance. However, balance does occur in the two "who" clauses, though these are not parallel because they modify different nouns.

The Advantages of Balance

Balanced construction has several virtues. It is pleasing to our eyes and ears, and gives shape to the sentence, one of the essentials of good writing. It is memorable. And by playing key terms against each other, it opens up their implications. For example, the following sentence by Charles Dickens makes us consider the plight of those who lack the cash to turn their ideas to account:

Talent, Mr. Micawber has; capital, Mr. Micawber has not.

Anthony Hope implies a skeptical assessment of politicians and bureaucrats:

Ability we don't expect in a government office, but honesty one might hope for.

And here the movie critic Pauline Kael comments on the film *Love Story:*

In itself, a love idyll like this may seem harmless, but it won't be by itself very long.

Kael's complaint is that shlock films, if they are popular, usher in a host of even worse imitations. Notice how the sentence swings and advances on the phrases "in itself" and "by itself."

Beyond highlighting specific words and ideas, balance has a deeper significance. It expresses a way of looking at the world, just as freight-train or cumulative sentences express their own angles of vision. Implicit in the balanced style is a sense of objectivity, control, and proportion. In the following passage about Lord Chesterfield, the critic F. L. Lucas reinforces his argument by the reasonableness of his balanced sentences. The very style seems to confirm the fairness and lack of dogmatism suggested by such phrases as "seem to me" and "I think":

In fine, there are things about Chesterfield that seem to me rather repellant; things that it is an offense in critics to defend. He is typical of one side of the eighteenth century—of what still seems to many its most typical side. But it does not seem to me the really good side of that century; and Chesterfield remains, I think, less an example of things to pursue in life than of things to avoid.

Because the balanced style keeps a distance between writer and subject, it works well for irony and comedy. For instance, the novelist Anthony Trollope implies humorous disapproval of a domineering female character in this way:

It is not my intention to breathe a word against Mrs. Proudie, but still I cannot think that with all her virtues she adds much to her husband's happiness.

The balance suggests the objectivity of the author and increases the credibility of his criticism, while at the same time the second clause comically reveals him indulging in the very gossip he forswears in the first.

Comic, too, is the effect of this sentence from the autobiography of Edward Gibbon, the historian of *The Decline and Fall of the Roman Empire,* which describes an unhappy love affair of his youth, broken off at his father's insistence:

After a painful struggle I yielded to my fate: I sighed as a lover, I obeyed as a son; my wound was insensibly healed by time, absence, and the habits of a new life.

Writing from the calmer waters of age, when the tempests of twenty seem less catastrophic, Gibbon is smiling. The very parallelism and balance of this triadic sentence, as formal as a minuet, are a comment on the passions of youth.

Balance and parallelism do not communicate meaning by themselves. The primary units of meaning, of course, are words. But balanced and parallel constructions do reinforce and enrich meaning. Or, to be more exact, certain kinds of meaning. Not every sentence can be cast in this mold, or should be. Like every style, parallelism and balance have limitations as well as potentialities. Their very sanity, reasonableness, and control make them unsuitable for conveying the immediacy of raw experience or the intensity of strong emotion. Moreover, their formality is likely to seem too elaborate to modern readers, a less "natural" way of writing than the segregating style or the freight-train or cumulative sentences.

However, we ought not to equate formality with artificiality or to think naturalness the only ideal. All well-constructed sentences result from art, even those—perhaps especially those—like Hemingway's that create the illusion of naturalness. Remember, too, that *natural* is a tricky word. To men and women of the eighteenth century, parallelism and balance reflected nature, which they understood as a vast but comprehensible structure of ordered parts.

Perhaps the best lesson a modern writer can learn from the parallel and balanced styles is the necessity of giving shape to what he or she thinks and feels. The shape congenial to the eighteenth century seems unnatural to us. But while we no longer write like Thomas Jefferson or Samuel Johnson, we can still use parallelism and balance as ways of organizing some aspects of experience and knowledge, and as means of attaining economy, emphasis, and variety in our sentences.

For Practice

▷ The following sentences all exhibit balanced construction. Some exhibit a simple one-to-one balance; others are more complicated. Identify the general pattern of each, whether ——/——; ——/—— ——; —— ——/——; and so on.

I was enjoying the privilege of studying at the world's finest universities; Negroes at home were revolting against their miserable condition.   Stanley Sanders

As for me, I am no more yours, nor you mine. Death hath cut us asunder; and God hath divided me from the world and you from me.   Sir Walter Raleigh

For aristocrats and adventurers France meant big money; for most Englishmen it came to seem a costly extravagance.   Geoffrey Hindley

Then she shrieked shrilly, and fell down in a swoon; and then women bare her into her chamber, and there she made overmuch sorrow.   Sir Thomas Malory

Heaven had now declared itself in favour of France, and had laid bare its outstretched arm to take vengeance on her invaders.   David Hume

The more we saw in the Irishman a sort of warm and weak fidelity, the more he regarded us with a sort of icy anger.   G. K. Chesterton

Building ceases, births diminish, deaths multiply; the nights lengthen, and days grow shorter.   Maurice Maeterlinck

In a few moments everything grew black, and the rain poured down like a
cataract.   Francis Parkman

He could not keep the masses from calling him Lindy, but he convinced them that
he was not the Lindy type.   John Lardner

In literature there is no such thing as pure thought; in literature, thought is always
the handmaid of emotion.   J. Middleton Murry

▷ Choosing different subjects from those in the text, compose five balanced sentences
modeled upon examples in the preceding question.

The Subordinating Style

The sentence styles we have looked at thus far—segregating, freight-train,
cumulative, parallel, and balanced—are similar in one essential: all treat
their constituent ideas as more or less equally important. In much composition, however, it is necessary to show degrees of significance. This
calls for a different principle of structure: subordination. Subordination
means focusing on one idea (expressed in the main clause) and arranging
points of lesser importance around it, in the form of phrases and dependent
clauses.

There are four basic variations of the subordinating sentence, depending
on the relative positions of the main clause and the subordinate constructions:

1. *Loose* structure: the main clause comes first and is followed by the subordinate
   clauses and phrases.
2. *Periodic* structure: the subordinate constructions precede the main clause, which
   closes the sentence.
3. *Convoluted* structure: the main clause is split in two, opening and closing the
   sentence; the subordinate constructions intrude between the parts of the main
   clause.
4. *Centered* structure: the main clause occupies the middle of the sentence and is
   both preceded and followed by subordinate constructions.

The four patterns may be mixed in varying degrees and frequently are.
Even so, it is probably true that most subordinate sentences follow one
pattern or another.

The Loose Sentence

At its simplest the loose sentence contains a main clause plus a subordinate
construction:

We must always be wary of conclusions drawn from the ways of the social insects,
since their evolutionary track lies so far from ours.   Robert Ardrey

The number of ideas in loose sentences is easily increased by adding phrases and clauses, related either to the main constructions or to a preceding subordinate one:

I found a large hall, obviously a former garage, dimly lit, and packed with cots.   Eric Hoffer

I knew I had found a friend in the woman, who herself was a lonely soul, never having known the love of man or child.   Emma Goldman

As the number of subordinate constructions increases, the loose sentence approaches the cumulative style (discussed on pages 124–25). It is impossible to draw a line between loose and cumulative sentences. Indeed, cumulative sentences (or rather, most of them) are a special variety of the loose style. The difference is relative, depending on the length and weight of the subordinate constructions. In the cumulative sentence these take over, becoming more significant than the main clause, which serves primarily to introduce them. The following passage describing a Welsh town illustrates how loose structure evolves into a cumulative style:

Llanblethian hangs pleasantly, with its white cottages, and orchard and other trees, on the western slope of a green hill; looking far and wide over green meadows and little or bigger hills, in the pleasant plain of Glamorgan; a short mile to the south of Cowbridge, to which smart little town it is properly a kind of suburb.
                                                                          Thomas Carlyle

Loose sentences are appropriate for writing that aims to be colloquial, informal, relaxed. It puts first things first, as most of us do when we talk. On the other hand, loose structure lacks emphasis and easily becomes formless. Its unity derives not so much from a structural principle as from the coherence of thought. A loose sentence is well formed to the degree that it expresses a completed idea or perception. A good example is the following passage, which begins a description of the Brooklyn home belonging to the writer's grandmother:

Her house was a narrow brownstone, two windows to every floor except the ground, where the place of one window was taken by a double door of solid walnut plated with layers of dust-pocked cheap enamel. Its shallow stoop. . . .   William Alfred

Alfred's sentence is unified by what it describes—the facade of the house. When that perception ends and our eyes are turned upon the stoop, the writer wisely begins a new sentence. Of course, this question of when to stop, of knowing when one statement should end and another begin, applies to all kinds of sentences. But it causes special problems with loose structure, where the absence of a clear stopping place may tempt you to ramble on and on.

The Periodic Sentence

Periodic sentences reverse the pattern of loose structure, beginning with subordinate constructions and putting the main clauses at the end:

If there is no future for the black ghetto, the future of all Negroes is diminished.   Stanley Sanders

Given a moist planet with methane, formaldehyde, ammonia, and some usable minerals, all of which abound, exposed to lightning or ultraviolet radiation at the right temperature, life might start almost anywhere.   Lewis Thomas

There is no one formula for the periodic sentence. Often, however, the opening subordinate constructions are adverbial clauses, as in the example by Stanley Sanders, or participial phrases, as in that by Lewis Thomas.

Whatever kinds of subordination it uses, the periodic style is emphatic. Delaying the principal thought increases its importance. To the degree that more and more subordinate clauses and phrases are accumulated at the beginning, further postponing the main clause, the sense of climax increases (within limits, of course; too long a delay will cause confusion). Here is an instance of effectively postponing the main point:

Paralyzed by the neurotic lassitude engendered by meeting one's past at every turn, around every corner, inside every cupboard, I go aimlessly from room to room.   Joan Didion

The periodic style is also more formal and literary than the loose, suggesting a writer at a desk rather than a speaker in a relaxed social setting, a tone advantageous on formal occasions, though less so when informality is desired.

The Convoluted Sentence

In this type of periodic structure the subordinate elements split the main clause from the inside, often intruding between the subject and the verb and sometimes between verb and object or within the verb phrase:

White men, at the bottom of their hearts, know this.   James Baldwin

And once in a spasm of reflex chauvinism, she called Queen Victoria, whom she rather admired, "a goddamned old water dog."   William Alfred

Convoluted structure, as an occasional rather than habitual style, is a good way of achieving variety in sentence movement. It also establishes strong emphasis by throwing weight upon the words before and after the commas or dashes setting off the interrupting constructions:

Now demons, whatever else they may be, are full of interest.   Lytton Strachey

Here both "demons" and "full of interest" draw attention, expressing the principal idea more strongly than would loose or periodic structure:

Now demons are full of interest, whatever else they may be.

Whatever else they may be, demons are full of interest.

However, this fact does *not* mean that the convoluted style is inherently better than either the periodic or the loose. It is simply a convenient way of establishing emphasis on particular words when that emphasis is desirable.

On the other hand, convoluted structure is formal, and it can tax readers' attention, especially as the interrupting elements grow longer and more complicated:

Even the humble ambition, which I long cherished, of making sketches of those places which interested me, from a defect of eye or of hand was totally ineffectual.   Sir Walter Scott

The life story to be told of any creative worker is therefore by its very nature, by its diversion of purpose and its qualified success, by its grotesque transitions from sublimation to base necessity and its pervasive stress towards flight, a comedy.   H. G. Wells

These are good sentences, carefully articulated and precise; but they are not easy to read. They demand attention; readers must recognize when a construction is suspended and when it is resumed and be able to put the pieces together. Used sparingly, the long convoluted sentence has the virtue of the unusual: it draws attention to itself and, more important, to what it says, and it can challenge and stimulate the reader. A steady diet of such challenges, however, very soon grows tiresome.

The Centered Sentence

The type of subordinate structure that places the main clause more or less in the middle of the sentence, with subordinate elements on either side, has no common name. It has been called "circuitous" and "round composition"; we shall say "centered." Whatever we call it, we see it often. (In the three examples that follow in this section, the main clauses have been italicized.)

Having wanted to walk on the sea like St. Peter *he had taken an involuntary bath,* losing his mitre and the better part of his reputation.   Lawrence Durrell

Standing on the summit of the tower that crowned his church, wings upspread, sword lifted, the devil crawling beneath, and the cock, symbol of eternal vigilance, perched on his mailed foot, *Saint Michael held a place of his own in heaven and on earth* which seems, in the eleventh century, to leave hardly room for the Virgin of the Crypt at Chartres, still less for the Beau Christ of the thirteenth century at Amiens.   Henry Adams

While not as emphatic as periodic or as informal as loose construction, the centered style has several advantages, especially in long sentences with numerous subordinate elements. It enables a writer to place those elements more clearly. If half-a-dozen or more phrases and dependent clauses all precede the main construction (as in the periodic style), or all follow it (as in the loose), some may seem to float free. The link becomes obscure, especially when writing about ideas. The chance of obscurity is reduced if the main clause can be placed in the middle of the subordinate elements.

Another advantage of the centered sentence is that it is easier to arrange sentence elements to reflect the natural order of the event or the ideas. Jonathan Swift does exactly this in the following passage criticizing England's participation in the War of the Spanish Succession (1701–1714):

After ten years' fighting to little purpose, after the loss of above a hundred thousand men, and a debt remaining of twenty millions, *we at length hearkened to the terms of peace,* which was concluded with great advantage to the empire and to Holland, but none at all to us, and clogged soon after with the famous treaty of partition.

Allowed a broad and uncritical meaning of "idea," we may say that Swift's sentence contains nine of them: (1) the "ten years' fighting"; (2) the "little purpose," or lack of result; (3) the "loss" of the men; (4) the "debt remaining"; (5) the "hearkening" to peace; (6) the conclusion of the peace; (7) the "advantages" that followed for England's allies; (8) the absence of such advantages for England herself; and (9) the "clogging" of the peace. Here the order of the sentence mirrors events. In reality, as in the sentence, the fighting comes first, then the absence of positive results, the loss of life, the debt, and so on. Effecting a workable compromise between the natural order of thought or of events on the one hand, and the grammatical order of the sentence on the other, is one of the most difficult tasks a writer faces. When you are dealing with a long and complicated subject, the centered sentence may prove the easiest solution to the problem.

The Fragment

A fragment is a single word, a phrase, or a dependent clause standing alone as a sentence. It is considered fragmentary rather than a grammatical sentence because it is not grammatically independent and may not contain a subject and a finite verb. In formal writing fragments are generally a fault, though occasionally valuable for emphasis or variety. Before looking at examples of such positive fragments, we need to understand the common forms that fragments may take and how, when they are a fault rather than a virtue, they may be corrected.

As an instance of a single-word fragment, consider this answer to a question:

Do you understand?

Perfectly.

If we were to see the word *perfectly* printed all by itself, we should be puzzled. We know what the word means, but completely isolated it makes no sense. It is not *grammatically* meaningful. Of course we rarely encounter words in such utter isolation. Usually they occur in the context of other words (or of clarifying social situations), and we can easily supply what is needed to complete the meaning:

[I understand] perfectly.

Fragments in composition are less likely to be single words than phrases or clauses, usually modifiers detached from the words they modify. Three very common cases are the participial phrase, the adjectival clause, and the adverbial clause; each is italicized in the examples below:

DETACHED PARTICIPIAL PHRASE: I saw her. *Going down the street.*
DETACHED ADJECTIVAL CLAUSE: Everyone left except John. *Who decided to stay.*
DETACHED ADVERBIAL CLAUSE: It was very late. *When the party broke up.*

Awkward fragments such as these can be fixed in one of two ways. Either the fragment may be made part of the sentence where it acts as a modifier:

I saw her going down the street.
Everyone left except John, who decided to stay.
It was very late when the party broke up.

Or, the fragment may be kept as a separate statement but made grammatically complete, either by removing the word or words which render it subordinate or by supplying, if necessary, a subject and verb:

I saw her. She was going down the street.
Everyone left except John. He decided to stay.
It was very late. The party broke up.

Though these alternative corrections result in grammatical sentences, they have slight differences in meaning. ("Slight" differences in meaning are often the difference between good and mediocre writing.) Turning the fragment into a complete sentence gives it more emphasis.

A final type of fragment is the verbless statement:

All people, whether they live in the city or the country.

Here modifiers surround a noun ("people"). But this noun, presumably the intended subject of a sentence, has no verb; the writer never predicates anything about "people." Cases like this may require more extensive revision. Sometimes, if the noun is followed by a modifying clause, the verb of the clause may be adapted as the main verb:

All people live in the city or the country.

In this instance, the correction is too simpleminded to be what the writer intended. He or she needs to think out the idea and supply an appropriate predication, perhaps something like:

All people, whether they live in the city or the country, want the conveniences of modern life.

Effective Fragments

Fragments are very likely to be awkward and unclear when they are unintended, the result of carelessness or uncertainty about what a grammatical sentence is. But used skillfully, they are eye-catching, unusual, and emphatic:

"Many a man," said Speer, "has been haunted by the nightmare that one day nations might be dominated by technical means. That nightmare was almost realized in Hitler's totalitarian system." Almost, but not quite.   Aldous Huxley

Sweeping criticism of this type—like much other criticism—throws less light on the subject than on the critic himself. A light not always impressive.   F. L. Lucas

Obviously, the effectiveness of fragments like these depends upon their being uncommon. It is best, then, to employ fragments very occasionally in formal composition, and only when you wish to draw attention to the idea they express.

For Practice

▷ Which of the following statements are fragments? Revise them in two ways: first by turning the fragment into a grammatically complete sentence in its own right, and second by incorporating it into a sentence within which it serves as a modifier:

1. In the morning when the sun came up. The party broke camp.
2. Most people are honest. Making an effort, for example, to find the owner of a wallet they picked up on a busy street.
3. That girl is very nice. The one you introduced me to.
4. School is not so difficult. If you don't let your work pile up.
5. Not everyone likes football. My brother, for instance.
6. Older people who lived through the Depression and the Second World War. And experienced great changes in our society.
7. The boy climbing the tree. That's my cousin.
8. Although he wasn't at fault. Everybody blamed him.
9. That man running down the street. He stole this lady's purse.

20

The Well-Written Sentence: (1) Concision

Aside from being grammatical, a well-written sentence must be clear and interesting. Clarity means that it says to the reader what the writer intended to say; interesting, that it reads well, attracting us by its economy, novelty, sound, and rhythm. To a considerable degree these virtues are a matter of diction, that is, of word choice; and in the section on diction we shall look at them again from that point of view. But they also depend on sentence structure. In this chapter and the next we consider how sentence structure in itself contributes to clarity and interest. It does so by aiming at concision, emphasis, rhythm, and variety.

Concision is brevity relative to purpose. It is not to be confused with absolute brevity. A sentence of seven words is brief; but if the idea can be conveyed with equal clarity in five, the sentence is not concise. On the other hand, a sentence of fifty words is in no sense brief, but it is concise if the point can be made in no fewer words. Observing a few general rules of sentence construction will help you avoid certain kinds of wordiness.

▷ **Do Not Waste the Main Elements of the Sentence**

(In these and all following examples, the deadwood—that is, the unnecessary words—are italicized.)

WORDY   *The fact of* the war *had the effect of* causing many changes.

CONCISE   The war caused many changes.

The main elements of a sentence are its subject, verb, and object. They should convey the core of the thought. Suppose we abstract subject, verb, and object from the sentences above:

fact   had   effect
war   caused   changes

Clearly the revision—less than half the length of the original—uses the main elements more efficiently: from "war caused changes" a reader quickly grasps the nub of the idea. But who could guess the writer's point from "fact had effect"?

As you compose a sentence, then, get the essence of the thought into the subject, verb, and object. Not doing so often results from uncertainty about what your subject is. A sentence that starts out on the wrong foot will stagger under a load of excess verbiage as you struggle to get at what you mean:

The first baseman wears a special leather glove that is designed for easy scooping and long-range catching, while the catcher wears a large glove that is heavily padded to protect him from fast pitches.

The subject of the first clause is "the first baseman"; of the second, "the catcher." But these are the wrong subjects: the writer is contrasting the gloves, not the players. If the true subject ("glove") is used, the sentence steps off properly and moves along easily:

The first baseman's glove is designed for easy scooping and long-range catching, while the catcher's is large and heavily padded to protect him from fast pitches.

Awkward Anticipatory Construction

This is a special case of failing to use the main sentence elements effectively:

WORDY   *This is the kind of golfer that* is called a hacker.

CONCISE   This kind of golfer is called a hacker.

In an anticipatory sentence the notional subject—that is, what the sentence is really about—is not the grammatical subject. Instead it is introduced (or "anticipated") by a pronoun *(it, this, that, these, those, there)* which functions as the grammatical subject. (The *there*-construction is different grammatically but for all practical purposes works the same way.) A verb like *is, are,* or *seems* links the notional subject to the pronoun, and an adjectival phrase or clause, modifying the notional subject, tells us what is being predicated about it:

This is the man who witnessed the accident.

There are many property owners who object to new schools.

Those are the people from Chicago.

Anticipatory constructions require more words than comparable direct statements. Sometimes the construction is legitimized by emphasis or idiom; then the extra words are certainly not deadwood. But unless there is such a purpose, a direct statement is preferable. *Seems* and its close relative *appears* are especially frequent in awkward anticipatory sentences. Some writers, whether excessively cautious or polite, habitually hedge their bets, preferring a hesitant claim like

It seems that this professor did not prepare his lectures very well.

to the bolder assertion:

This professor did not prepare his lectures very well.

About any anticipatory construction, then, ask yourself whether idiom or emphasis justifies it. Sometimes one or the other will. Changing "It is true that we did not like the idea at first" to "That we did not like the idea at first is true" saves one word but results in a stiff sentence, too formal for many occasions. Similarly, revising "This is the man who witnessed the accident" to "This man witnessed the accident" deemphasizes the point, hardly an improvement *if* the writer wants to make a strong statement. But sometimes you will find that no such reason justifies an anticipatory construction. Then it is simply wordy, and you ought to replace it with a more direct statement.

▷ Express Modifiers in the Fewest Possible Words

WORDY   He acted *in an unnatural way.*
CONCISE   He acted unnaturally.

WORDY   The organization of a small business can be described *in a brief statement.*
CONCISE   The organization of a small business can be briefly described.

WORDY   She prefers wines *having a French origin.*
CONCISE   She prefers French wines.

WORDY   American exploration was rapid considering the means *which the pioneers had available to them.*
CONCISE   American exploration was rapid considering the means available to the pioneers.

WORDY   The targets *that are supplied in skeet shooting* are discs *made of clay.*
CONCISE   Skeet targets are clay discs.

Adverbs and adjectives ought to link as directly as possible with what they modify. The writers of the first two examples above are afraid of adverbs. (Many people are, perhaps made timid by uncertainty about the *-ly* ending.) "Unnatural" really describes "acted," but instead of directly connecting it to that verb, the writer hangs it on the empty word "way" in an unnecessary prepositional phrase. Similarly, the adverbial phrase "in a brief statement" can be rendered with equal clarity and far more economy by "briefly." The other three sentences labor under ponderous adjectival phrases or clauses when much briefer constructions will do.

Use Participles

WORDY   It leaves us *with the thought* that we were hasty.
CONCISE   It leaves us thinking that we were hasty.

WORDY   This is the idea *that was suggested* last week.
CONCISE   This is the idea suggested last week.

Wordy modification often results from failing to use participles. In cases like the first example an abstract noun ("thought"), which requires a preposition and an article, can be replaced by one word, "thinking." The second example here shows how to prune an adjectival clause consisting of a relative word ("that") + a linking verb ("was") + a participle ("suggested") or other predicative term. By dropping the relative word and the linking verb, you can move directly from the noun to the participle (or predicative word).

Sometimes an entire adverbial clause can be cut back to the operative participle:

WORDY   *Because they were tired,* the men returned to camp.
CONCISE   Tired, the men returned to camp.

And sometimes an independent clause or sentence can be trimmed:

WORDY   These ideas are already old-fashioned, *and they are not* frequently met with.
CONCISE   These ideas are already old-fashioned, infrequently met with.

WORDY   The women of the settlement would gather together at one home to work on the quilt. *They would* bring their children *with them* and spend the entire day, chatting gaily as they worked.
CONCISE   The women of the settlement would gather together at one home to work on the quilt, bringing their children and spending the entire day, chatting gaily as they worked.

Use Predicate Adjectives

WORDY   Riots became frequent *affairs*.
CONCISE   Riots became frequent.

WORDY   Mr. Martin is a quiet, patient, and cautious *person*.
CONCISE   Mr. Martin is quiet, patient, and cautious.
WORDY   The day was a perfect *one*.
CONCISE   The day was perfect.

A *predicate adjective* stands after the noun it notionally modifies, connected to it by a linking verb (*is, are, was, were, seems, becomes*, and so on), like "large" in this sentence:

The house is large.

An *attributive adjective* stands before the noun it modifies:

the large house

Predicate adjectives are not necessarily better. But it is better not to restate a word or idea pointlessly as the above examples do. "Affairs," "person," and "one" are empty words, hooks on which to hang an attributive adjective. Why not use the adjective predicatively? Then the empty word is no longer needed. And even more important, the adjective will get the emphasis it deserves.

▷ **Do Not State What Sentence Structure
Itself Makes Clear**
Use Colon or Dash for Announcement

WORDY   There were many reasons for the Civil War, *which include* slavery, economic expansion, states' rights, cultural differences, and sectional jealousies.
CONCISE   There were many reasons for the Civil War: slavery, economic expansion, states' rights, cultural differences, and sectional jealousies.
WORDY   Pitchers are divided into two classes. *These classes are* starters and relievers.
CONCISE   Pitchers are divided into two classes—starters and relievers.

In sentences like these, the colon or dash says: "Here comes a series of particulars." If you let the punctuation mark talk, you won't need deadwood like "which include" or "these classes are." (The only difference between the colon and the dash in this function is that the colon is a bit more formal. However, each mark has other, very different tasks in which they are not equivalents.)

The colon or dash can also set up an important idea delayed for emphasis:

WORDY   But a counterforce has been established within the weapons platoon.
           This counterforce is the anti-tank squad.
CONCISE   But a counterforce has been established within the weapons platoon—
           the anti-tank squad.

Use Ellipses

WORDY   He is taller than his brother *is*.
CONCISE   He is taller than his brother.

WORDY   When *you are* late, you must sign yourself in.
CONCISE   When late, you must sign yourself in.

WORDY   He lost his wallet; she *lost* her pocketbook.
CONCISE   He lost his wallet; she, her pocketbook.

An *ellipsis* (plural, *ellipses*) is the omission of words implied by the grammar but not necessary to complete the sense. The writer using an ellipsis assumes that readers can supply the missing words from the context.

Ellipses often secure concision with no loss of clarity or emphasis. They may even enhance those qualities. In the first example above, the sense does not require the second "is"; moreover, the revision allows the sentence to end on the key term "brother." In the second, the concise version stresses "late" and avoids repeating "you"; while in the third, dropping "lost" from the second clause makes a striking statement.

The unusual quality of some ellipses, however, limits their usefulness. For example, "He lost his wallet; she, her pocketbook" has a literary flavor that might seem odd in a matter-of-fact, colloquial passage.

Use Parallelism

WORDY   These books are not primarily for reading, but *they are used* for refer-
           ence.
CONCISE   These books are not primarily for reading but for reference.

WORDY   The beginner must work more slowly, *and he must work* more con-
           sciously.
CONCISE   The beginner must work more slowly and more consciously.

Parallelism means that two or more words, phrases, or clauses are grammatically related in the same way to the same thing. In "The man and the boy came in together," "man" and "boy" are parallel because each acts as a subject of the same verb ("came in"). Or in "She stood and raised her hand," "stood" and "raised" are parallel because each is a verb of the same subject ("She").

Parallelism is like factoring in mathematics; instead of repeating a in $2ax + 3ay + az$, the mathematician writes $a(2x + 3y + z)$. In a grammatically parallel construction the governing term need not be stated two or three times. In the first example, the phrase "for reference," by being made parallel to "for reading," does duty for the entire second clause.

But at times parallelism improves nothing. Emphasis or rhythm often justifies a certain amount of repetition. Thus in the second example above, the so-called "wordy" version would be preferable if the writer wished to stress "he must work."

CHAPTER 21

The Well-Written Sentence:
(2) Emphasis

In speech we achieve emphasis in a variety of ways: by talking loudly (or sometimes very softly); by speaking slowly, carefully separating words that ordinarily we run together; by altering our tone of voice or changing its timbre. We also stress what we say by nonvocal means: a rigid, uncompromising posture; a clenched fist; a pointing finger; any of numerous other body attitudes, gestures, facial expressions.

Writers can rely upon none of these signals. Yet they too need to be emphatic. What they must do, in effect, is to translate loudness, intonation, gesture, and so on, into writing. Equivalents are available. Some are merely visual symbols for things we do when talking: much punctuation, for example, stands for pauses in speech. Other devices, while not unknown in speech, belong primarily to composition. Some of these we shall look at in this chapter.

First, though, we need to distinguish two degrees of emphasis—*total emphasis*, which applies to the entire sentence, and *partial emphasis*, which applies only to a word, or a group of words, within the sentence. As an example of total emphasis, consider these two statements:

1. An old man sat in the corner.
2. In the corner sat an old man.

Sentence (1) is matter of fact, attaching no special importance to what it tells us. Sentence (2), however, like a closeup in a film, suggests that the fact is important. Now this distinction does *not* mean that the second version is superior to the first: simply that it is more emphatic. Whether or not the emphasis makes it better depends on what the writer wants to say.

By their nature strong sentences (that is, those having total emphasis) cannot occur very often. Their effectiveness depends on their rarity. Writing in which every sentence is emphatic, or even every other, is like having somebody shout at you.

Partial emphasis (emphasis within the sentence), however, is characteristic of all well-written sentences. Usually one word (or phrase or clause) is more important than the others. Consider these two variations of the same statement:

1. It suddenly began to rain.
2. Suddenly, it began to rain.

If we suppose that the writer wished to draw our attention to "suddenly," sentence (2) is better. By moving it to the opening position and isolating it with a comma, the writer gives the word far more weight than it has in sentence (1). Again there is no question of an absolute better or worse. Each version is well-suited to some purpose, ill-suited to others.

The Emphatic Sentence

There are a number of ways of stressing a statement in its totality.

▷ Announcement

An announcement (in the sense it has here) is a preliminary statement which tells the reader, "Watch out, here comes something important":

Finally, last point about the man: he is in trouble.   Benjamin DeMott

The construction receiving the stress should be phrased concisely and vigorously and separated from the preceding announcement by a colon or dash (though sometimes a comma will do).

Anticipatory constructions, which we saw on page 141 as a potential source of deadwood, can function effectively as a form of announcement. They are low-key, reducing the introduction to little more than a pronoun (or *there*) + a verb:

This was the consequence we feared.   Evelyn Jones

It's tragic—this inability of human beings to understand each other.   Joy Packer

The Fragment

A *fragment* is a construction which, like a sentence, begins with a capital and ends with full-stop punctuation, but which does not satisfy the traditional definition of a sentence.[1] While they are often serious grammatical faults, fragments can be used positively as a means of emphatic statement, drawing attention because of their difference:

And that's why there's really a very simple answer to our original question.
  What do baseball *managers* really do?
  Worry.
  Constantly.
  For a living.   Leonard Koppett

Going off her diet, she gained back all the weight she had lost. Also the friends.   Student

The Short Sentence

Short sentences are inherently emphatic. They will seem especially strong in the context of longer, more complicated statements. Often the contrast in length reinforces the contrast in thought:

As Thompson and the *Transcript* man had said, Vanzetti was naturally and quietly eloquent. So he was electrocuted.   Phil Strong

Again, it's an incontrovertible fact that, in the past, when contraceptive methods were unknown, women spent a much larger proportion of a much shorter life pregnant, or nursing infants whom they had borne with little or no medical help. And don't believe that that's a natural, a healthy thing for human beings to do, just because animals do it. It isn't.   Elizabeth Janeway

The Imperative Sentence

At its simplest the imperative sentence is a command:

Come here!
Listen to me!

Its distinguishing feature—usually—is that it drops the subject and begins with the verb, although some commands use a noun of address or an actual subject:

John, come here!
You listen to me!

  While commands are rare in composition, imperative sentences can be emphatic in other ways:

1. See page 112 for that definition.

Insist on yourself; never imitate.   Ralph Waldo Emerson

Let us spend one day as deliberately as Nature, and not be thrown off the track by every nutshell and mosquito's wing that falls on the rails.   Henry David Thoreau

Consider, for example, those skulls on the monuments.   Aldous Huxley

Aside from being strong, imperative sentences also link writer and reader. Emerson does not say "men and women must insist on themselves"; he addresses *you*. Thoreau urges *you* to participate in a new way of life, and Huxley invites *you* to look with him at the statuary he is examining. Huxley's sentence also illustrates another use of the imperative: moving readers easily from one point to another.

The Inverted Sentence

Inversion means putting the main elements of a sentence in an order other than subject-verb-object. Some patterns of inversion signal questions ("Are you going into town today?"); some signal condition contrary to fact ("Had I only been there"). Other inversional patterns indicate emphasis. The most frequent is the sentence that opens with an adverbial word or phrase (to which further modification may be attached) and follows it with the verb and subject:

And in one corner, book-piled like the rest of the furniture, stood a piano.
                                                                          Kenneth Grahame

Less commonly, emphatic inversion follows the pattern object-subject-verb:

Wrangles he avoided, and disagreeable persons he usually treated with a cold and freezing contempt.   Douglas Southall Freeman

Inversions are tricky, subject to subtle conventions of idiom, too numerous and complex to bother with here. If you aren't sure whether a particular inverted sentence will work, read it out loud and trust your ear. If it sounds un-English, it probably is.

The Interrupted Sentence

Normally a sentence moves from subject to verb to complement. Interruption breaks that flow by inserting constructions between the main elements and forcing pauses. As we shall see later in this chapter, interruption is an important means of emphasizing particular words. But it can also render an entire statement emphatic:

And finally, stammering a crude farewell, he departed.   Thomas Wolfe

The sentence could be expressed straightforwardly:

And he finally departed, stammering a crude farewell.

But while more natural, the revision is weaker. (Not therefore "poorer"; it depends on purpose.)

Interrupted movement makes demands on the reader, especially when the interrupting constructions grow numerous and long. But kept reasonably short and simple, interruption is an effective technique of emphasis.

The Periodic Sentence

A periodic sentence (sometimes called a *suspended* sentence) does not complete its main thought until the end:

If you really want to be original, to develop your own ideas in your own way, then maybe you shouldn't go to college.   Student

It differs from a loose sentence, which places its main clause at the beginning and then adds subordinate ideas:

Maybe you shouldn't go to college if you really want to be original, to develop your own ideas in your own way.

Periodic sentences can be constructed in various ways. Many are built by beginning the sentence with adverbials, like the "if"-clause in the example above. Others start off with a noun clause:

That John Chaucer was only an assistant seems certain.   John Gardner

That the author of Everyman was no mere artist, but an artist-philosopher, and that the artist-philosophers are the only sort of artists I take seriously will be no news to you.   George Bernard Shaw

However they are constructed, periodic sentences make stronger statements than do loose, requiring that we pay attention and suspend understanding until the final words pull everything together. But this type of sentence has limitations. It quickly grows tiresome, for the alertness it demands wearies readers. Furthermore, periodic structure has a formal, literary tone, unsuitable for informal occasions. Yet despite these limitations an occasional periodic sentence supplies valuable emphasis and has the further advantage of varying your style.

The Rhetorical Question

In discussing paragraphs (page 68) we saw that rhetorical questions can serve as topic sentences. They can also establish emphasis. Most emphatic rhetorical questions are, in effect, disguised assertions:

A desirable young man? Dust and ashes! What was there desirable in such a thing
as that?   Lytton Strachey

The question says, of course, that he was *not* "a desirable young man."

Some emphatic questions are more complicated in meaning, combining
an implicit avowal with an actual query:

Yet this need not be. The means are at hand to fulfill the age-old dream: poverty
can be abolished. How long shall we ignore this under-developed nation in our
midst? How long shall we look the other way while our fellow human beings
suffer? How long?   Michael Harrington

Even here, however, Harrington is trying not so much to elicit an answer
as he is to convince us that allowing poverty to continue is indefensible.
(Notice, incidentally, that each of those two examples also contains other
kinds of emphatic statement: short sentences, fragments, repetitions.)

Negative-Positive Restatement

Here emphasis is achieved by stating an idea twice, first in negative terms,
then in positive:

Color is not a human or personal reality; it is a political reality.   James Baldwin

This is more than poetic insight; it is hallucination.   J. C. Furnas

The poor are not like everyone else. They are a different kind of people. They think
and feel differently; they look upon a different America than the middle class looks
upon.   Michael Harrington

Generally the same sentence contains both the negative and the positive
statements (as in the first two examples here). In an extended passage, negative and positive may be expressed in separate sentences (the third example).

Less commonly the progression may be from positive to negative, as in
this sentence by G. K. Chesterton about social conventions:

Conventions may be cruel, they may be unsuitable, they may even be grossly superstitious or obscene, but there is one thing they never are. Conventions are never
dead.

All this could be put more briefly:

Although conventions may be cruel, unsuitable, or even grossly superstitious or
obscene, they are never dead.

But not put so well.

Rhythm and Rhyme

Rhythm—primarily a pattern of stressed and unstressed syllables—is an inevitable aspect of prose, though rarely as regular or as obvious as in poetry. Since rhythm of some sort is inescapable, good writers are aware of it and make it work for them. Later, in Chapter 22, we shall look at prose rhythm a bit more closely, considering how it is controlled and how it contributes to meaning. One contribution we touch upon here—emphasis. Probably the most common ways in which rhythm conveys emphasis are by clustered stresses and metrical runs.

A stressed syllable is spoken relatively loudly, an unstressed one more softly. Stressed syllables are marked by /, unstressed by x, as in

x   /
above.

A metrical run consists of a number of stressed and unstressed syllables recurring in a more or less regular pattern. This, of course, is common in poetry, but much less so in prose.

Clustered Stresses

x   /   /   /   x   x   /
The Big Bull Market was dead.   Frederick Lewis Allen
x   /   x   /   /   /   /   /   /   x
He speaks and thinks plain, broad, downright, English.   William Hazlitt

Clustering stresses simply means constructing a sentence so that three or four or more stressed syllables occur successively. Obviously such clustering cannot be extensive or frequent. Done skillfully, as in the examples above, it endows an idea with considerable importance. It can also contribute to meaning in subtle ways. For example, the rhythm of Allen's sentence reinforces the sense of unalterable finality conveyed by "dead."

Metrical Runs

x   /   /   /   x   x   /   x   /   x   x   /   x   /   x   /   x
For one brief moment the world was nothing but sea—the sight, the sound, the
/   x   /   x   /   x   /
smell, the touch, the taste of sea.   Sheila Kaye-Smith

The rhythmic regularity of that sentence not only makes it memorable but also enhances the emotional intensity of the experience.

Like clustered stresses, metrical runs cannot be maintained for very long or employed very often. Otherwise prose begins to sound awkwardly poetic. It is a mistake, however, to suppose that such passages have no place in prose, that prose must avoid any rhythmic effects at all. As we suggested, rhythm is *always* there, but it should be unobtrusive, directing a reader's response, but without drawing attention to itself.

Rhyme
Rhyme, the repetition of identical or very similar sounds, is, like rhythm,
a technique we associate more with poetry than with prose. When it does
occur in prose it is usually a way of emphasizing particular words within
the sentence (we shall see examples later in the chapter). Occasionally,
however, rhyme serves to unify and emphasize an entire sentence, most
commonly in the form of alliteration (the repetition of successive or near-
successive initial sounds):

Reason will be replaced by Revelation.   W. H. Auden

Emphasis Within the Sentence

Emphatic sentences are only occasionally needed. But it is usually necessary to establish appropriate emphasis upon particular words within the
sentence. Good writers do this subtly. Rather than scattering exclamation
points, underlinings, and capitals, they rely chiefly upon the selection and
positioning of words.

Modifiers

Modifiers are an important source of emphasis. A special class called *inten-*
sives do nothing but stress the term they modify: *great, greatly, extremely,*
much, very, terribly, awfully, and many, many more. But on the whole
intensives are not very satisfactory. They quickly become devalued, leading
to a never-ending search for fresh words. Imaginative writers can and do
discover unusual and effective ones, as in this description of the modern
superstate:

These moloch gods, these monstrous states. . . .   Susanne K. Langer

Still it is best not to rely upon intensives as a primary device of emphasis.

Pairing and Piling Modifiers
As we shall see in a few pages, adjectives and adverbs can be made emphatic by where they are placed and how they are punctuated. But aside
from that, they may be paired and piled up (that is, grouped in units of
two or of three or more). Here are a few instances of paired modifiers:

They [a man's children] are his for a brief and passing season.   Margaret Mead

This antiquated and indefensible notion that young people have no rights until they
are twenty-one . . .   Evelyn Jones

[Lady Mary Wortley Montague was like] a dilapidated macaw with a hard, piercing
laugh, mirthless and joyless, with a few unimaginative phrases, with a parrot's powers
of observation and a parrot's hard and poisonous bite.   Edith Sitwell

Working as a team, paired adjectives impress themselves upon the reader. And they often do more, reinforcing a point by restatement ("a brief and passing season") or suggesting subtle contrasts and amplifications of meaning, as Sitwell's sentence leads us to think about the distinction between "mirth" and "joy" and about how a laugh can be both "hard" and "piercing."

Adjectives may also be accumulated in groups of three or more; as in this description of an Irish-American family:

. . . a wilful, clannish, hard-drinking, fornicating tribe.   William Gibson

Or this one of a neighbor taking a singing lesson:

A vile beastly rottenheaded foolbegotten brazenthroated pernicious piggish screaming, tearing, roaring, perplexing, splitmecrackle crashmegiggle insane ass . . . is practicing howling below-stairs with a brute of a singingmaster so horribly, that my head is nearly off.   Edmund Lear

Passages like these, especially the second, are virtuoso performances in which exaggeration becomes its own end. Of course, exposition cannot indulge itself like this very often. But sobriety needs relief, and verbal exuberance dazzles and delights. Whatever may be the objective truth of such fusillades of modifiers, they bring us into startling contact with the thoughts and feelings of the writer—that is the essence of communication.

Position

Two positions in a clause or sentence are more emphatic than any others—the opening and the closing. Elsewhere emphasis must depend on inversion, isolation, modification, restatement, and so forth. (Of course these techniques may work in harness with positioning to give even greater strength to opening and closing words.)

Opening with key words has much to recommend it. Immediately, readers see what is important. E. M. Forster, for example, begins a paragraph on "curiosity" with the following sentence, identifying his topic at once:

Curiosity is one of the lowest human faculties.

Putting the essential idea first is natural, suited to a style aiming at the simplicity and directness of forceful speech:

Great blobs of rain fall. Rumble of thunder. Lightning streaking blue on the building.   J. P. Donleavy

Donleavy's sentences mirror the immediacy of the experience, going at once to what dominates his perception—the heavy feel of rain, thunder, lightning. (The two fragments also enhance the forcefulness of the passage.)

Beginning (or ending) with the principal idea is advantageous in developing a contrast, which is strengthened if the following clause or sentence opens with the opposing term:

Science was traditionally aristocratic, speculative, intellectual in intent; technology was lower-class, empirical, action-oriented.   Lynn White, Jr.

Postponing a major point to the end of the sentence is more formal and literary. The writer must have the entire sentence in mind from the first word. On the other hand, the final position is more emphatic than the opening, perhaps because we remember best what we have read last:

So the great gift of symbolism, which is the gift of reason, is at the same time the seat of man's peculiar weakness—the danger of lunacy.   Susanne K. Langer

Like the opening position, the closing is also useful for reinforcing contrasts and iterations:

We can never forget that everything Hitler did in Germany was "legal" and everything the Hungarian freedom fighters did was "illegal."   Martin Luther King, Jr.

But Marx was not only a social scientist; he was a reformer.   W. T. Jones

Inexperienced writers often waste the final position. Consider, for instance, how much more effective is the revision of this statement:

As the military power of Kafiristan increases, so too does the pride that Dravot has.
REVISION: As the military power of Kafiristan increases, so too does Dravot's pride.

In topic sentences, finally, the closing position is often reserved for the idea the paragraph will develop (if it can be done without awkwardness). Here, for instance, is the opening sentence of a paragraph about Welsh Christianity:

The third legacy of the Romans was Welsh Christianity.   George Macaulay Trevelyan

Isolation

An isolated word or phrase is cut off by punctuation. It can occur anywhere in the sentence but is most common—and most effective—at the beginning or end, positions, as we have seen, emphatic in themselves:

Leibnitz, it has sometimes been said, was the last man to know everything.
                                                                        Colin Cherry

Children, curled in little balls, slept on straw scattered on wagon beds.
                                                                    Sherwood Anderson

If the King notified his pleasure that a briefless lawyer should be made a judge or that a libertine baronet should be made a peer, the gravest counsellors, after a little murmuring, submitted. Thomas Babington Macaulay

And then, you will recall, he [Henry Thoreau] told of being present at the auction of a deacon's effects and of noticing, among the innumerable odds and ends representing the accumulation of a lifetime, a dried tapeworm. E. B. White

It is also possible to use both ends of a sentence. See how neatly this sentence isolates and emphasizes the two key terms "position" and "difficult":

The position—if poets must have positions, other than upright—of the poet born in Wales or of Welsh parentage and writing his poems in English is today made by many people unnecessarily, and trivially, difficult. Dylan Thomas

Isolating a word or phrase in the middle of the sentence is less common but by no means rare:

I was late for class—inexcusably so—and had forgotten my homework.
Emily Brown

Whether the isolated expression comes first, last, or in between, it must be set off by commas, dashes, or a colon. (As isolating marks, colons never go around words within a sentence; usually they precede something at the end, though they may also follow an initial word.) Generally, dashes mark a longer pause than commas and hence imply stronger stress: "Suddenly—it began to rain" emphasizes the adverb a little more than does "Suddenly, it began to rain." A colon before a closing term is stronger than a comma, but about the same as a dash.

Isolation involves more, however, than just punctuating a word or phrase you wish to emphasize. The isolation must occur at a place allowed by the conventions of English grammar. In the following sentence "Harry" may properly be split from its verb and isolated by an intruding adverbial phrase:

Harry, it was clear, was not the man for the job.

But it would be un-English arbitrarily to place a comma between "Harry" and the verb:

Harry, was not the man for the job.

The emphasis gained by isolation—like emphasis in general—does more than merely add strength to particular words: it conveys nuances of meaning. Suppose, for instance, that the sentence by Macaulay quoted above were to end like this:

. . . the gravest counsellors submitted, after a little murmuring.

The words are the same and the grammar and the logic, but not the implications. Macaulay, while admitting that the counsellors of Charles II occasionally protested, stresses their submissiveness; the revision, while acknowledging that they submitted, makes their protest more important. In short, the two sentences evaluate the king's ministers differently.

As one final example of how isolation can endow a word with special meaning, read this sentence by Lewis Thomas:

There was a quarter-page advertisement in *The London Observer* for a computer service that will enmesh your name in an electronic network of fifty thousand other names, sort out your tastes, preferences, habits, and deepest desires and match them up with opposite numbers, and retrieve for you, within a matter of seconds, friends.

Balance

A balanced sentence (see pages 128 ff.) divides into roughly equal parts on either side of a central pause. Usually the pause is marked by a comma or other stop, though now and then it may be unpunctuated. The halves of a balanced sentence are often independent clauses, but sometimes one will be a dependent clause or even a long phrase. In any case, the two parts must be roughly the same in length and of comparable significance, although they need not be of the same grammatical order.

In balanced construction words are stressed by being positioned so that they are played against one another:

It is a sort of cold extravagance; and it has made him all his enemies.
G. K. Chesterton

Till he had a wife he could do nothing; and when he had a wife he did whatever she chose.   Thomas Babington Macaulay

Chesterton draws our attention to the connection between a "cold extravagance" and making "enemies." Macaulay, playing "do nothing" against "did whatever she chose," comments wryly on the freedom of the married man.

Polysyndeton and Asyndeton

Despite their formidable names, polysyndeton and asyndeton are nothing more than different ways of handling a list or series. *Polysyndeton* places a conjunction *(and, or)* after every term in the list (except, of course, the last). *Asyndeton* uses no conjunctions and separates the terms of the list with commas. Both differ from the conventional treatment of lists and series, which is to use only commas between all items except the last two, these being joined by a conjunction (with or without a comma—it is optional):

CONVENTIONAL   We stopped on the way to camp and bought supplies: bread,
                   butter, cheese, hamburger, hot dogs, and beer.
POLYSYNDETON   We stopped on the way to camp and bought supplies: bread and
                   butter and cheese and hamburger and hot dogs and beer.
ASYNDETON   We stopped on the way to camp and bought supplies: bread,
                   butter, cheese, hamburger, hot dogs, beer.

The conventional treatment of a series emphasizes no particular item, though the last may seem a little more important. In polysyndeton emphasis falls more evenly upon each member of the series, and also more heavily:

It was bright and clean and polished.   Alfred Kazin

It is the season of suicide and divorce and prickly dread, whenever the wind blows.   Joan Didion

In asyndeton too the series takes on more significance as a whole than it does in the conventional pattern. But the stress on each individual item is lighter than in polysyndeton, and the passage moves more quickly:

His care, his food, his shelter, his education—all of these were by-products of his parents' position.   Margaret Mead

Polysyndeton and asyndeton do not necessarily improve a series. Most of the time the usual treatment is more appropriate. However, when you do wish a different emphasis remember that polysyndeton and asyndeton exist.

Repetition

In a strict sense, repetition is a matter more of diction than of sentence structure. But since it is one of the most valued means of emphasis we shall include it here.

Repetition is sometimes a virtue and sometimes a fault. Drawing the line is not easy. It depends on what is being repeated. Important ideas can stand repetition; unimportant ones cannot. When you write the same word (or idea) twice, you draw the reader's attention to it. If it is a key idea, fine. But if not, then you have awkwardly implied importance to something that does not matter very much. In the following examples, of course, we are concerned with positive repetition, involving major ideas.

Repetition may take two basic forms: restating the same idea in different terms (called *tautologia* by Greek rhetoricians) and repeating the same exact word (or a variant form of the same word).

Tautologia
In tautologia the synonyms are frequently stronger than the original term:

That's camouflage, that's trickery, that's treachery, window-dressing.   Malcolm X

A second term need not be strictly synonymous with the first, and often it is not. Rather than simply restating the idea, the new terms may add shades of meaning:

October 7 began as a commonplace enough day, one of those days that sets the teeth on edge with its tedium, its small frustrations.   Joan Didion

One clings to chimeras, by which one can only be betrayed, and the entire hope—the entire possibility—of freedom disappears.   James Baldwin

In Didion's sentence "frustrations" signifies a worse condition than "tedium," but the ideas relate to the extent that tedium may contribute to frustration. In Baldwin's, "possibility" implies a deeper despair.

Now and then, a writer uses an expression just so he or she can replace it with another:

That consistent stance, repeatedly adopted, must mean one of two—no, three—things.   John Gardner

Finally, repetition of an idea may involve simile or metaphor:[2]

It follows that any struggle against the abuse of language is a sentimental archaism, like preferring candles to electric light or hansom cabs to aeroplanes.   George Orwell

In [Henry] James nothing is forestalled, nothing is obvious; one is forever turning the curve of the unexpected.   James Huneker

The image contained in a simile or metaphor often both clarifies and emphasizes an idea by translating it into more concrete or familiar terms. Consider Orwell's sentence. (Incidentally, he is paraphrasing a view he does *not* agree with; he believes that abuses of language *should* be struggled against.) We cannot *see* a "sentimental archaism" (we may not even know what one is). But, familiar with candles and electric light, we can understand that a preference for candles is somehow perverse. And Huneker, practicing the very quality he praises in the novelist Henry James, startles us by the unexpectedness of his metaphor.

Repeating the Same Word
This is a very effective means of emphasis and susceptible to considerable variation. Greek and Roman rhetoricians distinguished about two dozen

2. A simile is a literal comparison commonly introduced by *like* or *as:* Robert Burns's famous line "my luv is like a red, red rose" contains a simile. A metaphor is a literal identification, as if Burns had written "my luv is a red, red rose." Sometimes metaphors simply use the second term to mean the first: "my red, red rose" = "my luv."

varieties of verbal repetition, depending on the positions and forms of the repeated terms. For example, the words may begin successive clauses, or end them, or even end one and begin the next; the words may be repeated side by side, or three or four times, or in variant forms. In ancient rhetoric each pattern had its own learned name. We needn't bother with those here. But you should realize that the patterns themselves are still very much in use. Nor are they used only by writers consciously imitating the classics. They are at home in the prose of men and women who belong to our world and have something to say about it. The patterns of repetition remain vital because we enjoy unusual and clever combinations. Here, then, are some examples of skillful verbal repetition, which not only emphasize important words but also are interesting and entertaining in themselves:

To philosophize is to understand; to understand is to explain oneself; to explain is to relate.
                                                                                    Brand Blanshard

I didn't like the swimming pool, I didn't like swimming, and I didn't like the swimming instructor, and after all these years I still don't.
                                                                                    James Thurber

When that son leaves home, he throws himself with an intensity which his children will not know into the American way of life; he eats American, talks American, he will be American or nothing.
                                                                                    Margaret Mead

I am neat, scrupulously neat, in regard to the things I care about; but a book, as a book, is not one of those things.
                                                                                    Max Beerbohm

Problem gives rise to problem.   Robert Louis Stevenson

Life is tragic simply because the earth turns and the sun inexorably rises and sets, and one day, for each of us, the sun will go down for the last, last time.
                                                                                    James Baldwin

She smiled a little smile and bowed a little bow.   Anthony Trollope

Visitors whom he [Ludovico Sforza, a Renaissance duke] desired to impress were invariably ushered into the Sala del Tesoro, they rubbed their eyes, he rubbed his hands, they returned home blinded, he remained at home blind.   Ralph Roeder

(While the literal meanings of "rubbed" are the same, their implications differ. Sforza's guests rubbed their eyes dazzled and amazed by his riches; he rubbed his hands proudly satisfied. Their blindness was a blurring of vision; his, a blindness of spirit.)

The average autochthonous Irishman is close to patriotism because he is close to the earth; he is close to domesticity because he is close to the earth; he is close to doctrinal theology and elaborate ritual because he is close to the earth.
                                                                                    G. K. Chesterton

Mr. and Mrs. Veneering were bran-new people in a bran-new house in a bran-new quarter of London. Everything about the Veneerings was spick and span new.
                                                                                    Charles Dickens

If there had never been a danger to our constitution there would never have been a constitution to be in danger.   Herbert Butterfield

(This is a frequent pattern of repetition called *chiasmus* or *antimetable*. It involves two terms set in the order *X–Y* in the first clause and in the order *Y–X* in the second.)

Mechanical Emphasis

Mechanical emphasis consists of exclamation points and of printing or writing words in an unusual way. Italic type is probably the most common method of calling attention to a word or phrase. (In handwriting or typing, the equivalent to italics is a single underline.)

It is so simple a fact and one that is so hard, apparently, to grasp: *Whoever debases others is debasing himself.*
                                                                      James Baldwin

Yet this government never of itself furthered any enterprise, but by the alacrity with which it got out of its way. *It* does not keep the country free. *It* does not settle the west. *It* does not educate.
                                                                      Henry David Thoreau

Worse yet, he must accept—how often!—poverty and solitude.
                                                                      Ralph Waldo Emerson

Other devices of mechanical emphasis include quotation marks, capital letters, boldface and other changes in the style or size of type, different colored links, wider spacing of words or letters, and lineation—placing key words or phrases on separate lines. Advertisements reveal how well all these techniques work.

In composition, however, they work less effectively. An experienced writer does not call upon exclamation points or underlining very often. They quickly lose their value, revealing that one does not know how to create emphasis and so has shouted.

Certainly in the examples above the italics and the exclamation point are effective. But in each case the mechanical device merely strengthens an emphasis already attained by more compositional means. Baldwin's sentence puts the key idea last and carefully prepares its way with a colon. Thoreau draws our attention to "it" not only by using italics but by repeating the word at the beginning of three brief, emphatic sentences. And Emerson stresses "how often" more by isolating it than by the exclamation point.

CHAPTER 22

The Well-Written Sentence: (3) Rhythm

When things that we see or hear are repeated in identical or similar patterns the result is rhythm. In prose there are two patterns, both involving words, or more exactly the sounds of words. The most obvious is *syllabic rhythm*, consisting of loud and soft syllables. Loud syllables are said to be *stressed* and for purposes of analysis are marked by /; soft syllables are *unstressed* and marked x.[1] Writers create syllabic rhythm by arranging stresses and nonstresses in more or less regular patterns, as in:

```
x   /   x  /    x   /     x    /
A lucky few escaped the fire.
```

The second pattern is *rhythmic intonation*. Intonation is a change in the pitch of the voice, a kind of melody important in speaking. Think, for example, of how many shades of meaning you can give to the words *yes* and *no*, not only by loudness and softness but by altering the rise and fall of your voice. Rhythm based on intonation is created by repeating phrases or clauses of similar construction so that the same "melody" plays several times. Here is an instance from a poem by Alfred Tennyson:

The long day wanes; the slow moon climbs; the deep
moans round with many voices.

---

1. Distinguishing only two degrees of loudness and softness is arbitrary. In actual speech innumerable gradations exist. However, limiting the number to two is convenient. Sometimes an intermediate stage, called *secondary stress,* is distinguished and marked `. The process of analyzing syllabic rhythm is called *scansion.*

We hear this sentence as a three-part construction with an identical pattern of intonation in the first two clauses. The third repeats the melody in the first four words but varies it in the concluding phrase. Intonational rhythm coexists with syllabic. Thus Tennyson's lines also show an almost perfect alternation of stressed and unstressed syllables:

```
x    /  \      /    x   /   \    /      x    /
The long day wanes; the slow moon climbs; the deep
 \     /   x   / x  /  x
Moans round with many voices.
```

Finally a word of caution: there is an inevitable subjective element in rhythm, which is, after all, something we hear. Even sensitive, experienced readers do not all "hear" the same sentence in exactly the same way. We cannot say, however, that rhythm is purely a matter of perception, different for each one of us. Writers can—and good writers do—regulate what their readers hear, not completely, but within fairly clear limits.

Effective Rhythm

Rhythm is effective when it pleases the ear. Even more important, good rhythm enters into what a sentence says, enhancing and reinforcing its meaning. A necessary condition of effective rhythm is that a passage be laid out in clear syntactic units (phrases, clauses, whole sentences); that these have something in common (length, intonation, grammatical structure); and that there be a loose but discernible pattern of stressed and unstressed syllables. Generally the syntactic units, while showing some similarities, are very far from exactly the same. Nor are the syllables laid out in precisely repeated patterns. In this respect prose rhythm is much looser than that of traditional accented poetry, which has a much more predictable arrangement of stressed and unstressed syllables.

Here are two examples of rhythm in prose:

```
    x    x  x   /  x  x  /  /    x  x   /   x  x   /  x  x  x    /   x   /
There was a magic, and a spell, and a curse; but the magic has been waved away,
   x   x    /   x  x  x    /    x x  /  x   /  x   /   x   /
and the spell broken, and the curse was a curse of sleep and not of pain.
                                                                    R. L. Duffus

   x    x   /  x  x   /  x   x   /   x   x / x   x    /     x    x   /
We came up on the railway beyond the canal. It went straight toward the town
 x  /  x  /   /    x   x   /  x  /  x x  / x  /  x  x   /  x  /
across the low fields. We could see the line of the other railway ahead of us.
                                                                    Ernest Hemingway
```

Duffus's sentence moves in carefully articulated parts: two primary clauses separated by the semicolon, and, within each of these, three secondary units marked by commas. Each of the six units has a similar pattern of stressed and unstressed syllables, a pattern regular enough to be sensed, yet not so relentless that it dominates the sentence, turning it into singsong. In the passage by Hemingway the basic units are simple sentences.

The syllabic rhythm is less obvious than in Duffus's case, partly because Hemingway's sentences are not further broken up and partly because the pattern of stresses and nonstresses is a bit more irregular.

Awkward Rhythm

Poor rhythm usually results from either or both of two causes: (1) the sentence is not organized so that phrases and clauses create a pattern out of which rhythm can evolve; (2) syllables are poorly grouped, being either so irregular that no pattern at all can be grasped, or so unrelievedly regular that a steady, obtrusive beat overrides everything else.

Consider this example of poor rhythm:

Each party promises before the election to make the city bigger and better, but what happens after the election?

There are two problems: first, the initial clause does not break into well-defined groups. This fault can be corrected by changing the position of the adverbial phrase, using it as a sentence opener or as an interrupter, and in either case punctuating it:

Before the election, each party promises to make the city bigger and better. . . .
Each party, before the election, promises to make the city bigger and better. . . .

Now the clause is organized into potential rhythmic units.

The second fault is that the writer has mixed a statement and a question in the same sentence. The different intonations clash, leaving the ear dissatisfied. It would be wiser to place the ideas in separate sentences:

Before the election, each party promises to make the city bigger and better. But what happens after the election?

Other improvements might be made. For instance, shortening the question to "But what happens afterwards?" would make it less repetitious and more emphatic. But just as it stands, adding no words and taking none away, our revision shows that poor rhythm can often be improved simply by rearranging the words.

Sometimes, however, mere rearrangement is not enough. Consider this case:

```
x   /   x   /   x   x x   /   x   /   x   /   x   /   x   /   x   /   x
The man was standing on the stairs and far below we saw the boy, who wore an
 /   x   /   x   /   x   /
old, unpressed, and ragged suit.
```

The sentence has one of the same difficulties as the first example: it needs to be divided more clearly (or at least its first two clauses do). But it also has a different problem: its syllabic rhythm is too regular. With one excep-

tion the sentence scans as a series of unvaried iambs.[2] The regularity dominates the sentence, obscuring shadings of emphasis.

If the iambic pattern is made less relentless the sentence sounds much
better:

```
 x    /    /   x  x    /    /  x  /    x   /   x    /      /    x   x  /
The man stood on the stairs; far below we saw the boy, dressed in an old,
 x    /    /   x   /
unpressed, ragged suit.
```

The changes—substituting "stood" for "was standing" and "dressed"
for "who wore," and replacing two "ands" with a semicolon and a comma—
break up the excessive sameness of the syllabic beat. Yet they leave pattern
enough to please the ear. Furthermore, the clustered stresses now focus the
reader's attention upon key points:

```
 /     /       /      /       /   x   /    /   x   /
man stood . . . boy dressed . . . old, unpressed, ragged suit
```

Meaningful Rhythm

Good rhythm enters into the meaning of the sentence, not only reinforcing
the words but often giving them nuances they might not otherwise have.

Mimetic Rhythm

Mimetic means "imitative." Mimetic rhythm imitates the perception a sentence describes or the feeling or ideas it conveys:

```
 x    /    /  x    /     /       /   x   / x  x    x   x /   x   /
The tide reaches flood stage, slackens, hesitates, and begins to ebb.
```
                                                                            Rachel Carson

The flowing tide is suggested by the very movement of this sentence, which
runs smoothly and uninterruptedly to a midpoint, slows down, pauses (the
commas), and then picks up and runs to its end. Here is a similar, somewhat longer, sentence about Niagara Falls:

```
 x  x    /    x  x  / x  x   / x   /     x   /  x   x  /   x    /    x   / x    /
On the edge of disaster the river seems to gather herself, to pause, to lift a head
 /   x  x  / x   x    /     x   x  /    /   x   x   /   x  x x x / x  /   x
noble in ruin, and then, with a slow grandeur, to plunge into the eternal thunder
 x     /     / x  x /
and white chaos below.
```
                                                                            Rupert Brooke

Mimetic rhythm may also imply ideas more abstract than physical movement, as in this passage describing the life of peasants:

```
                                                                 x    /
2. An *iamb* is a unit of two syllables, a nonstress and a stress, as in the word *above*. The one
                                                     x    x x    /
exception in the example is the four syllables "-ing on the stairs."
```

```
/      /      /     /      /      /     x  / x x    /       / x  /   x  /   x    x    /      /
```
Black bread, rude roof, dark night, laborious day, weary arm at sunset; and life ebbs
```
x   /
```
away.

The six unrelieved stresses at the beginning mirror the dreary monotony of the peasant's existence. Then nonstressed syllables become more numerous and the sentence picks up speed and runs to a close, just as life slips away (in Ruskin's view) from the peasant before he has held and savored it.

Metrical Runs

A metrical run is a relatively regular pattern of stresses and nonstresses. This is, of course, a feature of traditional poetry, but not common in prose. It is, as we have seen, a fault when it is not controlled. But used with restraint and skill, metrical runs are effective. Though not specifically meaningful, like mimetic rhythms, they make a sentence memorable and intensify its mood and meaning:

```
x   /   x  /   x   /   x     /   x    /    x  x    /   x    /
```
I love to lie in bed and read the lives of the Popes of Rome.   Logan Pearsall Smith

```
 /    x x   /  x x   x    /    x    /    x x   /    x  /    x   x  /    x   x
```
This is a story about love and death in the golden land, and begins with the
```
 /   x
```
country.
                                                                          Joan Didion

Smith and Didion achieve their metrical runs in part by using prepositional phrases. A typical prepositional phrase consists of a one- or two-syllable preposition, a noun marker (a, an, the, this, that, and so on), and an object of (usually) one or two syllables. Neither the preposition nor the marker is stressed, while the object (or one of its syllables) is, so that one of these metrical patterns is likely:

```
  x      /
```
at home
```
  x   x      /
```
in the house
```
  x   x     /   x
```
in the morning
```
  x   x   x    /
```
in the event

Such metrical patterns (or "meters") are said to be *rising* since the stress comes at or near the end. By adding modifiers or doubling the objects of a preposition or stringing together several phrases, it is possible to sustain a rising pattern over the whole or a portion of a sentence:

```
 x    x   /    x    /   x  x    /   x   /
```
about love and death in the golden land

Sometimes a metrical run occurs at the end of a sentence, bringing it neatly to a close:

Smoke lowering from chimneypots, making a soft black drizzle, with flakes of soot
                                                                              x
in it as big as full grown snow-flakes—gone into mourning, one might imagine, for
 x   /   x x   /
the death of the sun.   Charles Dickens

                                                  /   x   x   /   x   /   x
Beyond the blue hills, within riding distance, there is a country of parks and beeches
     x   /   x x   /   /   /
with views of the far-off sea.   Logan Pearsall Smith

                                                            x   /   x
There was the sea, sheer under me, and it looked grey and grim, and streaked with
 x   /   x x   /   x
the white of our smother.   John Masefield

To work at all, metrical runs must be uncommon. Their effect is subtly to draw our attention. Responding unconsciously to the rhythm, we feel that a sentence is important and we are more likely to remember it. Certainly a metrical run will not dignify something silly, but it will help us to think about something important.

Rhythmic Breaks

One advantage of maintaining a fairly regular rhythm is that you can alter it for special effect:

 x   /   x   x   /   x x   /   x   /   /   x x   /
The roses have faded at Malmaison, nipped by the frost.   Amy Lowell

There are four rising meters up to the comma, then an unexpected stress upon "nipped," which throws great weight upon that word, making it the center of the sentence. And it is a key word, for the sentence alludes to the sad story of Josephine, Napoleon's first wife, who was divorced by him for political reasons and who retired to her palatial home of Malmaison, famous for its roses.

And look, finally, once again at the sentence by Logan Pearsall Smith, quoted above:

 x   /   x   /   /   x x / x   /   x   x   x x   /   x x   /   x   /   x
Beyond the blue hills, within riding distance, there is a country of parks and beeches
     x   /   x x   /   /   /
with views of the far-off sea.

The rising meters which run throughout most of the sentence abruptly change at the end to three clustered stresses, making the "far-off sea" the climax of the vision.

Rhyme

Rhyme is the repetition of sounds in positions close enough to be noticed. It is not an aspect of rhythm; even so we shall glance at it. We associate rhyme chiefly with poetry, especially in the form of end rhyme—the closing of successive or alternate lines with the same sound:

The grave's a fine and private place,
But none, I think, do there embrace.
Andrew Marvell

Poetry also often uses inner rhyme—repeating sounds within a line, as with the *a* and *i* vowels and the *p*'s of Marvell's first line.

Despite its association with poetry, rhyme occurs in prose, usually as inner rhyme (prose writers rarely end sentences or clauses with the same sound). Like rhythm, rhyme can affect the ear both pleasantly and unpleasantly, and it can enhance meaning.

It seems unlikely that sounds have inherent, culture-free significance in themselves. Particular sounds may acquire loose meanings; for example, we seem to associate the *ee* sound with smallness *(teeny, weeny)*. But psychologists who have studied this phenomenon think that such "meanings" are culturally conditioned and will vary from one group to another.

Even if language sounds do not possess inherent universal meanings, it remains the fact that within a particular culture certain sounds can evoke particular attitudes. Even here, however, one must be careful in talking about "meaning." Such meaning is broad and resists precise interpretation. In the following description by Mark Twain of a town on the Mississippi, the frequent *l* sounds, the *s*'s, the *m*'s, and the *n*'s probably contribute to the sense of peace and quiet. Words like *lull, lullaby, loll, slow, silent, ssh, shush,* and *hush* have conditioned us to associate those sounds with quietness. But that is about all we can say.

After all these years I can picture that old time to myself now, just as it was then: the white town drowsing in the sunshine of a summer's morning; the streets empty or pretty nearly so; one or two clerks sitting in front of the Water Street stores, with their splint-bottomed chairs tilted back against the walls, chins on breasts, hats slouched over their faces, asleep—with shingle shavings enough around to show what broke them down; a sow and a litter of pigs loafing along the sidewalk, doing a good business in watermelon rinds and seeds; two or three lonely little freight piles scattered about the "levee"; a pile of "skids" on the slope of the stone-paved wharf, and the fragrant town drunkard asleep in the shadow of them; two or three wood flats at the head of the wharf, but nobody to listen to the peaceful lapping of the wavelets against them; the great Mississippi, the majestic, the magnificent Mississippi, rolling its mile-wide tide along, shining in the sun; the "point" above the town, and the "point" below, bounding the river-glimpse and turning it into a sort of sea, and withal a very still and brilliant and lonely one.

If we do not insist upon interpreting their "meaning" too exactly, then, it is fair to say that sounds can convey or reinforce certain moods.

They may also contribute to meaning in another, less direct way. By rhyming key words, writers draw attention to them. Here, for instance, Virginia Woolf intensifies an image by repeating *s* sounds and by the alliteration of the *h*'s and the *c*'s:

Dust swirls down the avenue, hisses and hurries like erected cobras round the corners.

And in the following case the writer emphasizes "wilderness" by repeating *w* and "decay" by repeating *d:*

Otherwise the place is bleakly uninteresting; a wilderness of wind-swept grasses and sinewy weeds waving away from a thin beach ever speckled with drift and decaying things—worm-ridden timbers, dead porpoises.   Lafcadio Hearn

Yet prose rhyme is risky. Hearn succeeds, but the alliteration (and other rhyme) in these passages seems a bit much:

Her eyes were full of proud and passionless lust after gold and blood; her hair, close and curled, seems ready to shudder in sunder and divide into snakes.
                                                                                    Algernon Charles Swinburne

His boots are tight, the sun is hot, and he may be shot.   Amy Lowell

Excesses like this have led some people to damn and blast all rhyme in prose. Undoubtedly a little goes a long way. But it does have a place. The trick is to keep the rhyme unobtrusive, so that it directs our responses without our being aware of its influence. Certain things should be avoided: obvious and jingling rhyme or inadvertent repetitions of sound that draw attention to unimportant words. More positively, rhyme pleases the ear and makes us more receptive to what the sentence says, as in this passage by John Donne (a seventeenth-century poet who also wrote great prose):

One dieth at his full strength, being wholly at ease, and in quiet, and another dieth in the bitterness of his soul, and never eats with pleasure; but they lie down alike in the dust and the worm covers them.

Thus rhyme is—or can be—a positive element in prose. It is less important, and less common, than rhythm, but it is far from negligible. Too great a concern with sound, too much "tone painting," is a fault in prose (in poetry too, for that matter). Controlled by a sensitive ear, however, the sounds of a sentence can enrich its meaning.

CHAPTER 23

The Well-Written Sentence: (4) Variety

The Art Cinema is a movie theater in Hartford. Its speciality is showing foreign films. The theater is rated quite high as to the movies it shows. The movies are considered to be good art.   Student

The Smith disclosures shocked [President] Harding not into political housecleaning but into personal reform. The White House poker parties were abandoned. He told his intimates that he was "off liquor." Nan Britton [Harding's mistress] had already been banished to Europe. His nerve was shaken. He lost his taste for revelry. The plans for the Alaska trip were radically revised. Instead of an itinerant whoopee, it was now to be a serious political mission.   Samuel Hopkins Adams

Both of those passages consist chiefly of short, simple sentences. The first uses them poorly, the second effectively. Where does the difference lie? The first writer has not grasped the twin principles of recurrence and variety which govern sentence style. Adams, a professional author, understands them very well.

Recurrence means repeating a basic sentence pattern. *Variety* means changing the pattern. Paradoxical as it sounds, good sentence style must do both. Enough sameness must appear in the sentences to make the writing seem all of a piece; enough difference to create interest.

How much recurrence, how much variety depend on subject and purpose. For instance, when you repeat the same point or develop a series of parallel ideas, the similarity of subject justifies—and is enhanced by—similarity of sentence structure. Thus Adams repeats the same pattern in his second through seventh sentences because they have much the same content, detailing the steps President Harding took to divert the scandal threatening his administration. Here the recurrent style evolves from the subject.

In the other passage, however, the writer makes no such connection between style and subject, and so the recurrence seems awkward and monotonous. The ideas expressed in the separate sentences are not of the same order of value. For example, the fact that the theater is in Hartford is less important than that it shows foreign films. The sentence style, in other words, does not reinforce the writer's ideas; it obscures them.

Nor has the writer offered any relief from his short, straightforward statements. Adams has. Moreover, Adams uses variety effectively to structure his paragraph, opening with a relatively long sentence, which, though grammatically simple, is complicated by the correlative "not . . . but" construction. And he closes the paragraph by beginning a sentence, for the first time, with something other than the subject.

Adams's brief sentences work because the subject justifies them and because they are sufficiently varied. Lacking similar justification or relief, the four sentences of the first passage are ineffective. They could be improved easily:

The Art Cinema, a movie theater in Hartford, specializes in foreign films. It is noted for the high quality of its films; in fact, many people consider them good art.

There is still recurrence: in effect the passage consists of three similar short clauses plus an appositive. But now there is more variety. In the first sentence an appositive interrupts subject and verb; in the second there are two clauses instead of one, the latter opening with the phrase "in fact." Subordinating the information about Hartford also keeps the focus where it belongs, on the films.

Of course, in composing a sentence that differs from others, a writer is more concerned with emphasis than with variety. But if it is usually a by-product, variety is nonetheless important, an essential condition of interesting, readable prose. Let us consider, then, a few ways in which variety may be attained.

Changing Sentence Length and Pattern

From the beginning she had known what she wanted, and proceeded single-minded, with the force of a steam engine towards her goal. There was never a moment's doubt or regret. She wanted the East; and from the moment she set eyes on Richard Burton, with his dark Arabic face, his "questing panther eyes," he was, for her, that lodestar East, the embodiment of all her thoughts. Man and land were identified.   Lesley Blanch

It is not necessary, or even desirable, to maintain a strict alternation of long and short statements. You need only an occasional brief sentence to change the pace of predominately long ones, or a long sentence now and then in a passage composed chiefly of short ones:

We took a hair-raising taxi ride into the city. The rush-hour traffic of Bombay is a nightmare—not from dementia, as in Tokyo; nor from exuberance, as in Rome; not from malice, as in Paris; it is a chaos rooted in years of practiced confusion, absent-mindedness, selfishness, inertia, and an incomplete understanding of mechanics. There are no discernible rules.   James Cameron

Dave Beck was hurt. Dave Beck was indignant. He took the fifth amendment when he was questioned and was forced off the executive board of the AFL-CIO, but he retained enough control of his own union treasury to hire a stockade of lawyers to protect him. Prosecution dragged in the courts. Convictions were appealed. Delay.   John Dos Passos

Sometimes variation in length can be used to emphasize a key idea. In the following passage the historian Herbert Butterfield moves through two long sentences (the second a bit shorter than the first) to a strong short statement:

The Whig historian is interested in discovering agency in history, even where in this way he must avow it only implicit. It is characteristic of his method that he should be interested in the agency rather than in the process. And this is how he achieves his simplification.

Fragments

Fragments, usually a special kind of short sentence, make for effective variation—easy to see and easy to use (italics highlight the fragments in the next examples):

Sam steals like this because he is a thief. *Not a big thief.* He tried to be a big thief once and everybody got mad at him and made him go away to jail. He is strictly a small thief, and he only steals for his restaurant.   Jimmy Breslin

Examinations tend to make me merry, often seeming to me to be some kind of private game, some secret ritual compulsively played by professors and the institution. I invariably become facetious in all the critical hours. *All that solemnity for a few facts!* I couldn't believe they were serious. I never quite understood it.
                                                                      Mary Caroline Richards

Used with restraint, fragments like these are a simple way to vary your sentences. They are, however, more at home in a colloquial style than in a formal one.

Rhetorical Questions

Like fragments or any other kind of unusual sentence, rhetorical questions are rarely used for variety alone. Their primary purpose is to emphasize a point or to set up a topic for discussion. Still, whenever they are employed for such ends, they are also a source of variety:

> But Toronto—Toronto is the subject. One must say something—*what* must one say about Toronto? What can one? What has anybody ever said? It is impossible to give it anything but commendation. It is not squalid like Birmingham, or cramped like Canton, or scattered like Edmonton, or sham like Berlin, or hellish like New York, or tiresome like Nice. It is all right. The only depressing thing is that it will always be what it is, only larger, and that no Canadian city can ever be anything better or different. If they are good they may become Toronto.   Rupert Brooke

Varied Openings

Monotony especially threatens when sentence after sentence begins the same way. It is easy to open with something other than the usual subject and verb: a prepositional phrase; an adverbial clause; a connective like *therefore* or an adverb like *naturally;* or, immediately following the subject and splitting it from the verb, a nonrestrictive adjectival construction. Take a look at this passage:

> In the first decade of the new century, the South remained primarily rural; the beginnings of change, in those years, hardly affected the lot of the Negro. The agricultural system had never recovered fully from the destruction of the old plantation economy. Bound to the production of staples—tobacco, cotton, rice, sugar— the soil suffered from erosion and neglect. Those who cultivated it depended at best upon the uncertain returns of fluctuating world markets. But the circumstances under which labor was organized, particularly Negro labor, added to those difficulties further hardships of human creation.   Oscar Handlin

Handlin's five sentences show considerable variety in their openings: a prepositional phrase, a subject, a participial phrase, a subject, and a connective word.

Interrupted Movement

Interruption—positioning a modifier or even a second, independent sentence between main elements of a clause so that pauses are required on either side of the intruder—nicely varies straightforward movement. Here the writer places a second sentence between two clauses (italics added):

> I had halted on the road. As soon as I saw the elephant I knew with perfect certainty that I ought to shoot him. It is a serious matter to shoot a working elephant— *it is comparable to destroying a huge and costly piece of machinery*—and obviously one ought not to do it if it can possibly be avoided.   George Orwell

PART V

Diction

CHAPTER 24

Meaning

To say that a word has meaning is to say that it has purpose. The purpose may be to signify something—that is, to refer to an object or person other than the writer, to an abstract conception such as "democracy," or to a thought or feeling in the writer's mind. On the other hand, the purpose may be to induce a particular response in the readers' minds or to establish an appropriate relationship between the writer and those readers. We shall consider each of these three uses of words—modes of meaning, we shall call them.

Before we do that, however, we need to glance at several misconceptions about words and also at two aspects of meaning fundamental to all the purposes for which words may be used. These aspects concern denotative and connotative meaning and the various levels of usage.

First the misconceptions.

Words Are Not Endowed with Fixed and "Proper" Meanings

When people object to how someone else uses a word, they often say, "That isn't its proper meaning." The word *disinterested*, for example, is frequently employed in the sense of "uninterested," and those who dislike this usage argue that the proper meaning of *disinterested* is "objective, unbiased."

In such arguments "proper meaning" generally signifies a meaning sanctioned by past usage or even by the original, etymological sense of the word. But the dogma that words come to us out of the past with proper meanings—fixed and immutable—is a fallacy. The only meanings a word has are those that the speakers of the language choose to give it. If enough speakers of English use *disinterested* to mean "uninterested," then by definition they have given that meaning to the word.

Those who take a conservative attitude toward language have the right, even the duty, to resist changes which they feel lessen the efficiency of English. They should, however, base their resistance upon demonstrating why the change does make for inefficiency, not upon an authoritarian claim that it violates proper meaning.

As a user of words you should be guided by consensus, that is, the meanings agreed upon by your fellow speakers of English, the meanings recorded in dictionaries. We shall look at what dictionaries do in Chapter 29. For now, simply understand that dictionary definitions are not "proper meanings" but succinct statements of consensual meanings.

In most cases the consensus emerges from an activity in which individual language users participate without knowing that they are, in effect, defining words. The person who says "I was disinterested in the lecture" does not intend to alter the meaning of *disinterested.* He or she has simply heard the word used this way before. In a few cases people do act deliberately to establish a consensual meaning, as when mathematicians agree that the word *googol* will mean "10 raised to the 100th power." In any case, meaning is what the group consents to. This is the only "proper meaning" words have, and any subsequent generation may consent to alter a consensus.

But while the unconscious agreement which establishes the meaning of a word is a group activity, it originates with individuals. Particular speakers began using *disinterested* in the sense of "uninterested" or *square* in the sense of "extremely conventional and unsophisticated." From the usage of individual people the change spreads through the group—for better or worse.

By such a process word meanings change, sometimes rapidly, sometimes glacially. Often the change occurs as a response to historical events. When the eighteenth-century historian Edward Gibbon writes of "the *constitution* of a Roman legion" he means how it was organized, not, as a modern reader might suppose, a written document defining that organization. The latter sense became common only after the late eighteenth century, with the spread of democratic revolutions and the formal writing down of a new government's principles.

Because words must constantly be adapted to a changing world, no neat one-to-one correspondence exists between words and meanings. On the contrary, the relationship is messy: a single word may have half a dozen meanings or more, while several words may designate the same concept or entity. Thus *depression* means one thing to a psychologist, another to an economist, and another still to a geologist. But psychological "depression" may also be conveyed by *melancholia, the blues,* or *the dismals, in the dumps, low,* and so on.

One-to-one correspondences do in fact exist in the highly specialized languages of science and technology and mathematics. To a chemist *sodium chloride* means only the compound NaCl, and that compound is always designated in words by *sodium chloride*. The common term *salt,* in contrast, has a number of meanings, and we must depend on the context (that is, the words around it) to clarify which sense the writer intends:

Pass the *salt.*
She's the *salt* of the earth.
They're not worth their *salt.*
He's a typical old *salt.*
Her wit has considerable *salt.*
The crooks intended to *salt* the mine.
They are going to *salt* away all the cash they can.

But while one-to-one correspondences might seem desirable, having a distinct word for every conceivable object and idea and feeling would not be practical. The vocabulary would swell to unmanageable proportions. And probably we would like it less than we suppose. The inexact correspondence of words and meanings opens up possibilities of conveying subtleties of thought and feeling which an exactly defined vocabulary would exclude. The fact that *sodium chloride* means one thing and only one thing is both a virtue and a limitation. The fact that *salt* means many things is both a problem and an opportunity.

Words, then, are far from being tokens of fixed and permanent value. They are like living things, complex, many-sided, and responsive to pressures from their environment. They must be handled with care.

Denotation and Connotation

Denotation and connotation are aspects of a word's meaning, related but distinct. *Denotation* is a word's primary, specific sense, as the denotation of *red* is the color (or, from the viewpoint of physics, light of a certain wavelength). *Connotation* is the secondary meaning (or meanings), associated with but different from the denotation. *Red,* for instance, has several connotations: "socialist," "anger," and "danger," among others.[1]

Using a circle to represent a word, we may show the denotation as the core meaning and the connotation as fringe meanings gathered about that core. The line enclosing the denotation (D in the diagram) is solid to signify that this meaning is relatively fixed. The line around the connotation (C) is broken to suggest that the connotative meanings of a word are less firm, more open to change and addition.

Connotations may evolve naturally from the denotation of a word, or they may develop by chance associations. *Rose* connotes "fragrant," "beautiful," "short-lived" because the qualities natural to the flower have been incorporated into the word. On the other hand, that *red* connotes

---

1. In logic *denotation* and *connotation* are used in somewhat different senses.

"socialist" is accidental, the chance result of early European socialists' using a red flag as their banner.

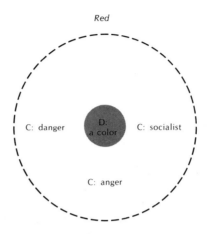

Sometimes a connotative meaning splits off and becomes a second denotation, the nucleus, in effect, of another word configuration. Thus "socialist" has become a new primary meaning of *red* when used as a political term. Around this second nucleus other connotations have gathered, such as (for most Americans) "subversive," "un-American," "traitorous," and so on:

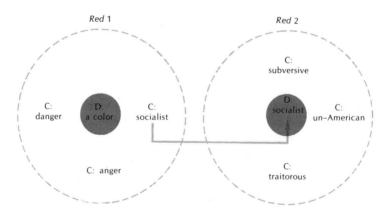

Often, though not inevitably, connotative meanings imply degrees of approval or disapproval and may arouse emotions such as affection, admiration, pity, disgust, hatred. Like positive and negative electrical charges, emotive connotations attract or repel readers with regard to the thing or concept the word designates (though the exact degree of attraction or repulsion depends on how particular readers are themselves charged concerning the thing or concept). These positive and negative charges are extremely important to a word's connotation, and in later diagrams we indicate them by + and − signs.

Individual words vary considerably in the relative weight of their denotative and connotative meanings. Most technical terms, for example, have very little connotation. That is their virtue: they denote an entity or concept precisely and unambiguously without the possible confusion engendered by fringe meanings: *diode, spinnaker, cosine.* We may think of such words as small and compact—all nucleus, so to speak. They have no circle of connotations around them.

Connotation looms larger than denotation in other cases. Some words have large and diffuse meanings. What matters is their secondary or suggestive meanings, not their relatively unimportant denotations. The expression *old-fashioned,* for instance, hauls a heavy load of connotations. It denotes "belonging to, or characteristic of, the past." But far more important than that central meaning is the connotation, or rather two quite different connotations, that have gathered about the nucleus: (1) "valuable, worthy of honor and emulation" and (2) "foolish, ridiculous, out-of-date; to be avoided." With such words the large outer, or connotative, circle is significant; the nucleus small and insignificant.

For many words denotation and connotation are both important aspects of meaning. *Rose* (in the sense of the flower) has a precise botanical denotation: "any of a genus (*Rosa* of the family Rosaceae, the rose family) of usu[ally] prickly shrubs with pinnate leaves and showy flowers having five petals in the wild state but being often double or semidouble under cultivation."[2] At the same time *rose* also has strong connotations: "beautiful," "fragrant," "short-lived," and so on.

Context

The denotation of any word is easy to learn: you need only look in a suitable dictionary. Understanding connotations, however, is more difficult. Dictionaries cannot afford the space to treat them, except in a very few cases. You can gain practical knowledge of a word's range of connotation only by becoming familiar with the contexts in which the word is used.

Context means the surroundings of a word. In a narrow sense, context is the other terms in the phrase, clause, sentence—a word's immediate linguistic environment. More broadly, context comprises all the other words in the passage, even the entire essay or book. It widens further to include a composition's relation to other works, why it was written, and so on. In speech, context in this inclusive sense involves the occasion of a conversation, the relationship between the talkers, even others who may be listening.

But one does not have to explore all the ramifications of context to get at a word's connotation. Usually the terms immediately around it supply the vital clue. *Real old-fashioned flavor* printed on an ice cream carton tells

---

2. *Webster's Seventh New Collegiate Dictionary* (Springfield, Mass.: G. & C. Merriam Company, 1963).

us that here *old-fashioned* connotes "valuable, rich in taste, worthy of admiration (and of purchase)." *Don't be old-fashioned—dare a new experience* in an ad for men's cologne evokes the opposite connotation: "foolish, ridiculous, out-of-date."

Linguistic context acts as a selective screen lying over a word, revealing certain of its connotations, concealing others. Thus "real" and "flavor" mask the unfavorable connotation of *old-fashioned*, leaving us aware only of the positive one. Here is a diagram of *old-fashioned* in the "real/flavor" context:

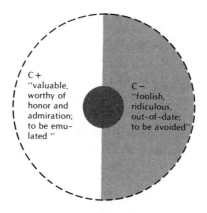

In the context of "don't/dare a new experience," the screening effect is just the opposite:

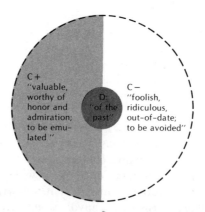

Not only does the linguistic context serve both to reveal and to hide certain of a word's connotations. It may also activate latent implications that ordinarily are not associated with a word. The meaning "rich in taste," for instance, is not one we customarily associate with *old-fashioned*. Yet in *real old-fashioned flavor* it comes to the surface.

Context also helps you determine whether a word is functioning primarily in its denotative or connotative sense. With words like *rose* that carry both kinds of meaning, only context reveals which is operating, or if both are in varying degrees. Clearly this sentence calls upon only the denotation of *rose:*

Our native wild roses have, in spite of their great variety, contributed little to the development of our garden roses.

But when the poet Robert Burns tells of his feelings for a young lady, while still denoting the flower, he uses the word primarily for its connotations:

O, my luv is like a red, red rose
    That's newly sprung in June.

In choosing words, then, you must pay attention both to denotative and to connotative meaning. With a purely denotative word like *cosine,* say, the problem is simple. If you make a mistake with such a word, it is simply because you do not know what it means and had better consult a dictionary (or textbook). But when words must be chosen with an eye to their connotations, the problem is more difficult. Connotative meaning is more diffuse, less readily looked up in a reference book, more subtly dependent on context. Here mistakes are easier to make. For instance, if you want readers to like a character you are describing, it would be unwise to write "a fat man with a red face," even though the words are literally accurate. *Fat* and *red* are negatively charged in such a context. More positive would be "a stout [*or* plump] man with rosy cheeks."

Levels of Usage

Level of usage refers to the kind of situation in which a word is normally used. Most words suit all occasions. Some, however, are restricted to formal, literary contexts, and others to informal, colloquial ones. Consider three verbs which roughly mean the same thing: *exacerbate, annoy, bug.* Talking among your friends, you would not be likely to say, "That person really exacerbated me." On the other hand, describing a historical episode you wouldn't (or shouldn't) write, "The Spartan demands bugged the Athenians." But you could use *annoy* on both occasions, without arousing derision in either friends or readers of your work.

The three words differ considerably in their levels of usage. *Exacerbate* is a literary word, appropriate to formal occasions. *Bug* (in this sense) is a colloquial, even slang, term appropriate to speech and very informal writing. *Annoy* is an all-purpose word, suitable for any occasion. When in the next chapter we discuss the practical problem of appropriateness, we shall use the labels *formal, informal,* and *general* to distinguish these broad levels of usage.

From the more theoretical viewpoint we are taking here, we may think of level of usage as a peripheral part of a word's connotation. As with connotation in general, it is not easy to look up the level of usage of any particular word. Dictionaries label an occasional term "colloquial" or "slang," but not in every case; and they do not label formal words like *exacerbate* at all. You have to depend on your own knowledge as a guide.

In recent years the line between formal and informal usage has blurred considerably (though not enough for Spartans to bug Athenians). The distinction still exists, however, and careful writers pay attention to it.

Telic Modes of Meaning

Finally, we shall discuss the point with which we began—the purpose a word is chosen to serve. This aspect we shall call the "telic mode" of meaning, from the Greek word *telos,* meaning "end," and the Latin *modus,* meaning "manner." Though the phrase sounds forbidding, it is a useful brief label for an obvious but important fact: that part of a word's meaning is the purpose it is expected to fulfill, and that words may serve different purposes.

To get a bit further into this matter it will help to look at a well-known diagram called the "communication triangle":

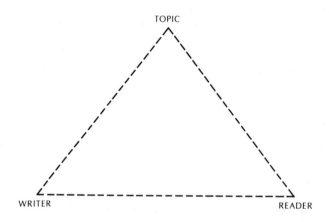

The diagram simply clarifies the fact that any act of communication involves three things: someone who communicates (for our purposes, a writer); something the communication is about (the topic); and someone to whom the communication is made (the reader). The broken lines joining these elements indicate an indirect relationship between them.

It is indirect because it must be mediated by words. Directly, each corner of the triangle connects only to words. The writer selects them, the reader interprets them, and the topic is expressed by them. Words thus occupy a central, essential, mediating position in the triangle:

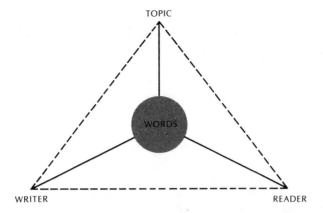

In selecting his or her words, a writer may be concerned primarily with any of the three areas of the triangle: writer-topic, writer-reader, or reader-topic. These areas correspond to the three "telic modes" of meaning. We shall call them respectively: "referential," "interpersonal," and "directive."

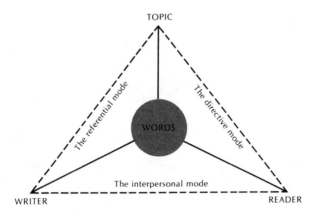

The Referential Mode

Referential meaning connects writer and topic. In this mode the writer chooses words for the exactness and economy with which they signify, or refer to, what he or she observes, knows, thinks, feels—in short, what is in his or her mind. Most writing involves chiefly this mode of meaning. Here are three examples:

Mary [Queen of Scots] had returned to Scotland in 1561, a young widow of nineteen, after an absence of thirteen years in France. . . .   D. Harris Willson

The principle of verification is supposed to furnish a criterion by which it can be determined whether or not a sentence is literally meaningful.   Alfred Jules Ayer

Calculus is a lousy subject.   Student

In all these cases the writers select words for their referential value, to make clear what is in their minds. The historian, aiming to be factually accurate, and the philosopher, aiming to be conceptually exact, chose diction on the basis of denotation: "in 1561," "a young widow of nineteen," "verification," "criterion." The student, expressing how he feels, selects "lousy" for its connotation; and while it would be more difficult to unravel all the implications of "lousy" than to explain the meanings of "widow" or "criterion," the word is exactly right.

In each case, of course, the diction will affect readers' attitudes toward both subject and writer, and to that degree the words will operate in the interpretive and interpersonal modes. Ayer's abstract diction may well bore people uninterested in philosophy, for instance. A mathematician, depending on his sense of humor, might be amused or annoyed by the student's characterization of calculus. But although such spill-over effects are very real, the fact remains that in all these examples the diction aims at referential accuracy and operates primarily in that mode of meaning.

The Interpersonal Mode

We choose words chiefly for their referential meanings. Those words, however, will also affect the link between readers and you. It follows that you should select even referential diction with an eye on the reader. You must consider what readers know and do not know, how they resemble you and how they differ, what degree of formality or informality you wish to establish with them. Such considerations may lead you, for example, to look for an easier word even though it is a bit less exact than a technical term.

But beyond showing a general concern for readers in choosing the words with which you discuss your topic, you may also wish occasionally to include words that will directly affect the readers' attitude toward you. Now you are in the interpersonal mode of meaning.

First, certain expressions create a favorable image of yourself. Inevitably you exist in your words—whether you wish to or not—as an unseen presence, a hidden voice of which readers are aware, sometimes dimly, sometimes with acute consciousness, and which we call the *persona* (see page 58). Since a persona is inevitable, you had better strive for an attractive one. Modesty, for instance, is generally a virtue in a writer. An occasional expression like *I think, it seems to me, to my mind* suggests to readers that here is a modest writer, undogmatic, aware of his or her fallibility. The following passages illustrate such interpersonal diction (the italics are added):

What, then, can one learn from [Samuel] Johnson in general? First, *I think*, the inestimable value of individuality.
F. L. Lucas

Whether this slowing-down of traffic will cause a great or a small loss of national income is, *I am told*, a point on which expert economists are not agreed.
Max Beerbohm

That this is so can hardly be proved, but it is, *I should claim,* a fact.   J. L. Austin

Such personal disclaimers are not always a virtue. At times modesty may strike a note that is weak or false. At times a subject may demand an impersonal point of view, making the use of *I, my, me* impossible. Even when modesty is called for and a personal point of view is possible, a few *I thinks* and *in my opinions* go a long way. Used in every second or third sentence they may well draw too much attention and annoy the reader. Still, occasionally acknowledging your limitations is one way of creating a favorable impression upon readers.

Beyond suggesting a diffident, nonassertive persona, you can also use words in the interpersonal mode which graciously acknowledge your readers' presence. Without being insincere or obsequious you can draw readers into your exposition so that they seem to share more directly in your ideas and feelings. The judicious use of *we, our, us,* for instance, implies a common ground of knowledge and values, subtly flattering to readers (again, in the examples that follow italics are added):

Let *us* define a plot.   E. M. Forster

No doubt, if one has more than one self (like most of *us*), it had better be one's better self that one tries to become.   F. L. Lucas

When *we* look more closely at this craft of philosophic expression, *we* find to *our* relief that it is less exacting than the art of the true man of letters.   Brand Blanshard

Any words, then, that refer to the writer in the role of writer or to the reader in the role of reader operate in the interpersonal mode of meaning. To the degree that such words create an attractive image of the former and graciously acknowledge the latter, they will add to the effectiveness of any piece of writing. In exposition, however, such diction, while important, necessarily remains infrequent.

The Directive Mode of Meaning

The last of the three modes of meaning relates to the reader-topic side of the communication triangle. Here you select words primarily for their value in assisting readers to understand or feel about the topic. Understanding and feeling are quite different responses: the first a function of intelligence, the other of emotion. Words concerned with facilitating understanding we shall call *constructive diction;* words intended to evoke emotion, *emotive diction.*

Constructive diction includes the various connectives and signposts which clarify the organization of a composition and the flow of its ideas: *however, even so, on the other hand, for example, in the next chapter,* and so on. While such words and phrases indicate real connections within the topic, their essential function is to help readers follow the construction of thought.

How much constructive diction you include in a composition depends both upon the amount of help you think readers need and upon your own preferences for spelling out logical relationships or leaving them implicit. You can overuse such diction, boring or even annoying readers with too many *howevers* and *therefores*. Most people, however, are more likely to err on the other side, giving readers too little help.

The other kind of interpretive diction aims at feeling. In emotive diction, connotations play a major role, especially those carrying strong negative or positive charges. Examples abound in advertising copy. The word *Brut* on a man's cologne tells us nothing referential, nothing about the product. *Brut* aims at our emotions. Cleverly combining strong macho connotations with others of sophistication and elegance, the name is intended to overcome masculine resistance to toiletries as "sissy" (or perhaps to appeal to women, who buy most of these products for their men).[3]

Emotionally loaded diction is also the stock-in-trade of the political propagandist. The Marxist who writes of "the *bourgeois lust* for personal liberty" uses *bourgeois* (a leftist sneer word for all things pertaining to capitalism) and *lust* for their capacity to arouse disapproval in a socialist audience. Similarly the conservative who complains of "*pinko liberals* in Washington" employs rightist sneer words. Diction may also be loaded positively, calling forth feelings of affection and approval: "*grass-roots* Americanism," "*old-fashioned* flavor," "an *ancient* and *glorious* tradition."

There is nothing wrong in trying to arouse the emotions of readers. It is the purpose for which the emotion is evoked that may be reprehensible, or admirable. The devil's advocate uses loaded diction, and so do the angels.

Many words operate in both the referential and directive modes simultaneously. In fact, it is not always easy to know which mode is paramount in particular cases. Both Marxist and conservative, for example, may believe that *bourgeois* and *pinko* really denote facts. Still, most of us feel that such words are largely empty of reference and have their meaning chiefly in their emotive force. On the other hand, some words work effectively in both modes, like those italicized in the following passage (the author is describing some fellow passengers on a bus tour of Sicily):

Immediately next to me was an aggrieved French couple with a small child who looked around with a *rat-like* malevolence. He had the same face as his father. They looked like *very cheap microscopes*.   Lawrence Durrell

Rat-like and *cheap microscopes* have genuine reference; they would help an illustrator drawing a picture of this father and son. At the same time the words arouse the emotional response that Durrell wants in the reader.

---

3. The sophistication and elegance derive from the French word *brut*—meaning "dry, unsweet"—which appears on fine champagne labels. The macho connotation follows from the fact that *brut* is pronounced "brute."

Conclusion

The relative importance of the three modes of meaning varies considerably from one kind of writing to another. Scholarly and scientific papers, for example, make the writer-topic axis paramount; advertising and political propaganda use that of reader-topic; applications for jobs and letters of appeal, for example, lie along the writer-reader axis. We can suggest such differences in emphasis in our triangular diagram by moving the circles representing words from the center of the triangle toward one or another of its sides. Some of the examples we have used might be visualized like this:

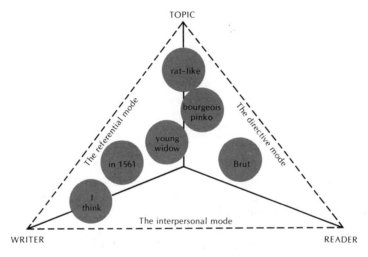

Some expressions (*in 1561,* for instance) are chosen solely for reference, that is to explain the topic; a few solely to influence readers' feelings about the topic *(Brut).* Other words function in two areas of meaning: either primarily within one but extending partially into another *(pinko, bourgeois, I think, young widow),* or more evenly balanced *(rat-like).*

But whether designed to serve a single end or several, diction succeeds only to the degree that it does in fact serve an end—enabling readers to comprehend your observations, ideas, feelings, and affecting their responses both to the topic and to you in ways that you wish. To the degree that it fails to achieve your purpose, your diction fails entirely.[4]

You must, finally, realize that words inherently have meaning in some or in all of the modes we have enumerated. If you do not choose words wisely, words will, in effect, choose you, saying things about the topic you do not intend and affecting readers in ways you do not want.

4. A purpose itself may be silly or stupid, of course, but then the fault lies in the writer's conception—what he or she wants to say—not in the diction—how it is said. Writers may use words well by a happy chance, that is, without really understanding their effect, and thus achieve a purpose they are blind to. But lucky prose is rare. The general truth holds: good diction is diction chosen to achieve a conscious purpose.

CHAPTER 25

Clarity and Simplicity

To be effective words must be precise. Precision means that words serve your purpose—that is, that they express exactly what you think or feel or see or hear. Precision also establishes an appropriate relationship between you and your readers and guides their responses. But in exposition precision is largely a matter of expressing your topic clearly.

That is more complicated than it sounds. It is not simply a question of deciding what you perceive or think or know or feel, and then of choosing appropriate words. The distinction between what goes on in our minds and how we put it into language is not that clear-cut. Words both limit and reveal reality. We do not so much "choose" words to fit our perceptions and ideas, as we see and think in terms of the words we know. To be more exact, the two processes—thinking, knowing, seeing, feeling, on the one hand; and using words, on the other—vitalize one another. Acquiring new words increases our capacity to understand ourselves and the world around us; and as our sensitivity to self and the world expands, we seek words that will express the subtler, more complicated persons we are becoming.

Diction—word choice—then, is the heart of writing. Sentences are important; paragraphing and clear organization are important. But words are fundamental. The essential virtue of words is that they be clear. At the same time it is desirable that they be simple, concise, and original. To a considerable degree these virtues overlap: words that are simple and concise will be clear. Yet there are occasions when these qualities of diction work at cross purposes. Sometimes, for example, the need to be exact will override the need to be simple or concise. But in general you should aim first at clarity, then strive for simplicity and concision.

In this and the next two chapters we'll consider how to use words well. First, we look chiefly at clarity and simplicity; next at concision; and finally at original, unusual diction which gives extraordinary power and perceptiveness to writing.

Here, then, are some things to keep in mind as you struggle—and struggle it is—to use words clearly and simply.

Concreteness and Abstraction

Abstract words signify things that cannot be directly perceived: *honor,* for instance, is an abstract word, as are *generosity* or *idea* or *democracy. Concrete* words refer to perceptible things: *a rose, a clap of thunder, the odor of violets.*

No hard-and-fast distinction exists between abstract and concrete. Often it is a matter of degree. Depending on its context the same term may now be used abstractly, now concretely, like *rose* in these sentences:

CONCRETE	On the hall table a single yellow tea rose stood in a blue vase.
LESS CONCRETE	Roses were growing in the garden.
ABSTRACT	The rose family includes many varieties.

The closer a word comes to naming a single, unique object the more concrete it is. When diction moves from the specific and perceptible to the general and imperceptible, it becomes abstract.

Do not suppose that abstract diction is necessarily a fault. If you deal with ideas, abstraction is inevitable. The following sentence is clear and concise, and almost all of its important words are abstract, yet they are essential to its clarity:

All too often the debate about the place, purpose, and usefulness of films as a means of instruction is clouded by confusion, defensiveness, and ignorance.
                                                                                            Sol Worth

Even when dealing with ideas, however, wise writers do not stay too long on high levels of abstraction, especially if aiming at readers who do not share their expertise. They know that many readers find it hard to enjoy or understand words remote from the eyes and ears. Occasionally, they make us "see" and "hear" ideas by using images in the form of examples, analogies, similes, or metaphors. In the following case the abstract notion—that the meeting of extremes is dull—is given concrete, visual reality in the image,[1] "a very flat country":

1. An image is a word that refers to something we can sense—that is, see, hear, touch, and so on. See pages 231 ff. for a fuller discussion.

It is often said truly, though perhaps not understood rightly, that extremes meet. But the strange thing is that extremes meet, not so much in being extraordinary, as in being dull. The country where the East and West are one, is a very flat country.

                                                                    G. K. Chesterton

And in the following description of a Japanese train crew, notice how the abstract terms "trim" and "dapper" are made perceptible:

Everything about them is trim and dapper; the stylized flourishes of the white-gloved guard, for instance, as he waves the flag for the train to start from Sano station, or the precise unfumbling way the conductor, in equally clean white gloves, clips one's ticket, arms slightly raised, ticket held at the correct angle and correct distance from the body, clipper engaged and operated in a sharp single movement.

                                                                    Ronald P. Dore

If unrelieved abstraction can be a fault even when writing about abstract subjects, it is a far worse fault when writing about a subject that is not abstract at all. When you describe what you see and hear, touch and taste, use the most specific, concrete words you know:

TOO ABSTRACT	The large coves are surrounded by various buildings.
MORE CONCRETE	The large coves are surrounded by summer cottages, boat houses, and piers jutting into the water.
EVEN BETTER	The large coves are surrounded by summer cottages, trimly painted, with bright red and blue and green shutters; by boat houses, a few seeming about to slide into the lake, but most still used and well-maintained; and by piers jutting into the water, in good repair with sturdy railings, from which hang clean white life-rings.

Inexperienced writers often complain, "I haven't anything to write about." There's plenty to write about; all you have to do is look and listen.

Specificity

Aside from being concrete or abstract, words may also be general or specific. Here, too, it is a matter of degree. A general word designates a class: *emotion*, for example, is a general (or generic) term for all kinds of feelings. *Fear* is more specific, and *terror*, a particular kind of fear, more specific still. It is a common error to pick words that mean too much, to name an entire class when what you wish to signify is something less:

Thrift is not one of their *attributes*. (For *virtues*)

The novel has far too many *people*. (For *characters*)

Hardy's poem *allows* the reader to experience the crashing of the iceberg and the ship. (For *forces* or *makes*)

On the other hand, there is nothing inherently wrong with general words. Sometimes you *do* want to refer to any or all feelings and then *emotion* is exactly the right word. If you mean humanity in general and not men or women or adults or Americans or Norwegians, then write

People differ considerably in their religious beliefs.

Ambiguity

Ambiguity means that a word can be read in either of two ways and the context does not make clear which way is intended. (The term *ambiguity* is sometimes also applied when three or more interpretations are possible.)

Ambiguity often is the result of a word's having two different senses:

It was a *funny* affair. ("Laughable" or "strange"?)

He's *mad*. ("Crazy" or "angry"?)

Large abstractions are often ambiguous, particularly if they involve value judgments. Words like *democracy, romantic,* and *Christian* encompass a wide range of meanings, some of them contradictory. A writer, or a reader, can easily make mistakes with such words, sliding unconsciously from one sense to another, an error which logicians call *equivocation.*

Pronouns may be ambiguous if it is not clear which of two possible antecedents they refer to:

Children often anger parents; *they* won't talk to *them*.

We sat near the heater, as *it* was cold. (The "heater" or the unmentioned "room"?)

Some connectives are prone to ambiguity. *Or*, for instance, can signify (1) a logical disjunction, that is, *A* or *B* but not both; and (2) an alternative name or word for the same thing: "The shag, or cormorant, is a common sea bird along the New England coast." *Because* after a negative statement may also be ambiguous:

We didn't go because we were tired. ("We did not go and the reason was that we were tired"; or, emphatically, "We did go and we certainly were *not* tired"?)

On other occasions ambiguity lurks, not in a single word, but in an entire statement:

I liked this story as much as I liked all his others. ("I like all his stories, including this one"; or "I don't like any of his stories, including this one"?)

So be it, until Victory is ours, and there is no enemy, but Peace. (". . . there is no enemy, and now we have Peace"; or ". . . there is no enemy except Peace"?)

Clever writers exploit ambiguity as a kind of irony, seeming to say one thing while meaning another. Joan Didion, in the following description of a wedding, wryly comments on marriage by using "illusion" both in its technical, dressmaking sense of a bridal veil and in its more commonplace meaning of a false hope or dream:

A coronet of seed pearls held her illusion veil.

And the nineteenth-century statesman and novelist Benjamin Disraeli had a standard response to all would-be authors who sent him unsolicited manuscripts:

Many thanks; I shall lose no time in reading it.

Connotation

The connotation of a word is its fringe or associated meanings, including implications of approval or disapproval. (See pages 179 ff.) When a connotation pulls awkwardly against the context, even though the basic meaning of the word fits, the term must be replaced. In the following sentence, for example, *unrealistic* has the wrong connotations for the writer's purpose:

In such stories it is exciting to break away from the predictable world we live in and to enter an unrealistic world where anything can happen.

The problem is that the writer approves of the story because it stimulates the imagination. But usually *unrealistic* connotes disapproval ("Don't be so unrealistic"; "Her plan is too unrealistic to work"). Thus while the basic meaning (or denotation) of *unrealistic* fits, its connotations do not. Such terms as *fantastic, unpredictable, imaginary, wonder-filled* would be more appropriate.

Barbarisms

A *barbarism* is either a nonexistent word or an existing one used ungrammatically. Inventing new words is not necessarily a fault; imaginative writers create them—*neologisms,* they are called. But a genuine neologism fills a need. When an invented word is merely an ungrammatical form of a term already in the language, it serves no purpose and is a barbarism:

She's always been a *dutifulled* daughter. (For *dutiful*)

Barbarisms are often spawned by confusion about suffixes, those endings which extend the meaning or alter the grammatical function of words—for example, as when -*ness* turns the adjective *polite* into the noun *politeness.*

Sometimes a barbarism is the result of adding a second, unnecessary suffix to a word to restore it to what it was in the first place:

He has great *ambitiousness*. (For *ambition*)

The story contains a great deal of *satiricalness*. (For *satire*)

Aside from nonexistent words, barbarisms also include legitimate ones used ungrammatically. Confusion of sound or appearance often causes this error:

Garbage is also used to fill holes *were* houses are to be built. (For *where*)

The average man is not *conscience* of his wasteful behavior. (For *conscious*)

I should *of* gone. (For *should've*)

A *women* stood on the corner. (For *woman*)

The chances of confusion are even greater with homonyms, different words pronounced the same (and sometimes spelled alike as well): *bear* ("carry"), *bear* ("animal"), and *bare* ("naked"). Especially prone to misuse are the forms *there* (adverb), *their* (possessive pronoun), and *they're* (contraction of *they are*); and *to* (preposition), *too* (adverb), and *two* (adjective).

Legitimate words may become barbarisms when misused in grammatical shifts. As we'll see in the next chapter, grammatical shifts can be valuable in writing. (It means changing the normal grammatical function of a word, turning a noun, for example, into a verb, as in "The car *nosed* down the street.") But if it serves no valid purpose, such a shift is simply a barbarism:

Our *strive* for greatness is one of our best qualities. (For *striving*)

They made their *deciding*. (For *decision*)

Awkward shifts are common with adjectives and adverbs. Usually the problem is leaving off a necessary *-ly*:

She dances *beautiful*. (For *beautifully*)

They did it *satisfactory*. (For *satisfactorily*)

A rough rule is that adverbs of three or more syllables end in *-ly* and that those having one or two syllables are rather idiomatic: some always end in *-ly (deadly)*, others never do *(well)*, and still others may be used either way *(slow* or *slowly, quick* or *quickly)*.

On the fringe of barbarism are many trendy words such as *finalize* and adverbs ending in *-wise* such as *weatherwise, universitywise, economywise*. There seems little justification for a word like *finalize*, which says nothing that *complete* or *finish* does not say. On the other hand, one can argue that *weatherwise* is at least more concise than the phrase *in regard to the weather.* One's tolerance for such terms depends on how liberal or conservative one is with regard to language (or languagewise).

Idiom

An idiom is a combination of words functioning as a unit of meaning, as in "to take the subway [bus, streetcar] home." Often one or more of the words has a special sense different from its usual meaning and confined to that idiom. Thus *to take* here means "to get on and travel in." In its idiomatic sense such a word cannot be replaced by any of its usual equivalents: we cannot "*carry, bring,* or *fetch* the subway home."

Idioms are always a difficulty in learning foreign languages. They are not easily reduced to rules and each must be memorized. Even native speakers make mistakes with idioms. The most frequent errors involve verb-preposition combinations:

I complained *with* my parents about their attitude.
IDIOMATIC: *complained to*

She concluded *in* saying. . . .
IDIOMATIC: *concluded by*

That is where we fool ourselves *of* our efficiency.
IDIOMATIC: *fool ourselves about*

They can't decide what to do *with* their problem.
IDIOMATIC: *do about their problem*

Errors like these probably come from confusing two idioms (*complain about* and *argue with,* for example), or from selecting an inappropriate one of several possible verb-preposition idioms (we do *with* physical objects— "What shall we do with this vase?"—but we do *about* problems, difficulties, abstractions of various kinds—"What shall we do about that crack in the vase?").

Although they are most likely with verbs and prepositions, mistakes in idiom occur with other grammatical patterns. Some verbs, for instance, do not combine idiomatically with certain objects:

People only *look out for* prestige. (Prestige is *looked for, valued, esteemed.*)

Robert Frost *gives* the image of a silken tent in a field. (Poets *create* or *develop* images.)

Adjectives and nouns also enter into idiomatic combinations:

We have a *great* standard of living.
IDIOMATIC: *high*

The English prefer *dining-room* comedy.
IDIOMATIC: *drawing-room comedy*

Colloquial and Pretentious Diction

Colloquialisms are expressions appropriate to informal, conversational occasions. In writing they may sound out of place:

We have a *swell* professor of mathematics.
BETTER: *nice, interesting, pleasant*

Colloquial words are a problem when they fit awkwardly with their contexts or when they are vague. And frequently colloquialisms *are* vague. (What, for example, does *swell* mean in the sentence above?) In speech we compensate for verbal vagueness by gestures, tone of voice, the common ground of knowledge and experience we share with our friends. None of these aids to communication is available to the writer.

On the other hand, some colloquialisms are remarkably expressive, and these are more acceptable now than they were a generation ago, when writers were more scrupulous about levels of usage. Today, we feel freer to mix formal words and colloquial ones. The result, if controlled by word sense and taste, is a clear gain in precision and variety (italics added in both cases):

Joan's voices and visions have *played tricks* with her reputation.
George Bernard Shaw

There's another *wrinkle* to this.   Elizabeth Janeway

An extreme form of colloquialism is slang. We all use slang, and we all recognize it. But we find it very difficult to define. Sometimes slang is an ordinary word given a special meaning: *heavy* in the sense of serious, or *cool* in the sense of unperturbed or a little better than all right. Other slang terms occur only as slang—*nerd,* for instance.

Slang tends to be short-lived: that of one generation sounds silly to the next. (There are exceptions; some slang terms are notably long-lived—*dough, okay.*) Slang tends also to be richly suggestive in meaning, conveying a wide range of attitudes and responses and values in a brief expression *(square, hep).* But the richness is likely to hide an imprecision: often we feel that a slang term says exactly what we want to say, but we find it very difficult to explain what that something is.

Even more than colloquialisms, slang has an air of informality. That tone can be useful, helping to create a good writer-reader relationship or a likeable persona. Used intelligently, an occasional bit of slang will not only say exactly the right thing but also please us by its novelty (italics added):

The authors had a reputation for being jealous of each other's fame and losing no opportunity of *putting the boot in* [kicking a fallen opponent]. . . .   Frank Muir

I don't mean to suggest that Segal is as *gaga* as this book [*Love Story*]—only that a part of him is.   Pauline Kael

Pretentiousness

Pretentiousness is using big words to no purpose (except perhaps to show off). It results in long-winded, wooden sentences filled with deadwood. Shorter, simpler words mean shorter, clearer sentences:

Upon *receiving an answer in the affirmative,* he *proceeded* to the bulletin board.
BETTER: Told yes, he went to the bulletin board.

Television shows which *demonstrate participation in physical exercise* will improve your muscle tone.
BETTER: Television exercise shows improve your muscle tone.

Remember, though, that not all unusual or learned terms are a flaw, even when they could be replaced by simpler ones. Skillful writers employ uncommon words to draw attention or to imply a subtlety. Here, for instance, a learned word wittily conceals a vulgar insult:

Among those who distrust the [literary] critic as an intrusive middleman, edging his vast steatopygous bulk between author and audience, it is not uncommon to wish him away, out of the direct line of vision.   Carlos Baker

Clichés and Jargon

A *cliché* is a trite expression, one devalued by overuse:

an agonizing reappraisal	the bottom line
at this point in time	the finer things of life
cool, calm, and collected	the moment of truth
history tells us	the voice of the people

Many clichés are simply stale figures of speech:

cool as a cucumber	Mother Nature
dead as a doornail	pleased as Punch
gentle as a lamb	sober as a judge
happy as a lark	the patience of Job
in the pink	the pinnacle of success
light as a feather	white as snow

Clichés are dull and unoriginal. Worse, they impede clear perception, feeling, or thought. Clichés are verbal molds into which we force experience. Instead of shaping reality for ourselves, we accept it, and pass it on, precast (and probably miscast).

Clichés, however, ought not to be confused with *dead metaphors.*

Expressions like *the key to the problem, the heart of the matter, the mouth of the river,* if they ever were clichés, are so no longer. They are simply old metaphors long dead and now useful, everyday diction. A cliché attempts to be original and perceptive but fails. A dead metaphor, on the other hand, makes no pretense to newness; it has dried and hardened into a useful expression for a common idea.

A special kind of cliché is the *euphemism,* which softens or conceals a fact considered improper or unpleasant. Euphemisms for death include *to pass away, to depart this life, to go to that big [whatever] in the sky*—all equally trite. Poverty, sexual matters, and diseases are often named euphemistically. Politicians, diplomats, advertisers are adept with euphemisms: *dedication to public service* = "personal ambition," *a frank exchange of views* = "continued disagreement," *tired blood* = "anemia."

Jargon

Jargon is technical language misused. Technical language, the precise diction demanded by any specialized trade or profession, is necessary when experts communicate with one another. It becomes jargon when it is applied outside the limits of technical discourse. Jargon is really a kind of pretentiousness, a learned and mysterious language designed to impress the nonexpert:

Given a stockpile of innovative in-house creativity for the generation of novel words, substituting members for the input of letters whenever feasible, and fiscally optimized by computer capacitization for targeting in on core issues relating to aims, goals, and priorities, and learned skills, we might at last be freed from our dependence on the past.

This is in fact a parody by Lewis Thomas, a biologist who does *not* write jargon. It catches the faults of jargon perfectly: the abstract, polysyllabic Latinism *(capacitization, optimized);* the trendy word *(creativity, in-house, input, core issues);* the pointless redundancy *(aims, goals, and priorities);* and the awesome combination of modifiers and headwords *(innovative in-house creativity, computer capacitization).*

At its worst jargon is incomprehensible. (The word originally meant the twittering of birds.) Even when it can be puzzled out, jargon is nothing more than puffed-up language, a kind of false profundity in which simple ideas are padded out in polysyllabic dress.

Awkward Figures

Figures of speech are words used less for their literal meaning than for their capacity to clarify or intensify feelings or ideas. For the writer of exposition the most common and important figures are the simile and metaphor.

A *simile* is a comparison, generally introduced by *like* or *as.* The essayist

Robert Lynd describes the bleak houses of a nineteenth-century city as looking "like seminaries for the production of killjoys." A *metaphor* is more complicated. For now let us say only that it expresses an implicit comparison, not a literal one (as a simile does):

When I walked to the mailbox, a song sparrow placed his incomparable seal on the outgoing letters.   E. B. White

White does not literally say that the bird's song is like a bright stamp or seal, but the comparison is there.

In Chapter 27 we look at figures at greater length and in a more positive light (see page 213 ff.). Here we are concerned with their misuse. A metaphor or simile can be faulty in any of three ways: it can be inappropriate, mixed, or overwhelming.

Mixed metaphors ask us to perceive simultaneously two things that simply cannot go together:

He put his foot in his mouth and jumped off the deep end.

We must feel with the fingertips of our eyeballs.

Inappropriate figures contain implications that do not fit the context and are likely to imply meanings the writer does not intend:

A green lawn spread invitingly from the road to the house, with a driveway winding up to the entrance like a snake in the grass.

Since the writer intended no sinister implications, comparing the driveway to a snake is misleading. Moreover, the simile, aside from being misleading and trite, is ridiculous. A snake in the grass is a kinetic image—one involving motion—and a wriggling driveway is silly.

Overwhelming figures ride roughshod over the main idea, as in the following sentence (about the considerable girth of the comedian Jackie Gleason):

Out of that flesh grew benign tumors of driving energy and unsatisfied appetite that stuck to his psyche and swelled into a galloping disease that at once blights and regenerates him.

False Hyperbole

Hyperbole (often shortened to *hype* in modern usage) is deliberate exaggeration intended to intensify importance or emotional force. Though no hyperbole is ever intended to be taken literally, we may properly call it false only when the exaggeration far outdistances the real value of the idea or feeling:

Football is the most magnificent sport ever developed by the mind of man. It tests physical skill, stamina, courage, and intelligence more thoroughly than any other human activity.

One shudders to think of what the world would have been like if Shakespeare had never written *The Tempest*.

Although these are silly exaggerations, hyperbole can be used legitimately. It is an old and useful figure of speech (though not as fashionable today as it once was). In the nineteenth century politicians delighted in spread-eagle oratory, and historians cultivated a hyperbolical style. In the following passage, for example, the American historian William H. Prescott writes about the ill effects of the gold which Spain had expropriated from the New World in the 1500s:

The golden tide, which, permitted a free vent, would have fertilized the region, through which it poured, now buried the land under a deluge which blighted every green and living thing.

Mark Twain was a master of hyperbole, as he reveals in this description of a tree after an ice storm:

. . . it stands there the acme, the climax, the supremest possibility in art or nature, of bewildering, intoxicating, intolerable magnificence. One cannot make the words strong enough.

Twain is at his best—at least to modern ears—when he uses hyperbole for comic effect:

[On the New England weather] In the spring I have counted one hundred and thirty-six different kinds of weather inside of four-and-twenty hours.

[On the music of Richard Wagner] Another time we went to Mannheim and attended a shivaree—otherwise an opera—called "Lohengrin." The banging and slamming and booming and crashing were beyond belief, the racking and pitiless pain of it remains stored up in my memory alongside the memory of the time I had my teeth fixed.

Repetitiousness

A word, unless it is important, will sound awkward if it is repeated too closely. It ought to be replaced by a synonym or a pronoun:

The auto industry *used* to produce cars that lasted, but they didn't make enough profit so planned obsolescence came into *use*.
BETTER: . . . came into fashion.

This *narrative* is *narrated* by a *narrator* whom we cannot completely trust.
BETTER: This story is told by a narrator whom we cannot completely trust.

However, repetitiousness must be distinguished from legitimate restatement, in which words are repeated for emphasis or clarity:

He [a lax governor] took things easy, and his fellow freebooters took everything easily.   Hodding Carter

[Oliver Goldsmith's "The Deserted Village" is] a poem written not in ink but in tears, a rich suffusion of emotion rising up in a grubby room in Grub street for a grubby little Irish village.   Sean O'Faolain

The line between awkward repetition and effective restatement is not easy to draw. As a general rule, a repeated word should be important, able to stand the attention readers will give it.

Awkward Sound

We choose words primarily for what they mean, but we must remember that words are also units of sound and rhythm. Even people adept at silent reading will be put off by awkward patterns of sound, though they may not realize exactly what bothers them. Most often the problem is an accidental repetition of the same sound:

There is a grow*ing* awareness of the slow*ing* down of growth affec*ting* our economy.
BETTER: There is a growing awareness that dimished rates of growth are affecting our economy.

Built-in obsole*scence* has become the es*sence* of our society.
BETTER: . . . has become the basis of our society.

At the top of the hill were three *fine pine* trees standing in a *line*.
BETTER: . . . three beautiful pine trees in a row.

But it is also true (as we saw on pages 153–54) that rhyme, the deliberate repetition of sound, has a place in prose, as in this example:

. . . those Hairbreadth Harrys of History [who] save the world just when it's slipping into the abyss.   Arthur Herzog

As is often the case with diction, it is not easy to separate vice from virtue. Generally, rhyme is awkward when it is accidental or when—even if deliberate—it is too obvious or heavy-handed. Effective rhyme involves key terms and does not shout.

The best guard against awkward repetition of sound is to read your work aloud. If words jar your ear, change them.

CHAPTER 26

Concision

Concision is brevity relative to purpose, as we saw in Chapter 20. There we looked at concision as an aspect of sentence structure. Here we consider it from the point of view of diction. When you fail to be concise the result is *deadwood,* words that perform no useful function and simply get in the way of those that do. This chapter is about where deadwood comes from and how it may be avoided.

Psychological Factors

Verbal profundity is the fallacy that words which look impressive must mean a lot. The person, for example, who exclaimed of a painting that it exhibits "orderly and harmonious juxtapositions of color patterns" seemed to be saying a great deal. But if the words mean anything more than "color harmony," it is difficult to see what.

Closely related to verbal profundity is the desire for *false elegance,* often a variety of what in the last chapter we called pretentious diction. A sentence like

A worker checks the watch's time-keeping performance.

is an attempt to cast a verbal spell over the job of quality control in a watch factory. This is shorter, simpler, and clearer:

A worker checks the watch's accuracy.

Confusion about the subject also leads to wordiness:

Music is similar to dress fads in that its styles change from time to time. Perhaps the change is subtle, but no one style of music will remain on top for a very long time. I am not talking about classical music, but rather about popular music that appeals to the majority of young people.

This writer did not begin with a word specific enough for his subject. He chose too general a term ("music"). The final sentence reveals that he himself felt the problem, for he spends twenty words explaining what kind of music he means. How much easier to have begun

Popular music is similar to dress fads. . . .

Sometimes deadwood stems from *ignorance of words.* That's the problem here:

In this novel, part of the theme is stated directly in so many words, and part is not so much said in specific words but is more or less hinted at.

Had the writer known the terms *explicit* and *implicit* he could have made the point more clearly and concisely:

In this novel, part of the theme is explicit, and part is implicit.

A limited vocabulary is no disgrace. We all suffer that handicap, and education is the process of overcoming it. But while it may be pardonable, not knowing the right word often results in obscurity and deadwood. It helps to keep a list of pairs like *explicit* and *implicit* which enable you to make distinctions quickly and neatly: *extrinsic/intrinsic, concrete/abstract, actual/ideal, absolute/relative* are other examples.

Finally, *excessive caution* contributes to deadwood. Some people are afraid to express anything as certain. They will write:

It seems that Columbus discovered the New World in 1492.

Certainly some things call for caution. But no one can lay down a blanket rule about when qualification is necessary and when it is verbose. We'll consider the question in closer detail later in the chapter; for the moment remember that extreme caution in writing is more often a vice than a virtue.

A false sense of what is significant, confusion about what you want to say, ignorance of words, and timidity, then, are some of the psychological factors leading to deadwood. In practice, they are manifested in either of two ways: *circumlocution,* using too many words to say something; and *pointlessness,* saying something that doesn't need to be said at all.

Circumlocution
▷ ## Avoid Meaningless Strings of Verbs

English often conveys subtleties by stringing verbs:

I *was going to go* tomorrow.

Here the verbs are justified by the meaning (that a planned future action is now uncertain or negated). But when a string of verbs says nothing that cannot be said with equal clarity or force in fewer words, the result is deadwood:

The current foreign situation *should serve to start* many Americans *to begin* thinking.
BETTER: . . . should start many Americans thinking.

Nucleonics investigates the smaller particles that *go to make up* the nucleus of the atom.
BETTER: . . . that make up the nucleus of the atom.

A special case of empty verb strings is the *awkward passive construction.* The focus of thought or tact may make the passive voice necessary. Generally, however, you should write in the active voice. Overuse of the passive lards sentences with empty words:

The writer's point *must be clearly stated by him* at the beginning of the paragraph.
BETTER: The writer must clearly state his point at the beginning of the paragraph.

The work *must be done* by her by tomorrow.
BETTER: She must do the work by tomorrow.

(In the last example, however, note that if one wished to emphasize "work," the passive would be justified.)

▷ ## The Best Modification Is Concise and Direct

In practice this principle often boils down to not using a phrase if a word will do:

She conducted herself *in an irrational manner.*
BETTER: She conducted herself irrationally.
BETTER YET: She acted irrationally.

He didn't take the advice *given to him by his doctor.*
BETTER: He didn't take his doctor's advice.

It leaves us *with the thought* that. . . .
BETTER: It leaves us thinking that. . . .

A common kind of adjectival wordiness is using a full relative clause to introduce a participle or adjective that could be attached directly to the noun:

This is the same idea *that was* suggested last week.
BETTER: This is the same idea suggested last week.

The family *who are* living in that house are my friends.
BETTER: The family living in that house are my friends.

In such clauses the relative word *(that, which, who)* acts as the subject and is immediately followed by a form of *be* which is, in turn, followed by a participle or adjective. The relative word and the verb contribute nothing except to hook the adjective or participle to the noun. Occasionally clarity, emphasis, or rhythm justify the whole clause. Mostly they do not.

The direct, economic use of participles is a resource of style that inexperienced writers underuse. The economy also applies to adverbial clauses, which can sometimes be boiled down to one or two operative words:

Because they lacked experience, they didn't do a good job.
BETTER: Lacking experience, they didn't do a good job.

Now and then, independent clauses or separate sentences may be pruned and subordinated by means of participles:

These ideas are out of date, *and they don't tell us anything new.*
BETTER: These ideas are out of date, telling us nothing new.

Participles are also more economical than gerunds (the nounal use of the *-ing* form of a verb; see page 114):

She worried about *the cooking of* the dinner.
BETTER: She worried about cooking the dinner.

Note, however, that you must consider meaning in such revisions. "She worried about the cooking of the dinner" would make sense if someone else were doing the cooking.

▷ Specificity Means Concision

Beginning with a word too general for your idea creates a need for wordy modification:

People who enter college for the first time find it difficult to adjust to the teaching.

"People" is too inclusive. To specify what kind of "people," the writer must add seven words. English provides no single term meaning "people who enter college for the first time" (except *matriculants*, a Latinism too forbidding for this writer's purpose). *Students,* however, would be more precise than *people*, and *freshmen*, more precise still (even though second-semester freshmen are not, strictly speaking, entering college for the first time). With *freshmen* only one modifier is needed:

College freshmen find it difficult to adjust to the teaching.

While most frequent with nouns, failure to be specific occurs with verbs as well:

The sudden change *motivated him into a rage.*
BETTER: The sudden change enraged him.

They *emerged victorious.*
BETTER: They won.

The too-general verb is often a form of *be, have,* or *seem.* When these merely link a noun or modifier to the subject, they can often be replaced by a more exact verb:

The people *were supportive of* conservation.
BETTER: The people supported conservation.

Officers have *to have a knowledge of* their men.
BETTER: Officers have to know their men.

▷ Keep Prepositions and Conjunctions Brief

Piled-up connectives grow like weeds if you do not pull them:

More than one game has been decided *on the basis of* a fumble.
BETTER: . . . decided by a fumble.

Wordy equivalents for *because, how,* and *so* are particularly common:

The bill failed *as a result of the fact that* the Senate was misinformed.
BETTER: . . . because the Senate was misinformed.

She will show us *the way in which* to do it.
BETTER: She will show us how to do it.

He becomes self-conscious *to the extent* that he withdraws into himself.
BETTER: He becomes so self-conscious that he withdraws into himself.

Pointlessness

Pointless words serve no purpose. They do not need to be made more concise; they need to be eliminated. There are two broad causes of pointless diction: (1) failing to credit readers' intelligence, and (2) failing to focus on the subject.

Failing to Credit Readers' Intelligence

Think about your readers, and avoid telling them what they already know or can easily infer from the context.

▷ *Don't Define What Is Common Knowledge*

Accountants sometimes function as auditors *(people from outside a company who check the books kept by the company's own accountants).*

All the italicized words in that sentence are dead. If readers understand "accountants," there is no reason to suppose that "auditors" requires definition. Gratuitous definitions not only make deadwood, but interfere with communication in another, more serious way—annoying readers by seeming to insult their intelligence.

Granted, it is not easy to decide when a word ought to be defined. In the following instance the naturalist Joseph Wood Krutch, writing for general readers, realizes that they will not understand geological terms and neatly explains what they need to know:

To even the most uninstructed eye a scorpion fossilized during the Silurian or Devonian epoch—say something like three hundred million years ago—is unmistakably a scorpion.

Ask yourself whether a definition is needed *by the reader whom you have in mind.* (And remember that it is not too much to ask people to look into a dictionary now and again.)

▷ *Don't Spell Out What Is Clearly Implied*
Unless there is a clear chance of confusion, you do not have to state what is entailed in a word's meaning (the deadwood is italicized):

Her dress was blue *in color.*

He was very tall *in height.*

Noun-adjectival combinations often contain deadwood caused by over-explicitness. In many cases the adjective is unnecessary:

There is considerable danger *involved.*

We question the methods *employed.*

The equipment *needed* is expensive.

The store stocks many products *to be sold.*

Each play has a special purpose *when it is used.*

This question has two sides *to it.*

Most countries *of the world* have their own coinage.

In other cases it is the noun that is dead:

They committed *an act of* burglary.

The quarterback is noted for his passing *ability.*

It has existed for a long *period of* time.

She was an unusual *kind of* child.

The punt return resulted in a fumble *situation.*

The last major barrier to the westward expansion *movement* was the Rocky Mountains.

Categorizing words such as *kind, sort, type, class,* and so on are especially prone to dead use. Emphasis or tone will sometimes justify "He is the kind of man who . . . ." Otherwise, the more concise "He is a man who . . ." is preferable.

Often in these noun-adjectival combinations, the adjectives can be used substantively, that is, as nouns:

On quilts, silk patches replaced *the homespun ones.*
BETTER: On quilts, silk patches replaced homespun.

Verbs, too, hide implicit meanings, which, whether expressed as a complement or a modifier, are often better left unsaid:

She always procrastinates *things.*

He tends to squint *his eyes.*

I have been told *by various people* that smoking is sophisticated.

Sometimes an idea is clearly implied by the total context rather than by any single word. Each of these phrases is dead:

Writing poetry requires experience as well as sensibility. A prerequisite *to writing poetry* is being able to write prose.

I dislike television. Most programs *on television* are unbelievable.

A good personality will help anyone, no matter what profession he or she chooses *in life.*

A special but frequent form of overexplicitness is the unneeded connective, especially common with conjunctive adverbs like *however, therefore, furthermore,* and so on. The following sentence does not really need the connective:

People think that stamp collecting requires money; *however,* it doesn't.
BETTER: People think that stamp collecting requires money; it doesn't.

The negated verb establishes the contradiction, and removing "however" even strengthens the point.

Probably it is true that inexperienced writers use too few conjunctive adverbs rather than too many. Even so, it pays to check *however*s and *thus*es and *consequently*s. Be sure that you really need them, or rather, that your readers really need them.

It can be wordy and tiresome to spell out all the connections of your ideas. The same impulse can make you heavy-handed in explaining your intentions—telling the reader what you're going to do next, or have just done, or won't do at all. Such explanations are like scaffolding around a new building. Scaffolding can be helpful in early drafts, enabling you to see where you're going. But when they revise, experienced writers dismantle most of these planks and ladders. Some should remain—enough to help readers where they need help. Where they do not, where they can follow your progress for themselves, scaffolding gets in the way, obscuring thought as staging around a new building conceals its shape.

Announcement—when it cannot be justified by emphasis—is a particularly awkward kind of scaffolding. An overworked formula is "Let me say" (variants: "Let me make clear," "Let me explain," "Let me tell you something"). Be on guard against pointless announcement at the beginning of a composition. Many readers react negatively to this sort of opening:

The essay that follows is about baseball. Specifically, it will deal with the business organization of a major league team.
BETTER: Supporting every major league baseball team is a complex business organization.

Good writers help their readers, but they do not assume that readers are helpless.

▷ *Avoid Empty Redundancy*
Empty redundancy is pointless repetition. It is often found in headwords and modifiers:

bisect *in half*
modern life *of today*
vital essentials
sufficiently satisfied
It is *clearly* evident that
He hanged himself, *thereby taking his own life.*

Unlike legitimate restatements for clarity or emphasis, such redundancies are awkward and illogical, special instances of not understanding what words mean. A phrase like "vital essentials" seems to imply that there are "essentials" which are not "vital," a contradiction. Can you "bisect" anything without cutting it "in half"? Can a man hang himself without "thereby taking his own life"? (Never mind the rope's breaking; *hang* in such a context means to cause death.)

Failing to Focus on the Subject

Here deadwood comes from wandering away from the topic, from pursuing irrelevancies:

▷ *Don't Open Up Topics You Will Not Develop*
Now an idea in itself may be interesting, but if it does not support your topic it is just deadwood:

The people had come to the new world for freedom *of several different kinds,* and had found injustice instead.

There is nothing inherently dead in "of several different kinds." But the writer does not discuss these kinds of freedom (nor does his subject require him to). To mention them at all, then, is a mistake. The phrase contributes nothing to the main point. Even worse, it mutes the contrast between the key terms "freedom" and "injustice" and misleads readers by pointing to a path of development they will not find.

▷ *Avoid the Distinction Without a Difference*
A pointless distinction is naming several varieties of something when those varieties do not matter for your purpose:

Under the honor system, teachers do not have to stand guard during *exams, tests, and quizzes.*

There are of course real differences among exams, tests, and quizzes, and had the writer been concerned with the various modes of testing students must endure, the distinctions would have been vital. But in fact the topic is the honor system, and the distinction is empty. One word would do, probably "tests," the most general.

▷ *Don't Overqualify*
It is worth saying again that excessive caution leads to deadwood:

Theater-in-the-round *somewhat* resembles an arena.

Why so cautious? *Resembles* does not mean "identical with"; it doesn't need the protection of "somewhat." Writing so timidly is like holding up one's trousers with belt, suspenders, and several huge safety pins. As we discussed on pages 106–8, qualification is often necessary if you are to treat ideas without ignoring their complexity. But pointless qualification is wordy foolishness.

The verbs *seem* and *tend* and the windy phrase *can be said to be* (in place of a simple *is*) often indicate overqualification:

After a square dance the people are pretty tired, but *it seems that* when they have tried it once they want more.
BETTER: . . . but when they have tried it once they want more.

This play *tends to be* a comedy.
BETTER: This play is a comedy.

Ethan *can be said to be* a tragic hero.
BETTER: Ethan is a tragic hero.

Another verb that is often deadwood is *would*. This auxiliary does have legitimate uses—to indicate a conditional action, for example:

I would have gone if I had known you were there.

Or to anticipate a future effect:

The defeat would ultimately prove disastrous.

But when there is no question of doubt or conditionality or an anticipated future, *would* is a wasted word (and sometimes subtly misleading):

That *would be* my brother at the door.
BETTER: That is my brother at the door.

CHAPTER 27

Figurative Language

Whenever language is simple, plain, direct, whenever it employs words in their conventional meaning, we say that it is literal. *Literal* comes from the Latin *litera*, "letter"; what is literal is according to the letter. Consider, for example, this statement: "A writer's style should be purposive, not merely decorative." It is to be read literally: the words mean nothing more, and nothing less, than what they say.

In figurative language the same idea has been expressed like this: "Style is the feather in the arrow, not the feather in the cap." *Figurative* means that a word has been stretched to accommodate a larger or even very different sense from that which it usually conveys. A writer can make this stretch because of a likeness between different concepts, a likeness the context reveals. Thus the literal meaning of "feather in the arrow" is the stabilizer that keeps the arrow straight; the figurative meaning is that style keeps prose on target.

A writer must provide clues for readers so they may understand figurative words. In speech, we signal such meanings by gestures, facial expressions, pronunciation, or tone of voice (think of how we say *generous* to twist its sense to "stingy" when we say of a cheap acquaintance, "He's a generous guy!"). In writing, the context—the rest of the sentence, paragraph, and even total composition—controls a figurative word, making it fly in an unusual direction.

Effective figures depend on total diction, on all your words. You do not improve writing by sticking in occasional similes or metaphors. They must be woven into prose. When they are, figures of speech add great richness. Look again at the comparison of style to the feathers of an arrow. It enhances meaning on at least four levels. First, it clarifies and concretizes an unfamiliar and abstract idea ("style") in a striking visual image. Second, it enlarges our conception of style, endowing style with the functions of the feather in the arrow (providing stability and guidance) and disassociating it from the qualities of a feather in a cap (vanity, pretentiousness, pointless decoration). Third, the figure implies judgment: that style in the "arrow-feather" sense is good, while style in the "hat-feather" sense is bad. Finally, the figure entertains: we take pleasure in the witty succinctness with which a complicated idea is made clearer and enriched by the image of the two feathers.

Thus figures clarify, they expand and deepen meaning, they express feelings and judgments, and they are pleasurable. We observe these virtues over and over as we look at the more common figures of speech. The most frequent and most useful are similes and metaphors. Similes first.

Similes

A simile is a brief comparison, usually introduced by *like* or *as*. The preposition *like* is used when the following construction is a word or phrase:

My words swirled around his head like summer flies.   E. B. White

The conjunction *as* introduces a clause, that is, a construction containing its own subject and verb:

The decay of society was praised by artists as the decay of a corpse is praised by worms.   G. K. Chesterton

A simile consists of two parts: tenor and vehicle. The *tenor* is the primary subject—"words" in White's figure, the "decay of society" and "artists" in Chesterton's. The *vehicle* is the thing to which the main subject is compared—"summer flies" and the "decay of a corpse" and "worms."

Usually, though not invariably, the vehicle is, or contains, an image. An *image* is a word or expression referring to something we can perceive. "Summer flies," for example, is an image, primarily a visual one, though like many images it has a secondary perceptual appeal: we can hear the flies as well as see them.

Vehicle commonly follows tenor, as in the two instances above. But the vehicle may come first, emphasizing the main subject by delay and also arousing our curiosity by putting the cart before the horse:

Like a crack in a plank of wood which cannot be sealed, the difference between the worker and the intellectual was ineradicable in Socialism.   Barbara Tuchman

Most similes are brief, but they may be expanded—usually by breaking the vehicles into parts and applying each to the tenor. A historian, writing about the Italian patriot Garibaldi, explains that

his mind was like a vast sea cave, filled with the murmur of dark waters at flow
and the stirring of nature's greatest forces, lit here and there by streaks of glorious
sunshine bursting in through crevices hewn at random in its rugged sides.

George Macaulay Trevelyan

Similes Clarify

Similes have many uses. One is to clarify an unfamiliar idea or perception
by expressing it in familiar terms:

Cold air is heavy; as polar air plows into a region occupied by tropical air . . . it
gets underneath the warm air and lifts it up even as it pushes it back. A cold front
acts physically like a cowcatcher.   Wolfgang Langewiesche

Finding familiar equivalents often involves *concretion,* which is turning
an abstraction into an image readers can imaginatively see or hear or touch.
It has been said, for example, that the plot of one of Thomas Hardy's
novels is

as complicated as a medieval mousetrap.   Virginia Woolf

Even though few of us have seen a medieval mousetrap, the phrase cleverly
suggests a labyrinthine Rube Goldberg contrivance.

Occasionally the process may be reversed so that a simile *abstracts,* that
is, moves from the concrete to the abstract:

The taste of that crane soup clung to me all day like the memory of an old sorrow
dulled by time.   John G. Neihardt

Then the apse [of a medieval cathedral] is pure and beautiful Gothic of the four-
teenth century, with very tall and fluted windows like single prayers.   Hilaire Belloc

Similes can also be emphatic, especially when they close a sentence or passage, like those by Neihardt and Belloc.

Similes Expand the Subject

Most similes—even those whose primary function is to explain—do more
than provide a perceptible equivalent of an abstract idea. Any vehicle comes
with meanings of its own, and these enter into and enlarge the significance
of the tenor. Belloc's phrase "single prayers" does not help us to see the
windows of the cathedral. But it does enlarge our conception of those windows, endowing them with the connotations we associate with *prayer:* the
upward lift of the spirit, the urge to transcend mortal limits.

Here are two other examples of similes rich in implication. The first is
about the "what-a-great-war" reminiscences of old soldiers:

The easy phrases covered the cruelties of war, like sand blowing in over the graves
of their comrades.   Thomas Pakenham

The image suggests the capacity of the mind to obscure the horror of war, even in those, perhaps especially in those, who endured it.

In this second example the novelist Isak Dinesen is discussing life on a farm in South Africa:

Sometimes visitors from Europe drifted into the farm like wrecked timbers into still waters, turned and rotated, till in the end they were washed out again, or dissolved and sank.

The image implies a great deal about such drifters: their lack of will and purpose, the futility with which they float through life, their incapacity to anchor themselves to anything solid, their inevitable and unmarked disappearance.

Clearly, one advantage of similes—and of other figures as well—is economy of meaning. Compressing a range of ideas and feelings into few words, similes deepen prose.

Similes Express Feelings and Judgments

Many similes are emotionally charged. Pakenham's image of sand blowing over the graves of fallen soldiers, for example, is heavily freighted with sadness. And in the following figure the naturalist Rachel Carson does more than describe the summer sea; she reveals its beauty:

Or again the summer sea may glitter with a thousand moving pinpricks of light, like an immense swarm of fireflies moving through a dark wood.

Emotional connotations often involve judgments. The poet Rupert Brooke, writing about a conversation with a salesman, imagines how the man's mind works:

The observer could see thoughts slowly floating into it, like carp in a pond.

This simile operates on several levels: it translates an abstraction (the process of thinking) into an arresting visual image. It suggests the slowness and ponderousness of this particular mind. And it implies a judgment, even if humorously: this is not a mind the writer admires.

One other example, more extended, of a judgmental simile. The historian Barbara Tuchman is talking about the attitudes of English Socialists just before World War I:

What was needed was a strong [Socialist] party with no nonsense and a business-like understanding of national needs which would take hold of the future like a governess, slap it into clean clothes, wash its face, blow its nose, make it sit up straight at table and eat a proper diet.

Tuchman's image of the bossy nanny nicely conveys the unyielding self-righteousness of some Socialists of the period—their smug self-assurance, their certainty that they alone knew what was best for humanity, and their conviction that it was their duty to impose the truth upon people too childish to know what was good for them. Fairly or not, Tuchman is passing judgment. Her mocking image uncovers the disdain for common people which she senses beneath the Socialists' reforming zeal.

The judgments implied by such similes are more than sober, objective opinions. The images by which they are delivered give them great persuasive force. Thus Tuchman plays upon the resentment we carry from childhood against those Brobdingnagian know-it-alls who forced us to live by their rules.

Similes Give Pleasure

All good writing gives pleasure. But figurative language is a special delight. Tuchman's simile, reducing imposing Socialists who would reform the world to bossy nannies pontificating in a nursery, is amusing (whether it is fair is something else). Here is another example:

There are fanatics who love and venerate spelling as a tomcat loves and venerates catnip. There are grammatomaniacs; schoolmarms who would rather parse than eat; specialists in the objective case that doesn't exist in English; strange beings, otherwise sane and even intelligent and comely, who suffer under a split infinitive as you and I would suffer under gastroenteritis. H. L. Mencken

Similes Intensify Our Awareness

Finally, beyond their capacity to familiarize the strange, to expand ideas, to express feelings and evaluations, and to give us pleasure, similes have an even greater power. They bring us more intimately in touch with reality by joining diverse experiences. Think about this description of an old woman's hands:

Their touch had no substance, like a dry wind on a July afternoon. Sharon Curtin

Curtin's simile does all the usual things—compares a less familiar experience to a more familiar one, implies something about the loneliness of old age, even passes a judgment on life. But it does more: it unifies perceptions that most of us would not have put together.

Similes may also cut across the boundaries that separate the senses:

There was a glamour in the air, a something in the special flavour of that moment that was like the consciousness of Salvation, or the smell of ripe peaches on a sunny wall. Logan Pearsall Smith

In that image two disparate sense perceptions blend into a unified experience, and the fused aroma and vision of the peaches and the sunlit wall connect with the writer's consciousness of religious mystery.

Metaphor

Like a simile, a metaphor is also a comparison. The difference is that a simile compares things explicitly; it literally says that X is *like* Y. A metaphor compares things implicitly. Read literally, it does not state that X is like Y; but rather that X *is* Y:

Cape Cod is the bared and bended arm of Massachusetts.   Henry David Thoreau

Thoreau writes "is," not "is like." However, we understand that he means the Cape resembles a human arm, not that it really is an arm. The metaphor has simply taken the comparison a step closer and expressed it a bit more economically and forcefully.[1]

A metaphor has the same two parts as a simile: tenor—or the main subject—and vehicle—the image introduced for comparison. In Thoreau's sentence the tenor is "Cape Cod" and the vehicle is "the bared and bended arm." In many metaphors both parts are stated. In some, however, the writer refers only to the vehicle, depending on the context to supply the full comparison. Such a figure is called an *implied* or *fused metaphor,* rather than a full one. Had Thoreau written "the bared and bended arm of Massachusetts" in a context which clearly indicated he meant Cape Cod, his metaphor would have been implied.

Fused metaphors may involve metonymy. *Metonymy* means substituting for one concept another that is associated with it. The novelist Joseph Conrad, discussing the difficulty of saying exactly what one wants to say, speaks of

the old, old words, worn thin, defaced by ages of careless usage.

Conrad does not actually say that words are coins, but he implies the full metaphor by the expressions "worn thin" and "defaced," qualities of old coins. The logic of the figure runs like this:

Words are (like) old coins.

Old coins are often worn thin by passing from hand to hand and their faces nearly rubbed away.

Therefore, words can be "worn thin" and "defaced."

Another figure often found in metaphors and closely related to metonymy is *synecdoche,* which is substituting a part for the whole, as when a ship is referred to as a "sail." In the following passage the religious revivals

1. It is sometimes argued that metaphors are more powerful figures than similes and even in some ways essentially different. Here we need not assume any greater virtue in metaphors. They are more economical and generally more emphatic. For these reasons they are sometimes preferable to similes. But on some occasions the explicit comparison of a simile is better.

staged by the evangelist Aimee Semple Macpherson are compared (implicitly) to an amusement park:

With rare ingenuity, Aimee kept the Ferris wheels and the merry-go-round of religion going night and day.   Carey McWilliams

The logic goes like this:

Aimee's revivals were (like) an amusement park.

An amusement park contains Ferris wheels and merry-go-rounds.

Therefore, events at the revivals were (like) Ferris wheels and merry-go-rounds.

Many metaphors use synecdoche and metonymy.[2] Usually a writer wants to introduce as precise an image as possible into the vehicle of a metaphor, thus appealing immediately to the reader's eyes or ears. "Ferris wheels" and "merry-go-rounds," for instance, are easier to visualize than the larger, more abstract "amusement park." And these images are richly meaningful, implying the park in its entirety, as well as evoking vivid pictures of revolving vertical and horizontal wheels.

The Uses of Metaphor

Metaphors have the same functions as similes. They clarify the unfamiliar and render abstractions in images:

[Science] pronounces only on whatever, at the time, appears to have been scientifically ascertained, which is a small island in an ocean of nescience.
                                                                        Bertrand Russell

Russell's image of a small island (science) in a wide and lonely sea (all that we do not know) vividly expresses the relationship between knowledge and ignorance.

Metaphors also enrich meaning by implying added dimensions of thought or feeling. Consider all that is suggested by the term "idol" in this metaphor:

We squat before television, the idol of our cherished progress.   Evelyn Jones

"Idol," signifying a false god, denies the progress television symbolizes and celebrates. The image implies as well the irrationality and subservience of its worshippers.

In the next example the judgmental quality of the metaphor is more pronounced. About the ancient Romans, the writer remarks that

2. Metonymy is sometimes treated as a figure distinct from metaphor. For our purposes it is convenient to regard it—along with synecdoche—as a variety of metaphor.

they were marked by the thumbprint of an unnatural vulgarity, which they never
succeeded in surmounting.   Lawrence Durrell

A dirty thumbprint, like one left on a china cup or a white wall—what a
graphic signature of crudeness. In the following metaphor the judgment is
ironic (the passage concerns Huey Long, a powerful Louisiana politician
of the 1930s, who, when he was elected to the U.S. Senate, passed on his
governorship to a political crony):

He designated his old benefactor, O. K. Allen of Winnfield, as the apostolic choice
for the next full term.   Hodding Carter

"Apostolic," alluding to Christ and his disciples, is a wry comment on
Long: on the power he wielded, on the veneration he was accorded by his
followers, and perhaps even on how he regarded himself.
    Like similes, metaphors may be emotionally charged, pleasantly or, as
in this example, unpleasantly (the writer is remembering a dose of castor
oil forced down him when he was a child):

. . . a bulge of colorless slime on a giant spoon.   William Gibson

Metaphors are also emphatic, particularly at the end of a statement, where
the figure not only clarifies and pictures a complex abstraction, but also
strongly restates it, leaving a memorable image in the mind:

What distinguishes a black hole from a planet or an ordinary star is that anything
falling into it cannot come out of it again. If light cannot escape, nothing else can
and it is a perfect trap: a turnstile to oblivion.   Nigel Calder

Finally, metaphors may be extended through several sentences or even
an entire paragraph. In fact, exploring and expanding a metaphor can be
an effective way of generating a piece of prose. Here is a brief example:

Man is born broken. He lives by mending. The grace of God is glue.
                                                                          Eugene O'Neill

And here are two longer ones. The first works out a metaphor comparing *Time* magazine to a tale told to little children:

Time is also a nursery book in which the reader is slapped and tickled alternately.
It is full of predigested pap spooned out with confidential nudges. The reader is
never on his own for an instant, but, as though at his mother's knee, he is provided
with the right emotions for everything he hears or sees as the pages turn.
                                                                          Marshall McLuhan

Notice how the metaphor determines the diction: "slapped and tickled,"
"predigested pap," "spooned out," "nudges," "never on his own," "mother's

knee," "provided with." Even the phrase "as the pages turn" suggests the passivity of a child for whom the babysitter turns the pages.

The other example of an extended metaphor returns us to the passage with which we began this section, Thoreau's comparison of Cape Cod to a bent arm. The image opens a paragraph in the book *Cape Cod:*

Cape Cod is the bared and bended arm of Massachusetts: the shoulder is at Buzzard's Bay; the elbow, or crazy-bone, at Cape Mallabarre; the wrist at Truro; and the sandy fist at Provincetown—behind which the State stands on her guard, with her back to the Green Mountains, and her feet planted on the floor of the ocean, like an athlete protecting her Bay—boxing with northeast storms, and, ever and anon, heaving up her Atlantic adversary from the lap of the earth—ready to thrust forward her other fist, which keeps guard the while upon her breast at Cape Ann.

The figure organizes the entire paragraph, which develops the image of "the bare and bended arm" both by analysis and by expansion. Thoreau breaks it down into its parts—"elbow," "wrist," "fist"—and applies each of these to Cape Cod. At the same time he expands the metaphor into the larger inclusive image of the boxer—"back," "feet," "other fist," "breast"— connecting each detail with other parts of Massachusetts.

If you wish to develop a metaphor (or simile), remember that you can work in either of these ways, or even, like Thoreau, in both: inwardly, differentiating the elements of the image and relating these to your main topic; or outwardly, exploring the larger entity to which the image belongs, as the "bared arm" is a natural part of a boxer in a defensive stance.

Finding Metaphors

There is no formula for creating metaphors. Sometimes the literal detail of a scene lends itself to figurative use, as in the following sentence explaining why the writer was not allowed into a large office to observe the regimented life of clerks:

I knew those rooms were back there, but I couldn't get past the opaque glass doors any more than I could get past the opaque glass smiles.   Barbara Garson

Another source of metaphor is metonymy, which describes something in terms of an associated quality. Here is a sentence about the coming of spring in which birdsongs are described as if they were, themselves, birds:

The birds have started singing in the valley. Their February squawks and naked chirps are fully fledged now, and long lyrics fly in the air.   Annie Dillard

More often, however, a metaphor or simile involves a comparison which, while apt and revealing, does not grow naturally out of the subject as do the images by Garson and Dillard. For instance one philosopher discusses the style of another like this:

The style is not, as philosophic style should be, so transparent a medium that one looks straight through it at the object, forgetting that it is there; it is too much like a window of stained glass which, because of its very richness, diverts attention to itself.
Brand Blanshard

But whether a metaphor arises from "inside" the subject or from "outside," its coming depends on imagination. There is no magic for discovering metaphors. It is a talent, and some people are more adept at seeing resemblances than the rest of us. Still, we can all profit from letting our minds run free from inhibitions. In a first draft don't be frightened of a simile or metaphor, even if it sounds far-fetched.

Using Metaphors Effectively

When you revise, however, become more detached and critical about figures of speech (as about all phases of your writing). To use metaphors and similes effectively, remember these principles:

▷ *Metaphors and Similes Should Be Fresh and Original*
Avoid trite figures: "quiet as a mouse," "white as a sheet," "the game of life," "a tower of strength." Clever humorists can make such clichés work for them, but only by playing upon their staleness. If you can think of nothing more original than "his face was white as a sheet," you are better off saying simply, "His face was very white."[3]

▷ *The Vehicle Should Fit the Tenor*
The vehicle of any simile or metaphor is likely to have several meanings. Be sure that none of them works against you. It is easy to focus so exclusively on the meaning you want that you overlook others which may spoil the comparison:

The town hall has been weathered by cold winds and harsh snows like an old mare turned out to graze.

While an old mare is an image of decrepitude, it has other characteristics which make it unsuitable as a vehicle for a building. Can you imagine a town hall in a pasture, nibbling grass and swatting flies with its tail?

▷ *Metaphors and Similes Should Be Appropriate to the Context*
Figures of speech have their own levels of formality and informality. Even when it does not possess specifically awkward connotations, a simile or

---

3. As mentioned on pp. 198–99, such trite similes and metaphors may be described as "dying," to distinguish them from figures already dead. Dead metaphors—"mouth of a river," for example—have passed beyond the figurative stage so that the vehicle has acquired a new literal sense. They are perfectly legitimate, and you should not feel doubtful about them. Once "mouth of a river" was probably a fresh and vivid image. Today "mouth" in this expression is not felt to be metaphorical at all; it is taken literally to mean the widening of a river as it ·mpties into a larger body of water.

metaphor must not be too colloquial or too learned for the occasion. It would not do to write in a paper for a history professor that "Napoleon went through Russia like a dose of salts."

▷ *Metaphors and Similes Should Not Be Awkwardly Mixed*
When several similes or metaphors appear in the same passage, they ought to harmonize in thought and image. Mixtures like the following are awkward at best and silly at worst:

The moon, a silver coin hung in the draperies of the enchanted night, let fall her glance, which gilded the roof tops with a joyful phosphorescence.

This sounds impressive—until one begins to think about the picture it so lushly describes. If the moon is a "coin" how can "she" "let fall [a] glance"? How can "silver" be used for gilding, which means to cover with gold? Why mix the three elements of silver, gold, and phosphorus? Can "phosphorescence" be "joyful"? Do "coins" hang in "draperies"?

Even dead metaphors and similes must be mixed carefully. Although such expressions no longer have figurative value, they can bring each other embarrassingly to life. The dead metaphors, "mouth of a river" and "leg of a journey," for instance, work well enough alone, but it would be clumsy to write that "the last leg of our journey began at the mouth of the river."

You must be careful, too, about the other, nonfigurative words you use with a simile or metaphor, even when these words are to be read literally. Because this writer was careless with his contextual diction, his metaphor fails:

The teacher leaves the students to develop the foundations of their education.

"Foundations," of course, are "built" or "laid," not "developed."

▷ *Metaphors and Similes Should Not Be Overworked*
Metaphors and similes ought not to be sprinkled about profusely, especially in expository writing. Even when they do not clash, too many are likely to cancel one another. Their effectiveness depends on their being relatively uncommon, for if every other sentence contains a simile or a metaphor, readers soon begin to discount them.

Personification

Personification, really a special kind of metaphor, is referring to inanimate things or to abstractions as if they were human. A simple instance of personification is the use of personal pronouns to refer to objects, as when sailors speak of a ship as "she." Here is a more subtle instance, a description of the social changes in an area of London:

As London increased, however, rank and fashion rolled off to the west, and trade, creeping on at their heels, took possession of their deserted abodes.

Washington Irving

"Rank" and "fashion" signify aristocratic Londoners; "trade" designates the merchant class. These abstractions are personified by the verbs: the aristocrats "roll off" elegantly in carriages, the tradesmen "creep" in with the deference of self-conscious inferiors.

The purpose of personification—like that of metaphor generally—is to explain, expand, vivify:

There is a rowdy strain in American life, living close to the surface but running very deep. Like an ape behind a mask it can display itself suddenly with terrifying effect. It is slack-jawed, with leering eyes and loose wet lips, with heavy feet and ponderous cunning hands; now and then when something tickles it, it guffaws, and when it is angry it snarls; and it can be aroused more easily than it can be quieted. Mike Fink and Yankee Doodle helped to father it, and Judge Lynch is one of its creations; and when it comes lumbering forth it can make the whole country step in time to its own irregular pulse beat.

Bruce Catton

Catton's personification (or perhaps "animalification") makes his point with extraordinary clarity and strength: mindless savagery is no abstraction; it is an ever-present menace.

Allusions

An allusion is a brief reference to a well-known person, place, or happening. Sometimes the reference is explicitly identified:

As it is, I am like that man in *The Pilgrim's Progress,* by some accounted man, who the more he cast away the more he had.

W. H. Hudson

More often the reference is indirect, and the writer depends on the reader's recognizing the source and significance:

We [Western peoples] tend to have a Micawberish attitude toward life, a feeling that so long as we do not get too excited something is certain to turn up.

Barbara Ward

A writer making an allusion should be reasonably sure that it *will be* familiar. Barbara Ward, for instance, could fairly refer to Mr. Micawber, confident that her readers know Dickens's *David Copperfield* well enough to remember Mr. Micawber, burdened by family and debt, yet cheerfully optimistic that some lucky chance will rescue him from ruin.

Some allusions are not to persons, but to well-known passages—a verse from the Bible, say, or a line from Shakespeare. The passage may be paraphrased or quoted literally, although it is not usually enclosed in quotation marks. There is no question of plagiarizing; the writer assumes readers know what he or she is doing. In this sentence, for instance, the allusion is to the Old Testament book of Ecclesiastes (3:1–8):

I didn't know whether I should appear before you—there is a time to show and a time to hide; there is a time to speak, and also a time to be silent.
                                                                      Norman O. Brown

While many allusions are drawn from literature, some refer to historical events or people, ancient or more recent:

These moloch gods, these monstrous states, are not natural beings. . . . [Moloch was an ancient Semitic diety to whom children were sacrificed.]
                                                                      Suzanne K. Langer

And it is not opinions or thoughts that *Time* provides its readers as news comment. Rather, the newsreel is provided with a razzle-dazzle accompaniment of Spike Jones noises. [Spike Jones was a popular orchestra leader of the 1940s, famous for wacky, comic arrangements of light classics and pop tunes. He used automobile horns, cow bells, steam whistles, and so on.][4]   Marshall McLuhan

Whatever the source of an allusion, its purpose is to enrich meaning by packing into a few words a complex set of ideas or feelings. Think, for instance, of how much is implied by describing a politician's career as "Napoleonic," or an accident as being "Titanic."

But remember that to work at all, allusions must be (1) appropriate to your point and (2) within the experience of your readers.

Irony

Irony consists of using words in a sense very different from their usual meaning. The simplest case occurs when a term is given its opposite value. Here, for example, a historian describes a party at the court of the English king James I:

Later the company flocked to the windows to look into the palace courtyard below. Here a vast company had already assembled to watch the King's bears fight with greyhounds, and mastiffs bait a tethered bull. These delights were succeeded by tumblers on tightropes and displays of horsemanship.   C. P. V. Akrigg

By "delights" we are expected to understand "abominations," "detestable acts of cruelty."

In subtler form, irony plays more lightly over words, pervading an entire passage rather than twisting any single word into its opposite. An instance occurs in this sentence (the writer is commenting on the decline of the medieval ideal of the knight):

4. The fact that it is necessary to explain who Spike Jones was indicates that allusions to contemporary people and events may quickly become dated.

In our end of time the chevalier has become a Knight of Pythias, or Columbus, or the Temple, who solemnly girds on sword and armor to march past his own drugstore.   Morris Bishop

None of Bishop's words means its reverse; the sentence is to be read literally. Still, Bishop intends us to smile at contemporary men playing at knighthood. The irony lies in the fact that some of the words ought *not* to be taken literally. Twentieth-century businessmen ought not to "solemnly gird on sword and armor," blithely unaware of the disparity between knightly ideals and modern life.

Disparity is the common denominator in both these examples of irony: the difference between the ideal and the actual, between what we profess and what we do, between what we expect and what we get. In stressing such disparities, irony is fundamentally different from simile and metaphor, which build upon similarity. The whole point of irony is that things are *not* what they seem or what they should be or what we want them to be. They are different.

Irony reveals the differences in various ways. One is by using words in a double sense, making them signify both the ideal and the actual ("delights"). Another is by juxtaposing images of what could be (or once was) and of what is (the chevalier girding on his sword and the neighborhood druggist). Either way, we are made conscious of the gap between "ought" and "is": people *ought* to treat dumb animals kindly; they *do* take pleasure in torturing them.

The writer employing irony must be sure that his or her readers will understand the special value of the words. Sometimes one can depend on the general knowledge and attitudes of the audience. The ironic sense of Akrigg's "delights" is clear because modern readers know that such amusements are not delightful.

But sometimes irony must be signaled, as in this passage by the historian Barbara Tuchman (she is discussing the guilt of the Nazi leaders):

When it comes to guilt, a respected writer—respected in some circles—has told us, as her considered verdict on the Nazi program, that evil is banal—a word that means something so ordinary that you are not bothered by it; the dictionary definition is "commonplace and hackneyed." Somehow that conclusion does not seem adequate or even apt. *Of course,* evil is commonplace; *of course* we all partake of it. Does that mean that we must withhold disapproval, and that when evil appears in dangerous degree or vicious form we must not condemn but only understand?

The specifically ironic words are "respected" and "considered verdict." The first is cued by the qualification "respected in some circles," with its barbed insinuation: "respected, but not by you or me." "Considered verdict" is pushed into irony not so much by any particular cue as by the total context. If "banality" is the only judgment the other writer can make, her judgment—Tuchman suggests—is hardly worth considering. "Verdict" has another ironic overtone. The word signifies a judicial decision, and

Tuchman implies that her opponent is presumptuous in delivering a verdict as if she were judge and jury.

In other ways, too, Tuchman reveals her feelings and thus contributes to the tone of irony. The repetition of the italicized "of course" implies the commonplaceness of the ideas. And the rhetorical question, stressing the undeniable truth of Tuchman's point, underscores the folly she is attacking.

Irony may be used in a variety of tones. Some irony is genial, amusing and amused, like that by Morris Bishop. Some is more serious (Akrigg) or even angry (Tuchman). But whatever its tone, irony contributes significantly to a writer's persona. It is a form of comment—though an oblique form. Thus it represents an intrusion of the writer into the writing. He or she stands forth, moreover, in a special way: as a subtle, complex, witty presence, deliberately using intellect to distance emotion. This does not mean that irony diminishes emotion. On the contrary: irony acts like a lens, concentrating the emotions focused through it. But it does mean that irony constrains emotion rather than allowing it to gush.

Irony, finally, may function in prose in two ways: (1) as a specific figure of speech, a device for expressing a particular judgment; or (2) as a mode of thought, an encompassing vision of people and events. In this broad aspect irony is the stance some writers take toward life. They alone may properly be described as ironists. The rest of us, though we are not ironists in this deeper sense, can profitably use irony now and then.

Overstatement and Understatement

Overstatement and understatement are special kinds of irony. Each depends on the disparity between the reality the writer describes and the words he or she uses. Overstatement exaggerates the subject, magnifying it beyond its true dimensions. Understatement takes the opposite tack: the words are intentionally inadequate to the reality.

Overstatement

The rhetorical name for overstatement is *hyperbole*, from a Greek word meaning "excess." Loosely speaking, there are two kinds of overstatement: comic and serious. Like caricature, comic hyperbole ridicules or burlesques by enlargement.

Comic overstatement has deep roots in American literature. It is a major element in the tall tales told by such folk heroes as Mike Fink and Davey Crockett. Much of Mark Twain's humor depends on overstatement. Here, for instance, is a passage from his essay "The Awful German Language," included in *A Tramp Abroad:*

An average sentence in a German newspaper, is a sublime and impressive curiosity; it occupies a quarter of a column; it contains all the ten parts of speech—not in regular order, but mixed; it is built mainly of compound words constructed by the writer on the spot, and not to be found in any dictionary—six or seven words compacted into one, without joint or seam—that is, without hyphens; it treats of fourteen or fifteen different subjects, each inclosed in a parenthesis of its own, with here and there extra parentheses which reinclose three or four of the minor parentheses, making pens within pens: finally, all the parentheses and reparentheses are massed together between a couple of king-parentheses, one of which is placed in the first line of the majestic sentence and the other in the middle of the last line of it—*after which comes the* VERB, and you find out for the first time what the man has been talking about; and after the verb—merely by way of ornament, as far as I can make out—the writer shovels in *"haben sind gewesen gehabt haben geworden sein,"* or words to that effect, and the monument is finished.

Serious overstatement differs only in its end, which is persuasion rather than laughter. The writer may wish to impress us with the value of something or to shock us into seeing a hard truth. Shock is the tactic of H. L. Mencken, who cudgels what he regarded as the venality, stupidity, and smugness of life in the 1920s:

It is . . . one of my firmest and most sacred beliefs, reached after an enquiry extending over a score of years and supported by incessant prayer and meditation, that the government of the United States, in both its legislative arm and its executive arm, is ignorant, incompetent, corrupt, and disgusting—and from this judgment I except no more than twenty living lawmakers and no more than twenty executioners of their laws. It is a belief no less piously cherished that the administration of justice in the Republic is stupid, dishonest, and against all reason and equity—and from this judgment I except no more than thirty judges, including two upon the bench of the Supreme Court of the United States. It is another that the foreign policy of the United States—its habitual manner of dealing with other nations, whether friend or foe, is hypocritical, disingenuous, knavish, and dishonorable—and from this judgment I consent to no exception whatever, either recent or long past. And it is my fourth (and, to avoid too depressing a bill, final) conviction that the American people, taking one with another, constitute the most timorous, sniveling, poltroonish, ignominious mob of serfs and goose-steppers ever gathered under one flag in Christendom since the end of the Middle Ages, and that they grow more timorous, more sniveling, more poltroonish, more ignominious every day.

Comic or serious, overstatement relies on several devices. It likes the superlative forms of adjectives, the hugest numbers, the longest spans of time, extremes of all sorts. It prefers sweeping generalizations: *every, all, always, never, none.* It admits few qualifications or disclaimers, and if it does qualify, it may turn the concession into another exaggerated claim (like Mencken's "and from this judgment I except no more than twenty living lawmakers"). It rides upon words with strong emotional connotations like "sniveling," "poltroonish," "ignominious," "knavish." Its sentence structure is likely to be emphatic, with strong rhythms and frequent repetitions. Short statements are stressed by being set beside longer ones.

In the hands of writers like Twain or Mencken, overstatement is powerful rhetoric, shocking, infuriating, hilarious. But this very power is a limitation. Overstatement is hard to take for very long and quickly loses its capacity to shock or amuse. Even worse, overstatement like Mencken's is often abused. It is, after all, assertion, not reasoned argument, and it easily degenerates into shrill name-calling.

Understatement

Understatement stresses importance by seeming to deny it. Like overstatement it can be comic or serious. Twain is being funny in this passage:

I have been strictly reared, but if it had not been so dark and solemn and awful there in that vast, lonely room, I do believe I should have said something which could not be put into a Sunday-school book without injuring the sale of it.

But here is a more serious case:

Last week I saw a woman flayed alive, and you will hardly believe how it altered her appearance for the worse.
Jonathan Swift

Understatement works a paradox: increasing emotional impact by carefully avoiding emotive language. It is a species of irony in that the deeper value of the words differs from their surface meaning. Swift's phrase "altered her appearance for the worse" seems woefully inadequate: no streaming blood, no frenzied screams, no raw, quivering flesh—just that "it altered her appearance for the worse." But Swift tricks us into imagining the scene for ourselves, and this makes the brutality real.

In the following paragraph Ernest Hemingway increases horror by denying the horrible, writing as if a cold-blooded execution were just routine. Which in time of war it is; *and that's the horror:*

They shot the cabinet ministers at half-past six in the morning against the wall of the hospital. There were pools of water in the courtyard. There were wet dead leaves on the paving of the courtyard. It rained hard. All the shutters of the hospital were nailed shut. One of the ministers was sick with typhoid. Two soldiers carried him downstairs and out into the rain. They tried to hold him up against the wall but he sat down in a puddle of water. The other five stood very quietly against the wall. Finally the officer told the soldiers it was no good trying to make him stand up. When they fired the first volley he was sitting down in the water with his head on his knees.

Sometimes words are unequal to reality. Then understatement may be the best strategy, rendering the event in simple, direct language:

In the heart of the city near the buildings of the Prefectural Government and at the intersection of the busiest streets, everybody had stopped and stood in a crowd gazing up at three parachutes floating down through the blue air.

The bomb exploded several hundred feet above their heads.

The people for miles around Hiroshima, in the fields, in the mountains, and on the bay, saw a light that was brilliant even in the sun, and felt heat.

Alexander H. Leighton

A special form of understatement is *litotes,* a term sometimes used as a synonym for understatement in general. More narrowly it means emphasizing a positive by doubling a negative as when we express admiration for a difficult shot in tennis by exclaiming, "Not bad," or stress someone's bravery by saying that he "did not play the coward."

Whatever we call it, understatement is a powerful figure of speech. To naive readers it sometimes seems callous or insensitive: some of Swift's contemporaries, for example, thought his irony to be mere cruelty. But when it really connects with subject and reader, understatement is more explosive than hyperbole.

Puns

A pun is a word employed in two or more senses, or a word used in a context that suggests a second term sounding like it. In either case the two meanings must interact, usually, though not necessarily, in a humorous way. In the first of the two following examples, the pun depends on different senses of the same word; in the second, on one word's sounding like another:

A cannon-ball took off his legs, so he laid down his arms.   Thomas Hood

During the two previous centuries musical styles went in one era and out of the other. . . .   Frank Muir

While puns resemble irony in simultaneously using words in different senses, they differ in important ways. For one thing, a pun is today almost exclusively a device of humor (though in earlier centuries poets and dramatists often employed puns for serious meanings). Here, for instance, Mark Twain makes a joke by punning on the expression "raising chickens":

Even as a schoolboy poultry-raising was a study with me, and I may say without egotism that as early as the age of seventeen I was acquainted with all the best and speediest methods of raising chickens, from raising them off a roost by burning Lucifer matches under their noses, down to lifting them off a fence on a frosty night by insinuating a warm board under their feet.

For another thing, puns reveal unexpected connections. In this they are less like irony than like simile and metaphor. A good pun not only amuses us, but also points to unrealized similarities. The humorist S. J. Perelman entitles one collection of essays *The Road to Miltown, or Under the Spreading*

Atrophy (Miltown was the brand name of a popular tranquilizer.) Punning on "a tree," the word "atrophy" echoes a famous phrase of sentimental poetry, "under the spreading chestnut tree"; and the participle "spreading" acquires a sinister implication, far removed from the pleasant connotations it has in Longfellow's poem, "The Village Blacksmith." In an age given to the wholesale swallowing of tranquilizers, atrophy may indeed be spreading.

Because they became a sign of "low" humor in the late nineteenth century, many people consider puns unseemly in anything but avowedly humorous writing. That judgment is a bit harsh. A bad pun *is* regrettable. But a good pun—one both clever and revealing—is worth making.

Zeugma

Zeugma (pronounced ZOOG-ma) is a special kind of pun involving a verb used with two or more objects, but with a difference of meaning. Here the novelist Lawrence Durrell is describing the plight of a maiden chased by lustful monks:

Joanna, pursued by the three monks, ran about the room, leaping over tables and chairs, sometimes throwing a dish or a scriptural maxim at her pursuers.

And here is a wry definition of a piano:

Piano, n. A parlor utensil for subduing the impenitent visitor. It is operated by depressing the keys of the machine and the spirits of the audience.
                                                                Ambrose Bierce

Zeugma, like puns generally, is a comic figure of speech. It is witty and amusing, and increases meaning by linking disparities: Durrell's pairing of dishes and scriptural maxims reveals their equal inefficacy in Joanna's plight.

Imagery

An image is a word or expression that speaks directly to one or more of the senses, as in this description of the Seine in Paris:

The river was brown and green—olive-green under the bridges—and a rainbow-coloured scum floated at the sides.   Jean Rhys

Images are classified according to the sense to which they primarily appeal. Visual images, like those in the sentence above, are the most common. Next in frequency, probably, are auditory images, directed to the ear:

The [medieval] house lacked air, light, and *comfort moderne;* but people had little taste for privacy. They lived most of their lives on the streets, noisy indeed by day, with pounding hammers, screaming saws, clattering wooden shoes, street cries of vendors of goods and services, and the hand bells of pietists, summoning all to pray for the souls of the dead.   Morris Bishop

Images can appeal to other senses: to smell, taste, touch, even to the muscular sense of movement and balance (these are called kinesthetic images). Here, for example, is an indictment of the odors of a modern city:

. . . [T]he reek of gasoline exhaust, the sour smell of a subway crowd, the pervasive odor of a garbage dump, the sulphurous fumes of a chemical works, the carbolated rankness of a public lavatory . . . the chlorinated exudation of ordinary drinking water. . . .   Lewis Mumford

Often an image stimulates two or more senses simultaneously, though it is directed primarily to one. Thus in Rhys's sentence about the Seine, the imagery, while essentially visual, also suggests the feel of the water and the smell of the scum.

At their simplest, images re-create sensory experience. Bishop makes us "hear" a medieval city. In the following passage the writer "images" the experience of walking in a small stream:

Exploring a streambed can be done on a purely sensual level. How it all feels— moss, wet rock, soft mud under feet; cold fast mountain water or the touch of a sun-warmed gentle brook; water wrapping itself around your ankles or knees, swirling in little eddies, sparkling in small pools, rushing away white and foamy over rapids, or calmly meandering over glistening pebbles.   Ruth Rudner

Rudner's description also shows how images may be mixed to appeal to several senses. Many of her words are tactile: "soft mud under feet," "the touch of a sun-warmed gentle brook," "water wrapping itself around your ankles or knees." Others are visual: "moss, wet rock," "swirling in little eddies," "sparkling," "glistening pebbles." Still others, kinesthetic: "swirling" again, "rushing away," "calmly meandering."

But images can be stretched to signify more than sensual experience. Here, for instance, is a description of a California landscape, scene of a murderous love affair:

The lemon groves are sunken, down a three- or four-foot retaining wall, so that one looks directly into their foliage, too lush, too unsettlingly glossy, the greenery of nightmare; the fallen eucalyptus bark is too dusty, a place for snakes to breed.   Joan Didion

Literally these images describe the trees and the bark-strewn ground. Yet they suggest unnaturalness and evil too, a morbid aura of death. We cannot say that they "mean" evil and death, as we may say that the vehicle of a metaphor signifies the thing for which it stands. Nonetheless the images have overtones that give the passage a sinister vibrato.

At times this sort of implication is carried so far that an image acquires symbolic value, rendering a complex, abstract idea in a sharp perception. At the end of the following sentence the novelist and essayist George Orwell turns an image into a symbol of judgment:

When one watches some tired hack on the platform mechanically repeating the familiar phrases—*bestial atrocities, bloodstained tyranny, free peoples of the world, stand shoulder to shoulder*—one often has the curious feeling that one is not watching a live human being but some kind of dummy: a feeling which suddenly becomes stronger when the light catches the speaker's spectacles and turns them into blank discs which seem to have no eyes behind them.

CHAPTER 28

Unusual Words and Collocations

Diction does not have to be figurative to catch our eye. Even literal language is memorable when it is unusual, whether in the form of uncommon words or of everyday ones used in odd senses or in striking collocations.

A *collocation* is a group of words considered as a unit of meaning. For example, in the sentence "Ambitious people seek a place in the sun" the phrase "a place in the sun" is a collocation, a conventional and predictable one in that context. In "Wise people seek a place in the shadows" the phrase "in the shadows" is, for the context, less usual, more surprising. Like a good simile or metaphor, an unpredictable word or combination of words—effectively used—conveys a fresh idea or feeling or perception. It stretches our minds to accommodate something new.

Urging the value of uncommon words may seem to contradict the principle of simplicity. Actually it only qualifies that principle. Simplicity of diction does not mean simplemindedness. It means that diction ought to be no more difficult than the writer's purpose requires. And sometimes only an uncommon word or collocation *will* serve the purpose of expressing a thought or of stimulating the reader.

Unusual Words

Often a striking word comes from a foreign language or is an antiquated English word:

The average autochthonous Irishman is close to patriotism because he is close to the earth.   G. K. Chesterton

For when the Commodore roused his starboard watch at 5:14—having given them an hour and a quarter as lagniappe—there was a good feeling of having turned a corner unaware. . . .   Christopher Morley

We stood there mumchance and swallowing, wondering what the devil this construction was.   Lawrence Durrell

Now each of these examples confirms an important principle: unusual words ought not to be used just because they are unusual, but because they are also precise and economic. *Autochthonous*—the condition of being a native, one born in a particular region—derives from Greek roots meaning, loosely, "the land itself." Thus the word is not simply a fancy equivalent to *native*; it stresses Chesterton's point that patriotism is rooted in soil. *Lagniappe*, common in Louisiana though not elsewhere, is borrowed from American Spanish and means something extra thrown in for goodwill, like the thirteenth roll in a baker's dozen; it has here the advantage of concision, of saying in a single word what otherwise would require a phrase of three or four terms. *Mumchance*, an older English word seldom heard today, means "silently," and implies a shocked, stunned silence.

Sometimes an unusual word is not foreign or archaic, but technical, made striking by being applied outside its normal context, like the business terms in this sentence by Rudyard Kipling:

Very minute are the instructions of the Government for the disposal, wharfage, and demurrage of its dead.

Here again we see that the unusual words are exactly right. Kipling implies the callousness of the British government toward those who died in its service in India: their coffins are merchandise, and the charges for loading and storage are carefully calculated.

Unusual Meanings

Uncommoness may reside not so much in the rarity of the word itself, as in the meaning it carries. A writer may evoke an older meaning, closer to the etymological sense. Robert Frost, writing about the United States, speaks of the "land realizing itself westward." We think of *realize* as meaning "to understand clearly," and we must pause a moment to grasp that Frost calls up the older sense of "to make real": the nation created its reality as it drove westward. And in the following sentence *imagination* does not have its common meaning of "creative faculty," but rather signifies the productions of that creativity:

Universities flourished; scholars wrote their profundities and novelists their imaginations.   Morris Bishop

Everyday words may also be made striking by being shifted out of their usual grammatical roles. Here a writer describing the coming of spring employs *indestructible* as a noun:

Under the spruce boughs which overlay the borders, the first shoots of snowdrops appeared, the indestructible.   E. B. White

Neologisms

Neologisms constitute a special class of rare words. Literally "new words," they are made up by the writer. Some are new in being original combinations of phonemes (that is, sounds). James Thurber invents several such neologisms to describe the family car being hit by a trolley:

Tires booped and whoosed, the fenders queeled and graked, the steering wheel rose up like a spectre and disappeared in the direction of Franklin Avenue with a melancholy whistling sound, bolts and gadgets flew like sparks from a Catherine wheel.

Thurber's coinages are *onomatopoeic* (imitating sound). In the next example the neologism is formed by adding a suffix which does not conventionally go with the word (and in the process making a pun):

But once there came to "the grey metropolis" a Finnish lady—a most perfect representative of non-Aryan beauty and anythingarian charm—to whom not only men, but what is more wonderful, most women, fell captive the moment they saw her.   George Saintsbury

But probably most neologisms are novel compound words. Barbara Tuchman describes the most remarkable quality of a particular statesman as his "you-be-damnedness"; and a traveler in Sicily complains of the crude duckboards placed for tourists around an excavation of beautiful mosaics:

It was a groan-making thing to do and only an archeologist could have thought of it.   Lawrence Durrell

Such constructions are called *nonce compounds,* which are distinct from the conventional compounds we all use, like *teenager* or *schoolboy.* Nonce compounds are usually hyphenated, unlike conventional compounds, some of which are hyphenated and some written as one unit. Occasionally a nonce compound consists of a number of words strung together in a phrase acting as a single grammatical part (usually a modifier) like the ten-word adjectival in this sentence (it modifies a three-word noun):

I doubt whether even the breathless, gosh-gee-whiz-can-all-this-be-happening-to-me TV-celebrity-author could cap this shlock classic with another.   Pauline Kael

Unusual Collocations

An unusual collocation is an unlikely combination of words, each commonplace in itself but rarely used with the other(s). This description of a midwestern steel plant is an example:

Republic Steel stood abrupt out of the flat prairie.   Howard Fast

We do not think of buildings as "standing abrupt," but for that very reason the diction is memorable, like the structures it describes rearing dominantly out of the flat land. Here are several other instances:

. . . the crackling sea. . . .   Dylan Thomas

The clammy hauteur of President Hoover. . . .   Arthur M. Schlesinger, Jr.

Under the trees, along the cemented paths go drifts of girls, sympathetic and charming. . . .
                                                                    William Golding

  Any grammatical nexus may be made unusual; a subject and verb, for instance:

But her smile was the *coup de grâce* and her sigh buried him deep.
                                                            W. Somerset Maugham

Or a verb and complement:

He smiles his disappointments and laughs his angers.   e. e. cummings

Unusual Verbs

Verbs are a fertile source of implied meanings when joined with unlikely subjects or objects:

But the weeks blurred by and he did not leave.   Willard R. Espy

. . . no birdsong splintered the sunflecked silence.   Joan Lindsey

  Often an unusual verb implies a comment:

The more we prattle about morality, the more the world shows us how complicated things really are.
                                                            Samuel C. Florman

The cops squealed with excitement.   Howard Fast

. . . and then the hideous mannequins galumphed with squeaky shoes on stage.
                                                            Nancy Mitford

Each of those verbs carries adverse connotations. "Prattle" suggests childishness; "squealed," a piglike quality; "galumph," comic awkwardness. And each enriches its passage, implying considerably more than it literally states.

Unusual Adjectives

Many other striking collocations involve a modifier (typically an adjective) and its headword, as in Dylan Thomas's "the crackling sea." One variety of such adjectives is known as a *transferred epithet*—a word customarily applied to a particular noun or class of nouns which is used instead to modify something associated with that noun, as in "a boiling kettle." Here is a more original example:

He would sit upstairs in his angry overalls, too angry to come down to luncheon.
                                                                                                   Harold Nicholson

Oxymoron and Rhetorical Paradox

When the oddity of a collocation becomes seemingly contradictory, it is called an *oxymoron*. A famous instance is John Milton's description of hell as "darkness visible." In an oxymoron the modifier appears to contradict its headword: "How," we wonder, "can 'darkness' be 'visible'?" Several other examples:

. . . a practical mystic. . . .   Lord Roseberry

. . . delicious diligent indolence. . . .   John Keats

A yawn may be defined as a silent yell.   G. K. Chesterton

A *rhetorical paradox* is an oxymoron writ large. (An oxymoron, in fact, has been defined as a "condensed paradox.") It too expresses an apparent contradiction, and differs only in being longer and in not condensing the contradiction into a headword and modifier:

His soul will never starve for exploits or excitement who is wise enough to be made a fool of.
                                                                                                   G. K. Chesterton

Oxymoron and rhetorical paradox must not be confused with the *logical paradox*, which asserts that something is simultaneously both true and not true, thus violating what logicians call the law of noncontradiction. A classic example is:

"All Cretans are liars," said a Cretan.

A rhetorical paradox, on the other hand, does not contain a true contradiction. It may seem to. Chesterton appears to be saying something that is logically paradoxical—can wisdom consist of being made a fool of? But the appearance vanishes when we understand that Chesterton is using "wise" and "fool" in special, though not unique, senses. By "wise" he means simple and pure in spirit, unworldly and good. By "fool," he means a trusting innocent, rather than a self-deluded egotist, the word's usual sense.

Another kind of rhetorical paradox is less an apparent self-contradiction than an actual contradiction of a commonly accepted belief:

Baseball is an interminable game played by overgrown boys who have nothing better to do for the amusement of loafers who have nothing to do at all.

That unlikely sentence contains no inner contradiction, apparent or real, but it violently disagrees with conventional attitudes.

Paradoxes of this sort may take the form of standing a cliché or popular maxim on its head. Someone remarked, for instance, that the German General Staff "has a genius for snatching defeat from the jaws of victory." Oscar Wilde mocked Victorian morality by reversing the smug judgment that "drink is the curse of the working class"; he put it that

. . . work is the curse of the drinking class.

Oxymoron and rhetorical paradox, finally, can be especially effective, if they grow naturally out of the subject and reveal an important truth about it.

Accumulation, or Piling Up

Accumulation, as we use it here, means stringing together a number of words, all the same part of speech and grammatically parallel, that is, connected to the same thing. Most commonly the words are a series of verbs serving the same subject or of adjectives attached to the same headword:

They glittered and shone and sparkled, they strutted, and puffed, and posed.
                                                                Beverley Nichols

He criticized and threatened and promised. He played the audience like an organ, stroked them and lashed them and flattered and scared and comforted them, and finally he rose on his toes and lifted his fists and denounced that "great betrayer and liar," Franklin Roosevelt.   Wallace Stegner

Lolling or larricking that unsoiled, boiling beauty of a common day, great gods with their braces over their vests sang, spat pips, puffed smoke at wasps, gulped and ogled, forgot the rent, embraced, posed for the dickey-bird, were coarse, had rainbow-coloured armpits, winked, belched, blamed the radishes, looked at Ilfracombe, played hymns on paper and comb, peeled bananas, scratched, found seaweed in their panamas, blew up paper bags and banged them, wished for nothing.   Dylan Thomas

Manipulative, industrious, strangely modest, inexorable, decent, stodgy, staunch, the Habsburgs had come out of Switzerland in 1273.   Frederic Morton

How, people are asking, could four mopheaded, neo-Edwardian attired Liverpudlian-accented, guitar-playing, drumbeating "little boys" from across the ocean come here and attract the immense amount of attention they did by stomping and hollering out songs in a musical idiom that is distinctly American?   John A. Osmundsen

The unusualness of such diction lies not in unconventional or paradoxical combinations but in sheer quantity, and of course, in quality.

Mixed Levels of Usage

Level of usage means the degree of formality or of informality associated with a word. Some words have a limited range of appropriateness. They are suitable, say, for formal but not informal occasions *(pedagogue)*. Contrarily, another word is at home in a colloquial atmosphere but not in a formal one *(prof)*. But of course most words are always acceptable *(teacher)*, and are not limited by usage restrictions.

It is possible to achieve unusual diction by mixing words from different usage levels so that learned literary terms rub elbows with colloquialisms and slang:

Huey [Long] was probably the most indefatigable campaigner and best catch-as-catch-can stumper the demagogically fertile South has yet produced.
Hodding Carter

American perceptions of empire have decline and fall built in. Decline and fall are both the outcome of and the alternative to empire. Which puts Americans in a fine pickle today.   James Oliver Robertson

The line between formal and informal styles is not now held so inflexibly as it used to be. Many writers mix literary and colloquial diction with a freedom that would have been frowned upon a generation or two back. This freedom is welcome. But it poses its own problems. The mix must work. It cannot be an artificial forcing of an occasional bit of slang to relieve relatively formal prose, or shouldering in a big word here and there to decorate a colloquial style. Words should always be chosen primarily because they say exactly what you want to say.

When the mix does work, a writer achieves not only precision but a variegated "speech" interesting in itself. Listen, for example, to this discussion of contemporary detective fiction:

The moral fabric of any age, of any society, is a tapestry in which there are strikingly different and even antithetical motifs. Our popular art forms show that the prevailing fashion in heroes runs to the extroverted he-man, the tough guy who saves the word with a terrific sock on the jaw of the transgressors, and the bang, bang of his pistol. But even this generation, so much exposed to philosophies of power, has its hankering for the light that comes from within; and in its folklore there appears, intermittently, a new kind of priest-hero—the psychoanalyst.
Charles J. Rolo

Rolo's language is generally literary (that is, belonging to formal, written prose): "moral fabric," "antithetical motifs," "transgressors," "philosophies of power," "intermittently," "priest-hero," "psychoanalyst." At the same time he works in colloquialisms: "he-man," "tough guy," "terrific sock on the jaw," "hankering." The diction is unpredictable. It surprises and thereby pleases us.

But the mix achieves surprise and novelty without sacrificing exactness or economy. Indeed both the literary and the colloquial terms are justifiable for their precision. "Priest-hero," for example, sets the detective story into the wider framework of literature and folktale. "He-man" nicely suits the flavor of the tough private-eye fiction Rolo is discussing.

It is possible to play off formal and colloquial language even more strikingly. In the following passage the journalist A. J. Liebling is describing fight fans, specifically those rooting for the other guy:

Such people may take it upon themselves to disparage the principal you are advising. This disparagement is less generally addressed to the man himself (as "Gavilan, you're a bum!") than to his opponent, whom they have wrongheadedly picked to win.

Liebling comically contrasts the deliberately inflated diction describing the fans' behavior ("disparage the principal you are advising") and the language they actually use ("Gavilan, you're a bum!").

CHAPTER 29

Improving Your Vocabulary: Dictionaries

Vocabulary is best extended by reading and writing. Memorizing lists of words has dubious value. The words are abstracted from any context, so that while you may learn the denotation you acquire little feeling for connotation and level of usage. Vocabulary should not be a forced plant but should grow naturally with learning and experience.

A good dictionary is the key to extending your knowledge of words. Try to keep one handy as you read. When you come upon a word you don't know, pause and look it up. If you can't stop or have no dictionary nearby, make a check in the margin (assuming the book is your own) or write the word on a piece of paper. Without such a reminder you will probably only remember that there was some word you intended to look up which now you can't recall.

As you write, don't be satisfied with thinking you know what a word means or how it is spelled or functions grammatically. If you aren't sure, open the dictionary. It's surprising how often what we think we know turns out to be wrong.

General Dictionaries

A general dictionary lists the words currently used by speakers and writers of a language or words readers are likely to come across in older literature. If it includes all such terms, it is *unabridged.* If it reduces the list by omitting many technical or archaic words, it is an *abridged* edition, sometimes called a desk dictionary.

Two unabridged dictionaries are standard for modern English: *Webster's*

Third New International Dictionary (G. & C. Merriam Company) and the *Oxford English Dictionary,* familiarly known as the *OED* (Oxford University Press). We'll return to these massive works a little later.

The abridged dictionary is of more immediate concern. Several good ones are available.[1] Whichever you own, take a little time to get familiar with its contents and organization. A typical dictionary consists of three parts: the front matter, the word list, and the back matter or appendixes.

Front matter, which includes everything preliminary to the word list, varies from work to work, but in all cases it explains how the word list is set up, how to read an entry, what the abbreviations mean, and so on. In addition front matter will likely contain general information, valuable to any writer, about English spelling, pronunciation, grammar, and usage.

Back matter, too, varies from book to book. *Webster's Seventh New Collegiate Dictionary,* for instance, discusses punctuation in its back matter and includes lists of famous persons, of important places, and of colleges in the United States and Canada. *The American Heritage Dictionary of the English Language* does not cover punctuation but includes people and places in the general word list.

Although the front and the back matter contain much important information, the chief part of a dictionary is its word list. To use the word list efficiently you need to understand how entries are organized and the kind of information they give. We'll look at two typical entries in some detail. But first a caution: while a dictionary is an authority, its authority is of a special and limited nature. It does not tell you how a word *should* be spelled or spoken or used; it simply tells you how it *is* spelled or spoken or used. The forms and meanings of words depend on the speakers and writers of English. Acting in unconscious collectivity, they—or rather we, all of us—constitute the "authority." Lexicographers collect hundreds, even thousands, of citations for each word they list. From these they determine how the word is actually pronounced and spelled, what meanings it is given, and any regional, social, or occupational facts affecting its use. If a lexicographer has personal feelings about spelling, pronunciation, or definition, he or she does not substitute these for what the citations reveal.

The exact arrangement of information in a typical entry will vary a bit among dictionaries. But they all list words according to a principle of alphabetization explained in the front matter, and they all indicate spelling (along with any variations), stress, syllabication, pronunciation, grammatical function (verb, noun, adjective, and so on), the different senses in which the word is used (the order of these may be historical or it may be according to frequency), and usually information about the word's etymology (that is, its origin and history).

1. *The American Heritage Dictionary of the English Language* (Houghton Mifflin Company); *The Random House College Dictionary, Revised Edition* (Random House); *Webster's New World Dictionary, Second College Edition* (Simon and Schuster); *Webster's Ninth New Collegiate Dictionary* (G. & C. Merriam Company); *Webster's II New Riverside University Dictionary* (Houghton Mifflin Company).

Here are two sample entries, each with explanations. The first is from *Webster's Seventh New Collegiate Dictionary:*

¹**hab·it** \'hab-ət\ *n* [ME, fr. OF, fr. L *habitus* condition, character, fr. *habitus,* pp. of *habēre* to have, hold—more at GIVE] **1** *archaic* : CLOTHING **2 a** : a costume characteristic of a calling, rank, or function **b** : RIDING HABIT **3** : BEARING, CONDUCT **4** : bodily appearance or makeup : PHYSIQUE **5** : the prevailing disposition or character of a person's thoughts and feelings : mental makeup **6** : a usual manner of behavior : CUSTOM **7 a** : a behavior pattern acquired by frequent repetition or physiologic exposure that shows itself in regularity or increased facility of performance **b** : an acquired mode of behavior that has become nearly or completely involuntary **8** : characteristic mode of growth or occurrence **9** *of a crystal* : characteristic assemblage of forms at crystallization leading to a usual appearance **10** : ADDICTION

   syn HABIT, HABITUDE, PRACTICE, USAGE, CUSTOM, USE, WONT mean a way of acting that has become fixed through repetition. HABIT implies a doing unconsciously or without premeditation, often compulsively; HABITUDE implies a fixed attitude or usual state of mind; PRACTICE suggests an act or method followed with regularity and usu. through choice; USAGE suggests a customary action so generally followed that it has become a social norm; CUSTOM applies to a practice or usage so steadily associated with an individual or group as to have the force of unwritten law; USE and WONT are rare in speech, and differ in that USE stresses the fact of repeated action, WONT the manner of it.

²**habit** *vt* : CLOTHE, DRESS

Main entry
  Superscript ¹ indicates that this is the first of two or more homographs (words having the same spelling and sound but used in different senses).
  The dot marks the syllabication. If you must split a word between lines, break it only at a point indicated by a dot.
Pronunciation
  In this dictionary the pronunciation is placed between slash marks and rendered in phonetic symbols (mostly similar in form to letters) whose values are listed at the bottom of each recto (right-hand) page.
  The mark ' indicates stress. It is placed before the accented syllable (that is, the one spoken with greatest force).
Part of speech
  n = noun.
Etymology
  Placed within brackets, the etymology uses capital abbreviations for languages and lower case abbreviations for other words: thus ME = Middle English, OF = Old French, L = Latin, fr. = from and pp. = past participle. Foreign words are italicized and their meanings are given in roman type without quotation marks.
  SMALL CAPS, here and elsewhere throughout the entry, signal that a term should be consulted in its alphabetical place in the word list for further information relevant to *habit.*
Definitions
  In this dictionary definitions are arranged in historical order. Different senses are distinguished by boldface arabic numerals; nuances within the same sense, by boldface lower case letters.
  Archaic is a status label indicating that a word or, as in this case, a particular sense of a word is used very rarely by contemporary speakers and writers.
  Of a crystal is a subject label indicating a special sense of the word in a particular subject or profession, here crystallography.
Synonyms
  A discussion of a group of words similar in sense but subtly different in meaning or usage. After the entry in the main word list of each of the terms in small caps following *habit,* there is a reference to this discussion. Thus at the end of the entry for *custom* you will find "*syn* see HABIT."
Homograph of *habit,* here a transitive verb meaning to clothe, to dress.

The second example comes from *The American Heritage Dictionary of the English Language:*

wake[1] (wāk) *v.* **woke** (wōk) or *rare* **waked** (wākt), **waked** or *chiefly British & regional* **woke** or **woken** (wō′kən), **waking, wakes**—*intr.* **1. a.** To cease to sleep; become awake; awaken. Often used with *up*. **b.** To be brought into a state of awareness or alertness. **2.** *Regional.* To keep watch or guard, especially over a corpse. **3.** To be or remain awake.—*tr.* **1.** To rouse from sleep; awaken. Often used with *up*. **2.** To stir, as from a dormant or inactive condition; rouse: *wake old animosities.* **3.** To make aware of; to alert. Often used with *to*: *It waked him to the facts.* **4.** *Regional.* **a.** To keep a vigil over. **b.** To hold a wake over.—*n.* **1. a.** A watch; vigil. **b.** A watch over the body of a deceased person before burial, sometimes accompanied by festivity. **2.** *British.* A parish festival held annually, often in honor of the patron saint. **3.** The condition of being awake: *between wake and sleep.* [Middle English *wakien* and *waken*, Old English *wacian*, to be awake and *wacan* (unattested), to rouse. See **weg-**[2] in Appendix.*]

Main entry
  The superscript [1] indicates that this is the first of at least two homographs, different words with the same spelling and pronunciation but different senses.

Pronunciation
  This is enclosed within parentheses and uses symbols and marks set out in a table at the beginning of the word list.

Part of speech
  v. = verb (*intr.* = intransitive and *tr.* = transitive); *n.* = noun.

Inflected forms
  For verbs these are the principal parts. (For nouns they would be the singular and plural, for modifiers the comparative and superlative forms.) As listed in this dictionary the principal parts, set in boldface, include the past preterite (*woke*), the past participle (*waked*), the present participle (*waking*), and the third person singular active indicative present (*wakes*). Alternate forms are given for the past and past participle, with the less common following the more common and labeled as *rare* or *chiefly British & regional* (that is, confined to the speakers of a particular geographical area rather than common to all users of English).

Definitions
  These are divided into the senses of the verb and of the noun. The former, in turn, are distinguished for both the intransitive and transitive uses of the verb. Within each category the various meanings are ordered, in this dictionary, by beginning with the most common or central. Different senses are marked by arabic numerals in boldface; subdivisions within a particular sense by lower-case letters in boldface. Where useful, brief examples of a sense are given in italics.

Etymology
  The etymology, set within brackets, traces the origin of the modern word. Foreign terms are italicized, and their meanings are in roman type without quotation marks. "Unattested" means that no actual record of a form exists,

Usage: The verbs *wake, waken, awake,* and *awaken* are alike in meaning but differentiated in usage. Each has transitive and intransitive senses, but *awake* is used largely intransitively and *waken* transitively. In the passive voice, *awaken* and *waken* are the more frequent: *I was awakened* (or *wakened*) *by his call.* In figurative usage, *awake* and *awaken* are the more prevalent: *He awoke to the danger; his suspicions were awakened.* *Wake* is frequently used with *up;* the others do not take a preposition. The preferred past participle of *wake* is *waked,* not *woke* or *woken: When I had waked him, I discovered that the danger was past.* The preferred past participle of *awake* is *awaked,* not *awoke: He had awaked several times earlier in the night.*

wake² (wāk) *n.* **1.** The visible track of turbulence left by something moving through the water: *the wake of a ship.* **2.** The track or course left behind anything that has passed: *"Every revolutionary law has naturally left in its wake defection, resentment, and counterrevolutionary sentiment."* (C. Wright Mills). **—in the wake of. 1.** Following directly upon. **2.** In the aftermath of; as a consequence of. [Probably Middle Low German *wake,* from Old Norse *vok,* a hole or crack in ice. See **wegw-** in Appendix.*]

though the form may be inferred from other evidence. *weg-²* refers to a list of Indo-European roots contained in an appendix following the word list. (Indo-European is the name given to the mother language of English and most other western languages, as well as of many in the Near East and India. That language does not exist in any written record. However, linguists can reconstruct many of its words or word elements, collectively called roots, from evidence in languages descended from Indo-European.)

Usage
A discussion of how the word and its various forms are actually used by contemporary speakers. The discussion is illustrated by typical cases, printed in italics.

Main entry of **wake²**
Wake², a homograph of **wake¹**, is a different word with a different meaning.

Quoted citation
Rather than a typical example, this is an actual employment of the word, attributed to a specific writer. It is an example of the kind of citation from which the dictionary maker works. Collecting hundreds or thousands of such specific examples, he or she frames the definition.

Idiom using the word.

Unabridged Dictionaries

Occasionally you will come across a word not in your desk dictionary. Turn then to an unabridged work. The standard for American English is *Webster's Third New International Dictionary* (G. & C. Merriam Company). This is the volume you find in most libraries, usually on its own stand and open somewhere near the middle. (It should be left that way to protect the binding.)

Webster's Third New International lists more than 450,000 words, including many older expressions and technical terms omitted from abridgments. In addition to the customary explanations, its front matter contains extensive discussions of spelling, punctuation, plural forms, the use of italics, and the handling of compound words. Accompanying the word list are thousands of illustrations (a few in the form of color plates) and numerous tables (the chemical elements, for instance, the Indo-European language family, radio frequencies, time zones, and so on).

Even more massive is the *Oxford English Dictionary*, published by the Oxford University Press in twelve volumes with four volumes of supplements. Several features distinguish the *OED*. It lists older words than the *Third New International* and arranges definitions in historical order, illustrating each sense by dated quotations (totaling about 1,800,000). These begin with the earliest known use of a word in a particular sense and include, if possible, at least one instance for every century thereafter until the present (or until the last known example in the case of obsolete words or meanings). The dated citations make the *OED* indispensable for scholars studying the history of words or ideas.

On the other hand, the *OED* is less useful for American English. For example, someone curious about the meaning of *Chicago pool* or the origin of *OK* will have to consult *Webster's Third New International*. Both unabridged dictionaries are necessary to a serious writer.

Special Dictionaries: Thesauri

Special dictionaries are restricted to a particular aspect of the general language or to the language of a specific group, profession, or region. There are hundreds of such works, many available in the reference section of most libraries. Informative introductions to special dictionaries and reference works in general can be found in *The Basic Guide to Research Sources*, edited by Robert O'Brien and Joanne Soderman (New American Library, 1975), *Reference Readiness: A Manual for Librarians and Students*, second edition (Linnet Books, 1977), or *A Guide to Library Research Methods*, by Thomas Mann (Oxford University Press, 1987).

Here we are interested only in one kind of special dictionary: the thesaurus or dictionary of synonyms. *Synonyms* are words in the same language having much the same meaning. *True*, or *identical*, *synonyms* have exactly the same definition and usually are simply alternative names for the same object. In sailboats, for instance, *mizzen* and *jigger* signify the same sail and are true synonyms. Most synonyms, however, are less than exact. For example, *pal* and *friend* overlap to a considerable degree, but are not exactly coextensive: any pal is a friend, but not any friend is a pal. In listing synonyms a thesaurus necessarily obscures this distinction between exact and near synonyms. To distinguish all shades of meaning would result in a vast work of many volumes, too expensive to buy and too cumbersome to use.

Roget's is probably the best-known thesaurus. (The word comes from Greek and means "treasure.") It was first published in 1852 by Mark Peter Roget, an American physician and professor, and entitled *A Thesaurus of English Words and Phrases, Classified and Arranged so as to Facilitate the*

Expression of Ideas and Assist in Literary Composition. Roget devised a system of grouping words in numbered and subdivided categories of ideas. Users searching for terms meaning, say, "friendship" could look under the appropriate category. To make his book usable from the other direction—that is, from word to category—Roget also included an alphabetized index of words, each keyed to its category by the appropriate number. Early in the twentieth century C. O. S. Mawson simplified Roget's scheme. Neither *Roget* nor *thesaurus* is copyrighted, and a number of *Roget's* are currently available—some revisions of Roget's original work, others of Mawson's modification, and still others consisting of alphabetical listings without Roget's categories.

Besides the various *Roget's,* there are other thesauri on the market: *The Random House Thesaurus* (Random House); *Webster's Collegiate Thesaurus* (G. & C. Merriam Company); *Webster's New World Thesaurus,* edited by Charlton Laird (World Publishing Company); and *Webster's II Thesaurus* (Simon and Schuster). (Like *Roget,* the name *Webster* is not copyrighted and is used by competing companies.)

The limitations of most thesauri are revealed in the directions given in one edition of *Roget:*

Turning to No. 866 (the sense required) we read through the varied list of synonyms . . . and *select the most appropriate expression.* [Italics added]

That matter of selection is critical, and a thesaurus does not offer much help. For example, among the synonyms listed in one *Roget* under the category *seclusion/exclusion* are *solitude, isolation, loneliness,* and *aloofness.* They are merely listed as alternates with no distinctions drawn, but, except in a very loose sense, these words are not synonymous and may not be interchanged indiscriminately. *Solitude* means physical apartness, out of the sight and sound of others, a condition not necessarily undesirable; in fact, *solitude* may be used with positive connotations, as in "She enjoys solitude." *Loneliness,* on the other hand, has a more subjective significance, relating to the feeling of being apart; it does not necessarily imply physical separation—one can be lonely in a crowd of Christmas shoppers—and it would never be given a positive sense. *Isolation* stresses physical separation, out of connection and communication with others, and is often used when that separation is not desired. *Aloofness,* finally, is self-chosen separation, a deliberate withdrawal from others, which may suggest a sense of superiority, though it does not have to.

To use these "synonyms" effectively you need to know considerably more about them than a thesaurus is likely to tell you. With many words—those in this example, for instance—a good abridged dictionary is more helpful. That is not to say that a thesaurus is a waste of money. Used wisely it can improve your working vocabulary. It may remind you of a word you have forgotten, or acquaint you with a new one. But before you employ that new word learn more about it.

A more useful source of synonyms is a work published by the G. & C. Merriam Company: *Webster's Dictionary of Synonyms.* It discusses meaning at greater length than does the typical thesaurus. For example, *Webster's Collegiate Thesaurus* uses about one inch of a column for *solitude,* the *Dictionary of Synonyms* spends more than seven inches, carefully distinguishing *solitude* from *isolation, loneliness,* and so on.

PART VI

Description and Narration

CHAPTER 30

Description

Description is about sensory experience—how something looks, sounds, tastes. Mostly it is about visual experience, but description also deals with other kinds of perception. The following passage, for example, uses sounds to describe the beginning of an act of revolutionary violence in China:

Five shots went off in a nearby street: three together, another, still another. . . . The silence returned, but it no longer seemed to be the same. Suddenly it was filled by the clatter of horses' hoofs, hurried, coming nearer and nearer. And, like the vertical laceration of lightning after a prolonged thunder, while they still saw nothing, a tumult suddenly filled the street, composed of mingled cries, shots, furious whinnyings, the falling of bodies; then, as the subsiding clamor was heavily choking under the indestructible silence, there rose a cry as of a dog howling lugubriously, cut short: a man with his throat slashed.   André Malraux

Whatever sense it appeals to, descriptive writing is of two broad kinds: objective and subjective. In *objective description* the writer sets aside those aspects of the perception unique to himself and concentrates on describing the percept (that is, what is perceived) in itself. In *subjective* (also called *impressionistic*) *description* a writer projects his or her feelings into the percept. Objective description says, "This is how the thing is"; subjective, "This is how the thing seems to one particular consciousness."

Neither kind of description is more "honest." Both are (or can be) true, but they are true in different ways. The truth of objective description lies in its relationship to fact; that of subjective in relationship to feeling or evaluation. The first kind of truth is more easily checked. We can generally decide which of two passages more accurately describes, say, a downtown office building. Subjective description, on the other hand, is "true" because it presents a valuable response, not because it makes an accurate report. If we do not agree with how a writer feels about something, we cannot say that the description is false. We can say only that it is not true for us—that is, that we do not share his or her feelings.

Nor are these two approaches hard-and-fast categories into which any piece of descriptive writing must fall. Most descriptions involve both, in varying degrees. Generally, however, one mode will dominate and fix the focus. In scientific and legal writing, for instance, objectivity is desirable. In personal writing subjectivity is more likely.

But in both kinds, success hinges on three things: (1) *details* that are sharply defined images, appealing to one or another of the senses; (2) *details* that are selected according to a guiding principle; (3) *details* that are clearly organized.

Objective Description
Selection of Detail

In objective description the principle which guides selection is the thing itself. The writer must ask: Which details are essential to seeing and understanding this object, event, person, experience? Which are accidental and of lesser importance? Essential details should make up the bulk of the description, those of secondary importance being included as the writer has space.

The following description of a freshwater fish by an eighteenth-century naturalist exemplifies the selection of essential detail:

The loach, in its general aspect, has a pellucid appearance: its back is mottled with irregular collections of small black dots, not reaching much below the *linea lateralis,* as are the back and tail fins: a black line runs from each eye down to the nose; its belly is of a silvery white; the upper jaw projects beyond the lower, and is surrounded with six feelers, three on each side; its pectoral fins are large, its ventral much smaller; the fin behind its anus small; its dorsal fin large, containing eight spines; its tail, where it joins the tail-fin, remarkably broad, without any taperness, so as to be characteristic of this genus; the tail-fin is broad, and square at the end. From the breadth and muscular strength of the tail, it appears to be an active nimble fish.   Gilbert White

White focuses on those features that enable us to recognize a loach: size and shape of tail and fins, number of feelers on each side of the jaw, and so on. Scientific description like this is a kind of definition, differentiating an entity from others similar to it.

Organization of Details

Objective description, especially the visual kind, often begins with a brief comprehensive view. It then analyzes this image and presents each part in detail, following an organization inherent in the object. Here, for instance, is a description of a lake in Maine:

In shape the lake resembles a gently curving S, its long axis lying almost due north-south. The shoreline is ringed by rocks of all sizes, from huge boulders to tiny pebbles—the detritus of the ice age. Beyond the rocks the forest comes almost to the water's edge. Mostly pine and hemlock, it contains a few hardwoods—maple, oak, birch. Here and there an old pine, its roots washed nearly clean of support, leans crazily over the water, seeming about to topple at any instant. But it never does; trees fall this way for years.

First we view the lake in its entirety, as a hawk might see it. Then we focus down and move progressively closer to shore. We see the rocks immediately at the water's edge, then the forest, then the various kinds of trees, and finally the old pine leaning over the water. The description, in short, is organized: it moves from general to particular, and it divides the visual experience of the lake into three parts—the lake as a whole, the shoreline, and the forest around.

To effect these changes in viewpoint, the writer does not waste time directing us. He does not say, "As we leave the bird's-eye view and come down for a closer look, we observe that the shoreline is ringed with rocks." It is awkward and wordy to turn tour guide. It is better to move about the object implicitly without holding the reader by the hand. Doing this usually requires an impersonal and omniscient point of view: impersonal in the sense that the writer does not refer to himself or herself; omniscient in that nothing is hidden, and he or she can range with complete freedom—above, below, around the object, inside and out. Readers will follow if the writer has clearly organized what they are supposed to see.

But he or she *must* organize. Writers of good description do not just "see." They analyze what they see and give it a pattern. Taking a perception apart in order to put it together can be seen in the following sentence by Joseph Conrad, which describes a coastal view. The angle of vision does not change as it did in the description of the lake, but there is a principle of organization:

Beyond the sea wall there curves for miles in a vast and regular sweep the barren beach of shingle, with the village of Brenzett standing out darkly across the water, a spire in a clump of trees; and still further out the perpendicular column of a lighthouse, looking in the distance no bigger than a lead pencil, marks the vanishing point of the land.

Our view shifts from near to distant. Our eyes move outward through a series of receding planes: the sea wall, the beach, the village with its spire and trees across the water, and the lighthouse in the offing.

Diction in Objective Description

In objective description words are chosen for exactness of denotation, not for forcefulness of connotation. Factual precision is what is most desired.

Gilbert White (page 254) says "six feelers, three on each side," not "several feelers." He carefully differentiates fins by concise technical names: "pectoral," "ventral," "dorsal."

Scientific description like this is not easy to write. Given enough time to observe and the training to know what to look for, anyone can compose a reasonably accurate description of a fish. But it requires more care to compose a description that is accurate and at the same time forceful, interesting prose. It is worth studying White's paragraph to observe how he organizes it and gives it vitality and movement by the short, direct clauses, constructed with just enough variety to avoid monotony.

Subjective Description

When describing objectively, the writer is a kind of camera, recording precisely and impersonally. When writing subjectively, he or she is no longer an impartial observer, but rather enters into what is perceived. Point of view—in most cases—becomes personal; and words have overtones of value and feeling that color the perception.

These evaluations and feelings are as much a part of the description as the object itself. In fact, more: they determine selection and organization. Sometimes writers state impressions directly, as in this paragraph about an Englishwoman's reactions to the citizens of Moscow:

I wandered about in the morning and looked at the streets and people. All my visit I looked and looked at the people. They seem neither happier nor sadder than in the West, and neither more nor less worried than any town dweller. (People in towns are always preoccupied. "Have I missed the bus? Have I forgotten the potatoes? Can I get across the road?") But they appear stupid, what the French call *abruti*. What do they think? Perhaps they don't think very much, and yet they read enormously. I never saw such a country of readers—people sitting on benches, in the metro, etc., all read books (magazines seem not to exist); on the trains they have lending libraries. They are hideously ugly. Except for a few young officers, I never saw a handsome man; there seem to be no beautiful women. They have putty faces, like Malenkov. It is nonsense to speak of Asiatics, Mongol Hordes and so on—the pretty little Tartar guards at Lenin's tomb were the only people I saw with non-European cast of features.   Nancy Mitford

Fixing the Impression in Images

While subjective description often states an impression directly, it cannot rest on abstract statement. Feeling must be fixed in images, in details appealing to the senses. Only details, emotionally charged, make the impression real.

No more dreary spectacle can be found on this earth than the whole of the "awful East," with its Whitechapel, Hoxton, Spitalfields, Bethnal Green, and Wapping to the East India Docks. The colour of life is grey and drab. Everything is helpless, hopeless, unrelieved, and dirty. Bath tubs are a thing totally unknown, as mythical as the ambrosia of the gods. The people themselves are dirty, while any attempt at cleanliness becomes howling farce, when it is not pitiful and tragic. Strange, vagrant odours come drifting along the greasy wind, and the rain, when it falls, is more like grease than water from heaven. The very cobblestones are scummed with grease.

Jack London

London, writing in 1902, begins by telling us what impression the slums of London's east end make on him: "no more dreary spectacle"; "the colour of life is grey and drab"; "everything is helpless, hopeless, unrelieved, and dirty." But we don't experience the impression until he renders it in images: "vagrant odours," "greasy wind," "rain . . . like grease," "cobblestones . . . scummed with grease."

You can see that details work differently in impressionistic description than in objective. Connotations are more important, and diction is charged with emotion. The writer wants to arouse in readers a response like his own. But he must do more than merely tell us how he feels. He must recreate the scene in a significantly altered manner, including this detail and omitting that, exaggerating one image and underplaying another, and calling up compelling similes and metaphors.

In short, the perception must be refracted through the writer's consciousness. It may emerge idealized, like a landscape by a romantic painter. It may be distorted and made ugly, like a reflection in a funhouse mirror. Idealization and distortion are perfectly legitimate. The writer of subjective description signs no contract to deliver literal truth. "Here," he or she says, "is how *I* see it." Yet the description may reveal a deeper truth than mere objective accuracy, and, like an artist's caricature, make plain a subtle reality.

To convey subjective truth, then, a writer must embody responses in the details of the scene. Often, in fact, he or she relies exclusively upon such embodiment, making little or no statement of feeling and, instead, forcing the perception to speak for itself. A simple case is catalogue description, in which the writer lists detail after detail, each contributing to a dominant impression. The following paragraph is a good example (it describes an outdoor market on Decatur Street in New Orleans):

The booths are Sicilian, hung with red peppers, draped with garlic, piled with fruit, trayed with vegetables, fresh and dried herbs. A huge man, fat as Silenus, daintily binds bunches for soup, while his wife quarters cabbages, ties smaller bundles of thyme, parsley, green onions, small hot peppers and sweet pimentos to season gumbos. Another Italian with white moustache, smiling fiercely from a tanned face, offers jars of green filé powder, unground all-spice, pickled onions in vinegar. Carts and trucks flank the sidewalk; one walks through crates of curled parsley, scallions piled with ice, wagonloads of spinach with tender mauve stalks, moist baskets of crisp kale; sacks of white onions in oyster-white fishnet, pink onions in sacks of old rose; piles of eggplant with purple reflections, white garlic and long sea-green leeks with shredded roots, grey-white like witches' hair. Boxes of artichokes fit their leaves into a complicated pattern. Trucks from Happy Jack, Boothville, and Buras have unloaded their oranges; a long red truck is selling cabbages, green peppers, squashes long and curled like the trumpets of Jericho. There is more than Jordaens profusion, an abundance more glittering in color than Pourbus. A blue truck stands in sunlight, Negroes clambering over its sides, seven men in faded jeans, washing-blue overalls; the last is a mulatto in a sweater of pure sapphire. A mangy cat steps across a roadway of crushed oranges and powdered oyster-shells.

John Peale Bishop

Not only the individual details, but their very profusion convey vitality and abundance far more effectively than would any plain statement. It is not possible to overestimate the importance of specificity to good description. Look back at how carefully Bishop names colors.

While details in catalogue descriptions are generally chosen according to an underlying feeling or evaluation, the selection is less rigorous than in some other kinds of subjective description. Thus Bishop includes the "mangy cat" and the "crushed oranges," even though these jar slightly with the attractiveness of the scene. More often the writer "edits" the perception, using fewer details and only those conducive to the impression. The novelist Thomas Wolfe, for example, draws this picture of an idealized, if modest, home:

On the outskirts of a little town upon a rise of land that swept back from the railway there was a tidy little cottage of white boards, trimmed vividly with green blinds. To one side of the house there was a garden neatly patterned with plots of growing vegetables, and an arbor for the grapes which ripened late in August. Before the house there were three mighty oaks which sheltered it in their clean and massive shade in summer, and to the other side there was a border of gay flowers. The whole place had an air of tidiness, thrift, and modest comfort.

The final sentence sums up the scene and states the impression directly, as to the modifiers "neatly," "clean," "gay," but on the whole the images create the sense of middle-class fulfillment. Any ugliness is excluded. If the lawn were disfigured by crabgrass, if weeds leered among the flowers, the facts are discreetly omitted.

Very different are the details—and the impression—in this account of the homes of miners in the north of England:

I found great variation in the houses I visited. Some were as decent as one could possibly expect in the circumstances, some were so appalling that I have no hope of describing them adequately. To begin with, the smell, the dominant and essential thing, is indescribable. But the squalor and the confusion! A tub full of filthy water here, a basin full of unwashed crocks there, more crocks piled in any odd corner, torn newspaper littered everywhere, and in the middle always the same dreadful table covered with sticky oilcloth and crowded with cooking pots and irons and half-darned stockings and pieces of stale bread and bits of cheese wrapped round with greasy newspaper! And the congestion in a tiny room where getting from one side to the other is a complicated voyage between pieces of furniture,

with a line of damp washing getting you in the face every time you move and the children as thick underfoot as toadstools!
George Orwell

Sometimes a writer concentrates on one or two images which symbolize the impression. In the following passage Alfred Kazin projects into two key symbols his childhood despair at being forced to attend a special school because of his stuttering:

It troubled me that I could speak in the fullness of my own voice only when I was alone on the streets, walking about. There was something unnatural about it; unbearably isolated. I was not like the others! At midday, every freshly shocking Monday noon, they sent me away to a speech clinic in a school in East New York, where I sat in a circle of lispers and cleft palates and foreign accents holding a mirror before my lips and rolling difficult sounds over and over. To be sent there in the full light of the opening week, when everyone else was at school or going about his business, made me feel as if I had been expelled from the great normal body of humanity. I would gobble down my lunch on my way to the speech clinic and rush back to the school in time to make up for the classes I had lost. One day, one unforgettable dread day, I stopped to catch my breath on a corner of Sutter Avenue, near the wholesale fruit markets, where an old drugstore rose up over a great flight of steps. In the window were dusty urns of colored water floating off iron chains; cardboard placards advertising hairnets, EX-LAX; a great illustrated medical chart headed THE HUMAN FACTORY, which showed the exact course a mouthful of food follows as it falls from chamber to chamber of the body. I hadn't meant to stop there at all, only to catch my breath; but I so hated the speech clinic that I thought I would delay my arrival for a few minutes by eating my lunch on the steps. When I took the sandwich out of my bag, two bitterly hard pieces of hard salami slipped out of my hand and fell through a grate onto a hill of dust below the steps. I remember how sickeningly vivid an odd thread of hair looked on the salami, as if my lunch were turning stiff with death. The factory whistles called their short, sharp blasts stark through the middle of noon, beating at me where I sat outside the city's magnetic circle. I had never known, I knew instantly I would never in my heart again submit to, such wild passive despair as I felt at that moment, sitting on the steps before THE HUMAN FACTORY, where little robots gathered and shoveled the food from chamber to chamber of the body. They had put me out into the streets, I thought to myself; with their mirrors and their everlasting pulling at me to imitate their effortless bright speech and their stupefaction that a boy could stammer and stumble on every other English word he carried in his head, they put me out into the streets, had left me high and dry on the steps of that drugstore staring at the remains of my lunch turning black and grimy in the dust.

In Kazin's description selection is extremely important. The passage focuses onto the images of THE HUMAN FACTORY and the two pieces of salami. Kazin tells us what his feelings were (he is quite explicit). But he *communicates* the despair of an alienated child in the salami with its "odd thread of hair . . . turning black and grimy in the dust," and the inhuman little robots endlessly shoveling food into a body that has become a machine. In a world symbolized by such images there is little room for humane values, for love and compassion and tender understanding.

Kazin's paragraph shows the importance of the "crystallizing image," the detail that precipitates the scene in the reader's mind. The writer must make readers see (or hear or taste or touch). He or she cannot achieve this merely by relentlessly listing every detail that falls within the perceptual field. Even in catalogue descriptions like that by John Peale Bishop, we are shown only a portion of what exists to be seen. The writer must select relatively few details but render these so vividly that a reader sees them in his mind's eye. These will then crystalize the perception, making it solid and true. It is rather like developing a photograph. The writer begins the process, carefully choosing details and expressing them in compelling images; readers, developing these images in the fluid of their own experience, complete the picture for themselves.

The point to remember is this: select only the details essential to the impression you want to convey; describe them precisely and concretely; then readers will perceive them.

Metaphor and Simile in Subjective Description

In addition to selecting and arranging details, the writer of description may also introduce comparisons, often in the form of metaphors or similes. In Bishop's paragraph about the Decatur Street Market, for instance, the proprietor is "fat as Silenus" (an ancient god of wine), the leeks "sea-green" with roots "like witches' hair," and the squashes "long and curled like the trumpets of Jericho."

Metaphor is even more central in the following passage about the Great Wall of China. The Wall assumes a monstrous power as it marches over and dominates the lands:

There in the mist, enormous, majestic, silent and terrible, stood the Great Wall of China. Solitarily, with the indifference of nature herself, it crept up the mountain side and slipped down to the depth of the valley. Menacingly, the grim watch towers, stark and four square, at due intervals stood at their posts. Ruthlessly, for it was built at the cost of a million lives and each one of those great grey stones has been stained with the bloody tears of the captive and the outcast, it forged its dark way through a sea of rugged mountains. Fearlessly, it went on its endless journey, league upon league to the furthermost regions of Asia, in utter solitude, mysterious like the great empire it guarded. There in the mist, enormous, majestic, silent, and terrible, stood the Great Wall of China.   W. Somerset Maugham

Exaggerating Details

An impression may be embodied in distorted and exaggerated details. Mark Twain, an adept at the art of hyperbole, or exaggeration, tells of a trip he took in an overland stage in the 1860s. The passengers have spent the night at a way station, and Twain describes the facilities for cleaning up before breakfast the next morning:

> By the door, inside, was fastened a small old-fashioned looking-glass frame, with two little fragments of the original mirror lodged down in one corner of it. This arrangement afforded a pleasant double-barreled portrait of you when you looked into it, with one half of your head set up a couple of inches above the other half. From the glass frame hung the half of a comb by a string—but if I had to describe that patriarch or die, I believe I would order some sample coffins. It had come down from Esau and Samson, and had been accumulating hair ever since—along with certain impurities.

We are not supposed to take this literally, of course. Twain is exercising the satirist's right of legitimate exaggeration, legitimate because it leads us to see a truth about this frontier hostel.

Process Description

A *process* is a directed activity in which something undergoes progressive change. The process may be natural, like the growth of a tree; or it may be humanly directed, like an automobile taking shape on an assembly line. But always something is happening—work is being done, a product being formed, an end of some kind being achieved.

To describe a process you must analyze its stages. The analysis will determine how you organize the description. In a simple case, such as baking a cake, the process has obvious, prescribed steps; the writer needs only to observe and record them accurately. On the other hand, complicated and abstract processes—for instance, how a law comes into being as an act of Congress—require more study and thought.

Here is a simple example of a process, a natural one—a small frog being eaten by a giant water bug:

> He didn't jump; I crept closer. At last I knelt on the island's winterkilled grass, lost, dumbstruck, staring at the frog in the creek just four feet away. He was a very small frog with wide, dull eyes. And just as I looked at him, he slowly crumpled and began to sag. The spirit vanished from his eyes as if snuffed. His skin emptied and drooped; his very skull seemed to collapse and settle like a kicked tent. He was shrinking before my eyes like a deflating football. I watched the taut, glistening skin on his shoulders ruck, and rumple, and fall. Soon, part of his skin, formless as a pricked balloon, lay in floating folds like bright scum on top of the water: it was a monstrous and terrifying thing. I gaped bewildered, appalled. An oval shadow hung in the water behind the drained frog; then the shadow glided away. The frog skin bag began to sink.   Annie Dillard

At the beginning of the description the frog is whole and alive, sitting in the creek; by the end it has been reduced to a bag of skin. This change is the process Dillard describes. It is continuous rather than divided into clearly defined steps. Yet it is analyzed. Verbs, the key words in the analysis, create sharp images of alteration: "crumpled," "collapse," "shrinking," "deflating," "ruck," "rumple," "fall." The similes and metaphors translate an unusual visual experience into more familiar ones: "like a deflating football," "formless as a pricked balloon."

The next example of process description involves an assembly line at a cosmetics plant:

Cream-jar covers joggle along a moving belt. Six iron arms descend to set paper sealers on sextuplicate rows of cream pots. Each clattering cover is held for a moment in a steel disk as a filled cream jar is raised by a metal wrist and screwed on from underneath.

At the mascara merry-go-round a tiny tube is placed in each steel cup—clink. The cups circle—ca-chong, ca-chong, ca-chong—till they pass under two metal udders. There the cups jerk up—ping—and the tubes are filled with mascara that flows from the vats upstairs in manufacturing. The cups continue their circle till they pass under a capper—plump. The filled, capped tubes circle some more till they reach two vacuum nozzles, then—fwap—sucked up, around and down onto a moving belt.

All along the belt women in blue smocks, sitting on high stools, pick up each mascara tube as it goes past. They insert brushes, tamp on labels, encase the tubes in plastic and then cardboard for the drugstore displays.

At the Brush-On Peel-Off Mask line, a filler picks an empty bottle off the belt with her right hand, presses a pedal with her foot, fills the bottle with a bloop of blue goop, changes hands, and puts the filled bottle back on the line with her left hand, as she picks up another empty bottle with her right hand. The bottles go past at thirty-three a minute.   Barbara Garson

Garson's description provides a fine example of how analysis determines paragraphing. Three products are involved—cream, mascara, and the "Brush-On Peel-Off Mask"—and each is treated in a separate paragraph. For the mascara two are used, marking the two-stage process of the tubes' being first filled and then packaged.

The sentences are also determined by the analysis. Thus the three sentences of the first paragraph distinguish (1) the covers on the conveyor belt, (2) the iron arms placing sealers on the pots, and (3) the fixing of the lids onto the jars. Notice, too, the long sentence in the fourth paragraph; it uses parallel verbs to analyze the filler's movements.

Process description may be either objective or subjective. Both the foregoing examples are relatively objective, though each suggests responses. Even though Dillard's subject is horrifying and she actually expresses her reaction ("it was a monstrous and terrifying thing"), her images are objective. Dillard concentrates on rendering the visual experience in and of itself (which in a case like this perhaps best communicates the horror).

Despite its objective surface, Garson's description also implies a reaction. Her diction—especially the words imitating sounds—suggests the inhuman quality of the assembly line. Her fourth paragraph cleverly hints her feelings about work on the line. The long elaborate first sentence describing the worker's mechanized movements is followed by a brief matter-of-fact announcement that "the bottles go past at thirty-three a minute." The implication makes sensitive readers wince.

CHAPTER 31

Narration

A *narrative* is a meaningful sequence of events told in words. It is sequential in that the events are ordered, not merely random. Sequence always involves an arrangement in time (and usually other arrangements as well). A straightforward movement from the first event to the last constitutes the simplest chronology. However, chronology is sometimes complicated by presenting the events in another order: for example, a story may open with the final episode and then flash back to all that preceded it.

A narrative has meaning in that it conveys an evaluation of some kind. The writer reacts to the story he or she tells, and states or implies that reaction. This is the "meaning," sometimes called the "theme," of a story. Meaning must always be rendered. The writer has to do more than tell us the truth he sees in the story; he must manifest that truth in the characters and the action.

Characters and action are the essential elements of any story. Also important, but not as essential, is the setting, the place where the action occurs. Characters are usually people—sometimes actual people, as in history books or newspaper stories, sometimes imaginary ones, as in novels. Occasionally characters are animals (as in an Aesop fable), and sometimes a dominant feature of the environment functions almost like a character (the sea, an old house).

The action is what the characters say and do and anything that happens to them, even if it arises from a nonhuman source—a storm, for instance, or a fire. Action is often presented in the form of a plot. Action is, so to speak, the raw material; plot, the finished product, the fitting together of the bits and pieces of action into a coherent pattern. Usually, though not invariably, plot takes the form of a cause-and-effect chain: event A produces event B; B leads to C; C to D; and so on until the final episode, X. In a well-constructed plot of this kind we can work back from X to A and see the connections that made the end of the story likely and perhaps inevitable.

Stories can be very long and complicated, with many characters, elaborate plots, and subtle interpenetration of character, action, and setting. In writing that is primarily expository, however, narratives are shorter and simpler. Most often they are factual rather than imaginary, as when an historian describes an event. And often in exposition an illustration may involve a simple narrative. Being able to tell a story, then, while not the primary concern of the expository writer, is a skill which he or she will now and again be called upon to use.

Organizing a Narrative

As with so much in composition, the first step in narration is to analyze the story in your own mind. In the actual telling, the analysis provides the organization. The simplest kind of narrative is the episode, a single event unified by time and place. But even an episode must be organized. The writer must break it down into parts and present these in a meaningful order.

In the following case the episode is the brief landing of a passenger ship at the Mediterranean island of Malta. After describing the setting in the first paragraph, the writer divides his story into two parts: the problems of getting ashore (paragraphs 2 and 3), and the difficulties of returning to the ship (4).

We called at Malta, a curious town where there is nothing but churches, and the only sound of life is the ringing of church bells. The whole place reminded me of the strange towns one often sees in the nightmares of delirium.

As soon as the ship anchored, a regular battle began between the boatmen for possession of the passengers. These unhappy creatures were hustled hither and thither, and finally one, waving his arms like a marionette unhinged, lost his balance and fell back into a boat. It immediately bore him off with a cry of triumph, and the defeated boatman revenged himself by carrying off his luggage in a different direction. All this took place amid a hail of oaths in Maltese, with many suggestive Arab words intermingled.

The young priests in the second class, freshly hatched out of the seminary, turned vividly pink, and the good nuns covered their faces with their veils and fled under the mocking gaze of an old bearded missionary, who wasn't to be upset by such trifles.

I did not go ashore, for getting back to the ship was too much of a problem. Some passengers had to pay a veritable ransom before they could return. Two French sailors, who had got mixed up with churches when looking for a building of quite another character, solved the matter very simply by throwing their grasping boatman into the sea. A few strokes with the oars, and they were alongside, and as

a tug was just leaving they tied the little boat to it, to the accompaniment of the
indignant shrieks from the owner as he floundered in the water.

Henry de Monfreid

In each of the two main parts of the story de Monfreid begins with a
generalization and then supports it with a specific instance. The effectiveness of his narrative lies both in the skill with which he analyzes the episode and the precision with which he renders characters and action. The
glimpses he gives us are brief, but vivid and filled with meaning: the tum-
bled passenger "like a marionette unhinged," "the mocking . . . missionary," the shrieking indignation of the greedy boatman thrown into the sea.

Their nightmare quality, which is the dominant note of the setting, unifies these details. But their causal connections are relatively unimportant.
For example, the sailors do not toss their boatman into the water because
of what other boatmen did earlier to the unfortunate passenger. The two
events relate not as cause and effect but more generally in showing the
greediness of the Maltese.

In more complicated stories, however, events may well be linked in a
plot of cause and effect. A brief example of such a plot appears in this
account of a murder in New York occasioned by the Great Depression of
the 1930s:

Peter Romano comes from a little town in Sicily. For years he kept a large and
prosperous fruit store under the Second Avenue elevated at the corner of Twenty-
ninth Street. A few years ago, however, he got something the matter with his chest
and wasn't able to work any more. He sold his business and put the money into
Wall Street.

When the Wall Street crash came, Peter Romano lost almost everything. And by
the time that Mrs. Romano had had a baby five months ago and had afterwards
come down with pneumonia, he found he had only a few dollars left.

By June, he owed his landlord two months' rent, $52. The landlord, Antonio
Copace, lived only a few blocks away on Lexington Avenue, in a house with a
brownstone front and coarse white-lace curtains in the windows. The Romanos
lived above the fruit store, on the same floor with a cheap dentist's office, in a little
flat to which they had access up a dirty oilcloth-covered staircase and through a
door with dirty-margined panes. The Romanos regarded Mr. Copace as a very rich
man, but he, too, no doubt, had been having his losses.

At any rate, he was insistent about the rent. Peter Romano had a married daughter, and her husband offered to help him out. He went to Mr. Copace with $26—
one month's rent. But the old man refused it with fury and said that unless he got
the whole sum right away, he would have the Romanos evicted. On June 11, he
came himself to the Romanos and demanded the money again. He threatened to
have the marshal in and put them out that very afternoon. Peter Romano tried to
argue with him, and Mrs. Romano went out in a final desperate effort to get together $52.

When she came back empty-handed, she found a lot of people outside the house
and, upstairs, the police in her flat. Peter had shot Mr. Copace and killed him, and
was just being taken off to jail.

Edmund Wilson

Chronology is the bony structure of Wilson's little story: "For years he kept . . . A few years ago . . . When the Wall Street crash came . . . By June . . . On June 11 . . . When Mrs. Romano came back. . . ." This temporal skeleton supports a cause-and-effect plot. The basic elements of such a plot are the exposition, the conflict, the climax, and the denouement.

The term *exposition* has a special meaning with reference to narration. The exposition is that part of the plot which gives us the background information about the characters, telling us what we need to know in order to understand why they act as they do in what is about to unfold. Exposition is usually, but not always, concentrated at or very near the beginning of a story. Wilson's exposition occupies the first three paragraphs, which locate Peter Romano in time and place and tell us necessary facts about his history.

Exposition gives way to *conflict,* the second part of a plot. Conflict involves two or more forces working at cross purposes. (Sometimes this takes place between a character and a physical obstacle such as a mountain or the sea; or it may be internalized, involving diverse psychological aspects of the same person.) In this story the conflict, obviously, occurs between tenant and landlord. The third part of a plot, the *climax,* resolves the conflict: here, the shooting. Finally the plot ends with the *denouement,* the closing events of the narrative: Peter Romano's being carried off to jail.

In the simple and often partial stories you are likely to tell in expository writing, it is not always necessary (or even desirable) that you develop all these elements of a plot in detail. You may need to spend your time on exposition and conflict—as Wilson does—and treat the climax and denouement very briefly. Or you may wish to slight the exposition and concentrate on the climax. But in any case you must be clear in your own mind about the structure of your plot and know much of each element your readers need in order to understand your narrative.

In organizing a story, then, you should ask these questions. (1) What is the plot? Specifically this comes down to: What is the climax? What events leading to the climax constitute the conflict? What should be included in the exposition? What events following the climax (the denouement) should be told? (2) What are the salient qualities of the characters and how can these best be revealed in speech and action? (3) What details of setting will help readers understand the characters?

Meaning in Narrative

How you answer those questions depends on what you want the story to mean. Meaning in narrative is a complex matter. Broadly there are three kinds: allegorical, realistic, and symbolic. In allegories the meaning is an abstract "truth"—moral, political, religious—which characters, plot, and setting are contrived to express. Often what happens in an allegory is not realistic or credible in terms of everyday experience. What it all means must be looked for on the abstract level of ideas. A Queen named Superba drawn in a magnificent carriage by six strangely assorted beasts begins to make sense only when we realize that Superba stands for the mortal sin of Pride and that the animals represent the other six deadly sins. We have to think theologically in terms of sin and damnation to understand what the poet Edmund Spenser was saying.

In realism, on the other hand, meaning exists in the surface events. We don't interpret characters or plot as emblems of thought or feeling. De Monfreid's account of the landing at Malta is an example. It has a meaning, or meanings: Maltese boatmen are greedy; their greed is punished; young priests are naive. But these are generalizations drawn from what literally happens.

In symbolic stories meaning is neither purely allegorical nor purely realistic. It is both at once. Such stories are realistic in that characters and events correspond to life as we know it, and we can generalize from them to real people. At the same time the stories—like allegories—point to another level of significance, more abstract and more inclusive. Edmund Wilson's tale, for instance, conveys both a particular (realistic) and a more abstract (allegorical) meaning. Read literally, the narrative is the tragedy of two men made desperate by economic frustration, and we may fairly apply it to similar men in similar circumstances. At the same time the story can be seen in Marxist terms as revealing the impersonal forces of the exploiting bourgeoisie and the dispossessed urban proletariat, each the victim of a capitalist economy, each the victimizer of the other.

In practice, many stories operate, so to speak, at intermediate points of meaning. The meaning of one narrative is realistic tending toward the symbolic; of another, symbolic tending toward the allegorical.

Whatever its mode, the meaning of a story, if it is to be truly communicated, has to be rendered in the characters and plot and setting. It may, in addition, be announced. That is, the writer may explicitly tell us what meaning he or she sees in the story. Sometimes such a statement of theme occurs at the end of a story (the "moral" at the end of a fable, for instance), sometimes at the beginning, sometimes in between. Thus the following account of the execution in 1618 of Sir Walter Raleigh begins with an announcement of its significance. But the writer does not rest content with telling us the theme. He is careful to select appropriate details of speech and action and to ground his theme in them:

Immortal in the memory of our race, the scene of Raleigh's death has come to us with its vividness undimmed by the centuries. Everything that had been mean, false, or petty in his life had somehow been sloughed off. The man who went to the block was the heroic Raleigh who all along had existed as Sir Walter's ideal and now was to become a national legend.

He had been lodged in the gatehouse at Westminster. At midnight his wife left him for the last time, and miraculously he lay down and slept for a few hours. Early in the morning the Dean of Westminster gave him his last communion. Afterwards he had his breakfast and enjoyed his last pipe of tobacco. At eight o'clock he started on his short journey to the scaffold erected in Old Palace Yard.

Raleigh, so completely a man of the Renaissance, was inevitably concerned at the time with thoughts of fame beyond death. In his speech from the scaffold he did what he could to protect that fame, assuring his hearers that he was a true Englishman who had never passed under allegiance to the King of France. He was concerned also that men should not believe the old slander that he had puffed tobacco smoke at Essex when the earl had come to die. At the end he concluded:

And now I entreat that you all will join me in prayer to that Great God of Heaven whom I have so grievously offended, being a man full of all vanity, who has lived a sinful life in such callings as have been most inducing to it; for I have been a soldier, a sailor, and a courtier, which are courses of wickedness and vice; that His Almighty goodness will forgive me; that He will cast away my sins from me, and that He will receive me into everlasting life; so I take my leave of you all, making my peace with God.

There followed the famous moment in which Raleigh asked to see the axe. The headsman was reluctant to show it. "I prithee, let me see it," said Raleigh, and he asked, "Dost thou think that I am afraid of it?" Running his finger along the edge he mused, "This is sharp medicine, but it is a sound cure for all diseases." There was some fussing about the way he should have his head on the block. Somebody insisted that it should be towards the east. Changing his position, Raleigh uttered a last superb phrase—"What matter how the head lie, so the heart be right?" He prayed briefly, gave the signal to the headsman, and died.

The headsman needed two strokes to sever the head. After holding it up for the crowd to see, he put it in a red leather bag, covered it with Raleigh's wrought velvet gown, and despatched it in a mourning coach sent by Lady Raleigh. Finally both head and body were buried by her in St. Margaret's Church, Westminster. C. P. V. Akrigg

Akrigg states his point in the opening paragraph: Raleigh died heroically. In the story itself Raleigh's own words and actions carry that theme. The writer wisely lets them speak for themselves. In effective narrative you must render scenes as you want readers to see them and not labor overlong on telling them why your story is significant. If you create real characters and action, readers will gather the meaning.

It is not even necessary to state the point at the beginning or end of the story (though sometimes, as in the example by Akrigg, it is desirable). Edmund Wilson, for instance, does not tell us what the story of Peter Romano and Mr. Copace means: it is clear enough. Similarly the following brief narrative by Ernest Hemingway, which we saw earlier as an example of understatement, leaves its meaning for readers to infer:

They shot the six cabinet ministers at half-past six in the morning against the wall of a hospital. There were pools of water in the courtyard. There were wet dead leaves on the paving of the courtyard. It rained hard. All the shutters of the hospital were nailed shut. One of the ministers was sick with typhoid. Two soldiers carried him down stairs and out into the rain. They tried to hold him up against the wall but he sat down in a puddle of water. The other five stood very quietly against the wall. Finally the officer told the soldiers it was no good trying to make him stand up. When they fired the first volley he was sitting down in the water with his head on his knees.

Hemingway's story exemplifies realistic meaning. For while one can read philosophical significance into the horrifying episode, there is no evidence that Hemingway intends us to jump to any philosophy. This, he implies, is simply the way things are; the story is its own meaning.

The narrative also exemplifies "objective" presentation. It concentrates on the surface of events, on what can be seen and heard. Such objectivity is not a refusal to see and convey meaning, as inexperienced readers sometimes suppose. It is rather a special way of communicating meaning.

It can be a very powerful way. Hemingway does not *tell* us that war makes men cruel. He shows us; he forces us to endure the cruelty. The meaning of his brief story is more than an idea we comprehend intellectually. It becomes a part of our experience—not as deep and abiding a part, probably, as if we had actually been there, but nonetheless a reality experienced.

This is what the writer of narrative does at his or her best: re-create events in an intense and significant manner and thus deepen and extend the reader's experience of the world. Of course, in narrative of this rich and powerful kind we are entering the realm of creative literature and leaving behind the simpler world of exposition. Still, all narrative, whether literary or serving the needs of exposition, must have meaning, and that meaning must be rendered in character, action, and setting.

Point of View and Tone in Narrative

Writers are always in the stories they tell, whether that presence is apparent or hidden. It is apparent in the first-person point of view—that is, a story told by an "I." The "I" may be the central character to whom things are happening. Or "I" may be an observer standing on the edge of the action and watching what happens to others, as de Monfried observes and reports the events at Malta but does not participate in them.

Even though a writer narrates a personal experience, however, the "I" who tells the tale is not truly identical with the author who writes it. The narrative "I" is a persona, more or less distinct from the author. Thus "I" may be made deliberately and comically inept—a trick humorous writers like James Thurber often employ—or "I" may be drawn smarter and braver than the author actually is. And in literary narrative "I" is likely to be even more remote from the writer, often a character in his own right like Huck Finn in Twain's great novel.

The other point of view avoids the "I." This is the third-person story, told in terms of "he," "she," "they." Here the writer seems to disappear,

hidden completely behind his characters. We know an author exists because a story implies a storyteller. But that presence must be guessed; one
never actually observes it.

Nonetheless the presence is there. Even if not explicitly seen as an "I,"
the writer exists as a voice, heard in the tone of the story. His words and
sentence patterns imply a wide range of tones: irony, amusement, anger,
horror, shock, disgust, delight, objective detachment.

Tone is essential to the meaning of a story. The tone of Hemingway's
paragraph, for example, seems objective, detached, reportorial on the surface. He avoids suggesting emotion or judgment—words like "pitiful,"
"horrible," "cruel," "tragic." Instead, his diction denotes the simple physical realities of the scene: "wet dead leaves," "paving," "rain," "shutters,"
"wall," "puddle," "water," "head," "knees."

The absence of emotive words actually intensifies the horror of the scene.
But the objectivity of Hemingway's style is more than rhetorical understatement—though it is that—the trick of increasing emotion by seeming
to deny it. The tone also presents a moral stance: a tough-minded discipline in the face of anguish. Men die and men kill one another, and we
must feel the horror, feel it deeply; but we must also accept its inevitability
and stand up to it and not be overwhelmed by it.

Now all this is implied in Hemingway's style—that is, in the tone of his
prose. It is obviously a very important part of what he is saying. Thus
style is not merely a way of conveying the meaning of a story; it is a part
of meaning, sometimes the vital part.

PART VII

Punctuation

Introduction

The Purpose of Punctuation

All punctuation exists, basically, to help readers understand what you wish to say. Mostly marks of punctuation do this by signaling the grammatical or logical structure of a sentence (usually these are the same):

In the long history of the world men have given many reasons for killing each other in war: envy of another people's good bottom land or of their herds, ambition of chiefs and kings, different religious beliefs, high spirits, revenge.   Ruth Benedict

The colon divides this sentence into its two principal parts: the introductory generalization and the list of specific reasons. The commas within the list mark each single reason. The period closes the total statement.

Less often punctuation marks stress an important word or phrase:

In 1291, with the capture of the last great stronghold, Acre, the Moslems had regained all their possessions, and the great crusades ended, in failure.   Morris Bishop

Bishop does not need the comma before the closing phrase to clarify the grammar or logic of the sentence. Its purpose is emphatic—to isolate and thus stress the phrase. (The other commas in the sentence, however, function in the more usual way, indicating grammatical and logical structure.)

Finally, punctuation may mark rhythm. Listen to this sentence closing an essay on General Robert E. Lee:

For he gave himself to his army, and to his country, and to his God.

W. K. Fleming

The commas separating the coordinated phrases have no grammatical necessity. In such coordinated series, commas are not usually employed with *and*. Here, however, the requirements of a closing sentence—that it be slow and regular in its rhythm—justify the commas.

Of course, these three functions of punctuation often overlap. Sometimes a comma or dash both signals grammatical structure and establishes emphasis. And anytime you put a comma into a sentence to help readers follow its grammar, you automatically affect emphasis and rhythm.

Still, keep in mind that these different reasons for punctuation exist. Asking yourself an unspecified question like "Is a comma needed here?" is not very helpful. Rather you must ask: "Is a comma needed here to clarify the grammar (or to establish a particular rhythm or stress)?" About Bishop's sentence we can answer that the comma before "in failure" is *not* required by grammar but *is* necessary for emphasis.

"Rules" of Punctuation

It would be nice if punctuation could be reduced to a set of clear, simple directions: always use a comma here, a semicolon there, a dash in such-and-such a place. But it cannot. Much depends, as we have just seen, on what you want to do. In fact, punctuation is a mixed bag of absolute rules, general conventions, and individual options.

For example, a declarative sentence is closed by a period: that is an inflexible rule. On the other hand, placing a comma between coordinated independent clauses ("The sun had already set, and the air was growing chilly") is a convention and not a rule, and the convention is sometimes ignored, especially if the clauses are short and uncomplicated. And occasionally a comma or other mark is used unconventionally because a writer wants to establish an unusual stress or rhythm (like the commas in the sentences by Bishop and Fleming).

But while punctuation as actually practiced by good writers may seem a melange of rule, convention, and idiosyncrasy, it does not follow that anything goes. To punctuate effectively you must learn when rules are absolute; when conventions allow you options (and, of course, what the options are); and when you may indulge in individuality without misleading the reader. Moreover, you must keep the reader in mind. Younger, less experienced readers, for instance, need more help from punctuation than older, sophisticated ones.

In the discussions of the various punctuation marks that follow, we shall try—as far as it is practical—to distinguish among rules, conventions, and unconventional but possible uses. At times the distinctions may seem a bit confusing. It is no good, however, making up easy rules about how to handle punctuation. Such directions may be clear, but they do not describe what really happens. Instead, we must look at what skillful writers actually do. To diminish some of the confusion, just remember that clarity of communication is the one simple "rule" underlying all effective punctuation.

Remember, too, that punctuation is not something you impose upon a sentence after you have written it out. Commas, semicolons, and the other marks are an intimate part of grammar and style. Often mistakes in punctuation do not simply mean that a writer broke an arbitrary rule; rather they signify his or her confusion about how to construct a sentence. To write well, you must punctuate well; but to punctuate well, you must also write well.

The Two Categories of Punctuation

It is convenient to divide punctuation into two broad categories: the stops and the other marks. *Stops* take their name from the fact that they correspond (though only loosely) to pauses and intonations in speech, vocal signals which help listeners follow what we say. Stops include the period, the question mark, the exclamation point, the colon, the semicolon, the comma, and the dash. We look at these first.

Then we look at the other marks. These more purely visual signals do not mark pauses (though on occasion some of them signal voice intonations). They include the apostrophe, the quotation mark, the hyphen, the parenthesis and bracket, the ellipsis, and diacritics (marks placed with a letter to indicate a special pronunciation). Along with these marks we consider capitalization and underlining (or use of italics), though, in a strict sense, these are not matters of punctuation.

CHAPTER 32

Stops

The Period

The period is called an "end stop" because it is used at the end of a sentence. More exactly, it closes declarative sentences—those which state a fact, perception, idea, belief, feeling—and it may also close an imperative sentence, or command (though these are often punctuated with an exclamation point).

Abbreviations

The period is used after many abbreviations: *Mr., Mrs., Ms., Dr.* When such an abbreviation occurs at the end of a sentence, the period does double duty, closing the sentence as well as marking the abbreviation.

Some abbreviations do not take periods: government agencies, for instance, such as the *SEC* (Securities and Exchange Commission) or the *GPO* (Government Printing Office). If you are uncertain about whether a particular abbreviation requires a period, consult a dictionary or an appropriate manual of style.

Not all abbreviations, incidentally, are allowable in composition. Some are perfectly acceptable: *SEC, GPO,* or *Mr., Mrs., Ms., Dr.* (Most professors, though, do not like *Prof.*) Others are not universally accepted. For example, many teachers prefer that instead of *&, i.e., etc.,* and *e.g.,* you write out *and, that is, and so on, for example.* Colloquial, slangy abbreviations are not acceptable at all: *econ* and *polysci* are legitimate enough in conversation, but you should use the full words in composition.

The Question Mark
Direct Questions

The question mark (also known as the "query" and the "interrogation point") is used after direct questions. A direct question is always marked by one or some combination of three signals: a rising intonation of the voice, an auxiliary verb inverted to a position before the subject, or an interrogative pronoun or adverb (*who, what, why, when, how,* and so on).

"Yes-no" questions (those answered by "yes," "no," or some variety of "maybe") are always signaled by a rising intonation, which may or may not be accompanied by the inversion of the auxiliary:

You're going downtown?
Are you going downtown?

In speech the intonation alone (without the inverted verb) is often felt to be sufficiently clear. In composition the auxiliary is generally inverted.

Informational questions (those requiring in answer a statement of fact, opinion, belief) do not have the rising intonation and may or may not have the inversion; but they contain, both in speech and in writing, an appropriate interrogative word:

Who is going downtown?
When are you going downtown?

Indirect Questions

Indirect questions do not close with a question mark but with a period. Like direct questions they demand a response, but they are expressed as declarations without the formal characteristics of a question. That is, they have no inversion, no interrogative words, and no special intonation. We can imagine, for example, a situation in which one person asks another, "Are you going downtown?" (a direct question). The person addressed does not hear and a bystander says, "He asked if you were going downtown." That is an indirect question. It requires an answer, but it is expressed as a statement and so is closed by a period, not a query.

Rhetorical Questions

A rhetorical question is a variety of direct question and must be closed by a question mark, no matter whether the writer intends to answer it—or to receive an answer—or not. (The notion that a rhetorical question does not require an answer is inaccurate. Rhetorical questions are often asked precisely so that the writer can compose the answer. And even when the writer does not state the answer, he or she expects the reader to supply it.)

Question Marks Within the Sentence

While question marks are primarily end stops, within the sentence they may signal doubt or uncertainty concerning a particular fact, idea, or feeling:

It was the Lord who knew of the impossibility every parent in that room faced: how to prepare the child for the day when the child would be despised and how to *create* in the child—by what means?—a stronger antidote to this poison than one had found for oneself.   James Baldwin

Occasionally a question mark in parentheses appears within a sentence after a word to indicate that the writer is uncertain either of the spelling of the word or of the accuracy of the idea. One does this only when no reasonable way exists of checking the spelling or the information. It is abusing a privilege to write: "In 1492 (?) when Columbus discovered America. . . ." Anyone not sure of that date can fairly be expected to look it up.

There is, finally, a problem connected with where a query must be placed relative to a closing quotation mark. But since the problem affects all the other stops as well, we treat it when we discuss the quotation mark in the next chapter.

The Exclamation Point

Exclamation points convey emphasis. Most often they close a sentence and signal the importance of the total statement. Used after imperative statements ("Come here!"), they suggest the tone of voice in which such a command would be spoken.

Even more frequently than queries, exclamation points are set within a sentence in order to stress the preceding word or phrase:

Worse yet, he must accept—how often!—poverty and solitude.
                                                                    Ralph Waldo Emerson

Interjections are usually followed by exclamation points:

Bah! you expect me to believe that?

As a device of emphasis the exclamation point is of limited value. Used very occasionally, it can be effective. But like most mechanical means of emphasis, it quickly loses force. It is far better to achieve stress by effective diction and sentence structure.

I. Period
   Closes all declarative sentences, whether grammatically complete or not
II. Question mark
   A. As an end stop
      Closes all direct questions, including rhetorical ones
   B. Within the sentence
      1. May mark a word or construction
      2. In parentheses may indicate uncertainty about a matter of fact or belief
III. Exclamation point
   A. As an end stop, marks a strong statement
   B. Within the sentence, stresses a word or construction

The Colon

The colon—along with the semicolon, the comma, and the dash—is an internal stop. That is, it is used only inside a sentence, never at its end.

In modern writing the most common function of the colon is to introduce a specification:

The first principle from which he [Hitler] started was a value judgment: the masses are utterly contemptible.   Aldous Huxley

Except for the size of the houses, which varies from tiny to small, the houses look like suburban housing for middle income families in any section of the country: flat, low, lots of wasted space, nothing in the design to please the eye or relieve the monotony.   Sharon R. Curtin

In both these sentences the first portion expresses a general idea (Hitler's "first principle"; "suburban housing for middle income families"). The second portion, introduced by a colon, particularizes the idea.

Sometimes the specification takes the form of a list or series:

There are three kinds of lies: lies, damned lies, and statistics.   Benjamin Disraeli

Occasionally the usual order is reversed, and the sentence begins with the specific word or phrase, which is followed by a colon:

Centering: that act which precedes all others on the potter's wheel.
                                                              Mary Caroline Richards

But usually the specific follows the general. Such constructions are emphatic. The specification—the key point—is put at the end of the sentence. The effect of the colon, which represents a relatively long pause, is to prepare us for something momentous. The emphasis is seen very clearly in these cases:

A once-defeated demagogue trying for a comeback, he tried what other dema-
gogues abroad had found a useful instrument: terror.   Wallace Stegner

Finally, last point about the man: he is in trouble.   Benjamin DeMott

What distinguishes a black hole from a planet or an ordinary star is that anything
falling into it cannot come out of it again. If light cannot escape, nothing else can
and it is a perfect trap: a turnstile to oblivion.   Nigel Calder

Notice in all these examples that it is not necessary that the construction
following the colon be a complete clause. It can be a phrase or even a single
word.

Colons are also used to introduce quotations (really a kind of specification), especially long, written ones:

A master expositor, W. K. Clifford, said of an acquaintance: "He is writing a book
on metaphysics, and is really cut out for it; the clearness with which he thinks he
understands things and his total inability to express what little he knows will make
his fortune as a philosopher."   Brand Blanshard

And sometimes rhetorical questions are introduced by a general statement followed by a colon:

The question is: How and to what purpose?   *Time* magazine

In such a construction it is common practice (but not an absolute rule) to
begin the question with a capital letter.

COLON
___

  I. Introduces specifications, often, though not always, in the form of a list or series
 II. Introduces quotations, particularly extended written ones
III. Occasionally introduces rhetorical questions
___

The Semicolon

The semicolon has two functions: to separate independent clauses and, under certain conditions, to distinguish the items in a list or series. The first
function is by far the more common.

Semicolon Between Independent Clauses

Independent clauses may be joined either by coordination or by parataxis.
In the first case they are linked by a coordinating conjunction *(and, but,
for, or, nor, yet, either . . . or, neither . . . nor, both . . . and, not only
. . . but)*, which is usually preceded by a comma. In the second they are
simply run together with no conjunctive word but are separated by a stop,
conventionally a semicolon:

Sentimentality and repression have a natural affinity; they're the two sides of one counterfeit coin. Pauline Kael

Paratactic compound sentences punctuated with semicolons are especially common when the second clause repeats the first:

The New Deal was a new beginning; it was a new era of American government. Arthur M. Schlesinger, Jr.

Wendell Willkie was publicly and privately the same man; he was himself.
 Roscoe Drummond

All of these newcomers—black and white—toiled under some degree of unfreedom; they were bound servants for greater or lesser terms. Oscar Handlin

Using *and* in such sentences would be subtly misleading, implying a change of thought where none in fact exists.

Parataxis is also effective between clauses expressing a sharp contrast of idea:

Languages are not invented; they grow with our need for expression.
 Susanne K. Langer

He [President Calvin Coolidge] knew precisely what the law was; he did not concern himself with what the law ought to be. Irving Stone

Groups are capable of being as moral and intelligent as the individuals who form them; a crowd is chaotic, has no purpose of its own and is capable of anything except intelligent action and realistic thinking. Aldous Huxley

Clauses like these could be joined by a comma and *but*. Omitting the conjunction and using a semicolon, however, makes a stronger statement, forcing readers to see the contrast for themselves.

Occasionally even coordinated clauses are separated by a semicolon. This is done at the discretion of the writer and is more common when the clauses are relatively long and complicated, containing commas within themselves. In that case a semicolon more clearly signals the break between them. The following sentence is an example (the Duke of Wellington is commenting with pleasant cynicism upon the capacity of young ladies to endure the absence of lovers gone to war):

They contrive, in some manner, to live, and look tolerably well, notwithstanding their despair and the continued absence of their lover; and some have even been known to recover so far as to be inclined to take another lover, if the absence of the first has lasted too long.

Even when the coordinated clauses are not very long, a semicolon may still replace the more conventional comma if the writer wants a significant pause for emphasis or rhythm:

Children played about her; and she sang as she worked.   Rupert Brooke

So the silence appeared like Death; and now she had death in her heart.

Ford Madox Ford

Run-on Sentences

A run-on sentence occurs when a semicolon has been omitted between uncoordinated independent clauses. Sometimes a comma is used instead (when it is, the error is often called a "comma fault"):

INCORRECT   It was late, we went home.[1]

And sometimes the clauses are simply run together with no stop of any kind:

INCORRECT   It was late we went home.

The most frequent cause of run-on sentences is mistaking the function of conjunctive adverbs—such words as *however, nonetheless, therefore, consequently, even so, on the other hand, for example.* These adverbs do not join clauses grammatically; they only show a relationship between the ideas in the clauses. In this they differ from coordinating conjunctions, which traditionally designate both a grammatical and a logical connection.

The difference may seem arbitrary. The coordinating conjunction *but* and the conjunctive adverb *however,* for instance, can be used almost interchangeably between appropriate clauses. Even so, the first is a conjunction and needs only a comma (or maybe even no stop at all); the second is an adverb and, when it is unaccompanied by a conjunction, requires a semicolon:

It was not late, but we went home.
It was not late; however, we went home.

It would result in a run-on sentence to punctuate it like this:

INCORRECT   It was late, however, we went home.

Run-on sentences may be corrected in several ways, though for any given case one way will probably be best. The simplest solution is to put a semicolon in the proper place. Or the clauses may be joined by an appropriate coordinating conjunction accompanied by a comma (though this stop may be omitted if the clauses are short and simple). Or the two clauses may be recast as two sentences. Finally, the clauses may be kept as parts of the same sentence with one being subordinated to the other, in which case a

---

1. Commas are sometimes effective in such cases, the so-called *comma link.* Comma links are discussed on pages 286–87.

comma may or may not be needed between them. Thus the run-on sentence "The search was fruitless, the men were discouraged" can be corrected:

The search was fruitless; the men were discouraged.
The search was fruitless, and the men were discouraged.
The search was fruitless. The men were discouraged.
Because the search was fruitless the men were discouraged.

Semicolon in Lists and Series

Semicolons are conventionally used to separate all the items in a list or series when any of the items contains a comma. This is done because the presence of a comma within one or more items requires a stronger stop to signal the distinction between one unit in the series and another. Look at this sentence about the rise of the Ku Klux Klan in the 1920s:

There were other factors too: the deadly tedium of small-town life, where any change was a relief; the nature of current Protestant theology, rooted in Fundamentalism and hot with bigotry; and, not least, a native American moralistic blood lust that is half historical determinism, and half Freud.   Robert Coughlan

Even when a comma occurs in only one item, consistency requires that semicolons be used between all the elements of the series:

He [Huey Long] damned and insulted Bigness in all its Louisiana manifestations: Standard Oil, the state's dominant and frequently domineering industry; the big corporations; the corporation lawyers.   Hodding Carter

Semicolon with Subordinate Clause

Now and then a semicolon separates a main clause and a subordinate one, a job conventionally assigned to the comma. The stronger semicolon is helpful when the clauses contain internal commas; it more clearly signals the break between the clauses and helps the reader to follow the grammar:

He [the white policeman] moves through Harlem, therefore, like an occupying soldier in a bitterly hostile country; which is precisely what, and where, he is, and is the reason he walks in twos and threes.   James Baldwin

SEMICOLON
_____

I. Between independent clauses
   A. Paratactic: semicolon is the conventional stop
   B. Coordinated: comma is conventional
            semicolon is optional for clarity or emphasis
II. In lists and series
    Semicolon between all items when any item contains a comma
_____

The Comma

The comma is the most frequent and the most complicated of all marks of punctuation. It is least reducible to rule and most subject to variation, depending on the need to be clear or emphatic, the preferences of individual writers, and even fashion.

▷ Coordinated Independent Clauses

Coordinated elements are grammatically identical constructions in the same sentence joined by a coordinating conjunction *(and, but, for, or, nor,* and the correlatives *either . . . or, neither . . . nor, both . . . and, not only . . . but).* Any part of a sentence may be coordinated: two subjects, two verbs, two objects, two adjectivals, two adverbials, two independent clauses.

As a very general rule, two coordinated independent clauses are punctuated with a comma; lesser elements, such as words, phrases, and dependent clauses, are not so punctuated. But exceptions occur, depending on the length and complexity of the constructions. Let's look at several examples.

Two coordinated independent clauses are usually separated by a comma, placed immediately before the conjunction:

It [history] is a story that cannot be told in dry lines, and its meaning cannot be conveyed in a species of geometry.   Herbert Butterfield

When such coordinated clauses are complicated and contain internal commas, the stronger semicolon may be used to separate them, as we saw on page 282. On the other hand when they are short, obviously related, and contain no internal commas, the comma between them may be omitted:

They tried to hold him up against the wall but he sat down in a puddle of water.   Ernest Hemingway

The Comma Link

A comma link is a comma used between independent clauses that are paratactic—that is, not joined by one of the coordinating conjunctions but simply run together. The semicolon is the conventional mark in such a construction (see pages 282–83), and employing a comma is generally regarded as a fault. Under certain circumstances, however, a comma may be used between paratactic clauses (though it is never obligatory). The clauses must be short and simple and contain no internal stops; the relationship of ideas should be immediately clear; and the sentences should move rapidly with only light pauses:

A memoir is history, it is based on evidence.   E. M. Forster

The crisis was past, the prospects were favorable.   Samuel Hopkins Adams

When three or more such short, obviously related independent clauses are joined paratactically, comma links are even more frequent:

Some of the people said that the elephant had gone in one direction, some said that he had gone in another, some professed not even to have heard of any elephant.   George Orwell

Sheep in the pasture do not seem to fear phantom sheep beyond the fence, mice don't look for mouse goblins in the clock, birds do not worship a divine thunderbird.   Susanne K. Langer

He becomes more callous, the population becomes more hostile, the situation grows more tense, and the police force is increased.   James Baldwin

The last sentence (about racial tensions in Harlem between white police-men and black residents) illustrates the particular advantage of comma links. By allowing rapid movement from clause to clause, the punctuation rein-forces our sense of the inevitability of social cause and effect.

Easy rules about when a comma link is effective and when it is a comma fault do not exist. Certainly long, complicated paratactic independent clauses (especially those containing commas) ought to be punctuated by semi-colons, not commas. And even when the clauses are not particularly long and contain no commas within themselves, the relationships among ideas may not be sufficiently close and obvious to allow a comma link. In this sentence, for instance, a semicolon would be clearer:

INCORRECT We are overloaded with garbage, in fact we have so much excess garbage that it is being used to make hills to ski on.

For the inexperienced writer the safest course is to use a semicolon be-tween uncoordinated independent clauses unless he or she is very sure that a comma will help the rhythm of the sentence and will not confuse the reader.

As the foregoing discussion suggests, the punctuation of independent clauses is not easily explained in a simple rule. Current practice is summed up in the following table:

PUNCTUATION OF INDEPENDENT CLAUSES

I. When coordinated:
    A. Conventional punctuation: comma
    B. Optional punctuation
        1. Semicolon
            a. If the clauses are long and internally punctuated
            b. If—even with short clauses—a long pause is effective
        2. No stop at all
            If the clauses are short, unpunctuated, clearly related, and a pause is not desirable
II. When paratactic:
    A. Conventional punctuation: semicolon
    B. Optional punctuation: comma
        If the clauses are short, clearly related, contain no commas, and fast movement is desirable
---

▷ The Comma with Coordinated Elements
   Other Than Independent Clauses

Two coordinated subjects, verbs, objects, or modifiers are not usually
punctuated:

Jack and Jill went up the hill.
NOT   Jack, and Jill went up the hill.

We saw them and were surprised.
NOT   We saw them, and were surprised.

He picked up his hat and books.
NOT   He picked up his hat, and books.

The men were tired and discouraged.
NOT   The men were tired, and discouraged.

However, commas may be helpful between the members of such coordinated pairs when the first is long or when the writer wants a pause for
emphasis. Thus in the following sentence the comma helps the reader to
distinguish the two long predicates that follow the subject ("the twentieth
century"):

The twentieth century finds this explanation too vapidly commonplace, and demands something more mystic.   George Bernard Shaw

   In the next examples the comma separating two coordinated verbs (while
not necessary because of their length) gives the idea more emphasis:

We turned to them, and paused.

At night we were stained by dew, and shamed into pettiness by the innumerable
silences of stars.   T. E. Lawrence

▷ The Comma with Lists and Series

A list or series consists of three or more grammatically parallel words or
constructions such as three of four subjects of the same verb, say, or three
verbs of the same subject, or four or five adjectives modifying the same
noun.
   The items in a list, or series, may be joined by coordinating conjunctions
("She bought bread and eggs and cheese") or by parataxis ("She bought
bread, eggs, cheese"). The most common method is to combine parataxis
and coordination, linking the last two items with *and, or,* or *but not,* and
joining the others paratactically: "She bought bread, eggs, and cheese."
   When a list or series is completely paratactic, commas are used between
the items:

Oriental luxury goods, jade, silk, gold, spices, vermilion, jewels, had formerly come
overland by way of the Caspian Sea. . . .   Robert Graves

When it is completely coordinated, the commas are usually omitted:

She was crying now because she remembered that her life had been a long succession of humiliations and mistakes and pains and ridiculous efforts.   Jean Rhys

In the combined method (the most frequent practice), a comma goes between each pair of paratactic elements and is optional between the final coordinated pair, the choice depending on the preference of the writer or the policy of an editor. The first of these examples uses the comma; the second does not:

Fifty years ago, when all type was set by hand, the labor of several men was required to print, fold, and arrange in piles the signatures of a book.   Carl Becker

His plan was to clinch his teeth, shut his eyes, whirl the club round his head and bring it down with sickening violence in the general direction of the sphere.
                                                                    P. G. Wodehouse

But whether you choose to place a comma between the final coordinated items or to leave it out, you should follow the same practice consistently in any piece of writing.

Finally about lists and series, remember that semicolons are conventionally used between all items when any item contains a comma within itself.

PUNCTUATING A SERIES

 I. Combined parataxis and coordination: commas and optional comma
       bread, eggs(,) and cheese
 II. Completely paratactic: commas
       bread, eggs, cheese
III. Completely coordinated
       A. Conventional punctuation: no stops
           bread and eggs and cheese
       B. Optional punctuation: commas for emphasis or rhythm
           bread, and eggs, and cheese
IV. Series with a comma in one or more items: semicolons
       bread, which she found too moldy; eggs; and cheese

▷ The Comma with Adjectivals

An adjectival is a word, phrase, or clause functioning as an adjective.

Single-Word Adjectives

Most single-word adjectives are restrictive—that is, essential to the meaning of the nouns they modify. A restrictive adjective is placed after the noun marker, if there is one (*a, an, the, some, this, any,* and so on), and is not punctuated (italics added in the following examples):

The *angry* man sat down abruptly.

However, adjectives are often used in a rather different sense, being either placed before the noun marker (when one is present) and followed by a comma, or after the noun and set off by commas:

Angry, the man sat down.
The man, *angry,* sat down.

They may even be pushed to the end of the clause and preceded by a comma:

The man sat down, *angry.*

In such patterns (especially common with participles acting as adjectives), the word really functions more like an adverb. It tells us something about the action (in this case, how or why the man sat down) rather than about the noun (the man himself). Such "adjectives" are punctuated.

Finally about single-word adjectives: when two or more are used together they are not usually punctuated if they are coordinated. However, should emphasis require it, the second of a pair of coordinated adjectives may be set off by commas:

It [England] always had a peculiar, *and a fond,* relationship with the papacy.

Paul Johnson

When two or more adjectives are run together without conjunctions, they must be punctuated for clarity:

A novel is in its broadest definition *a personal, a direct* impression of life. . . .
Henry James

Participial Adjectival Phrases
Used restrictively, participial phrases follow the noun and are *not* preceded by a comma:

A man *leading a horse* was walking inland from the sea.   W. S. Merwin

Often, however, participial phrases function nonrestrictively. They supply pertinent information about the noun they modify, but not information essential to understanding its meaning in the sentence. Nonrestrictive participles are always punctuated. They may precede their noun; follow it, introduced between it and the verb or remainder of the clause; or be postponed to the end of the clause. In any case they must be followed, set off, or preceded by commas:

Born to lowly circumstances, he came up the easy way.   Samuel Hopkins Adams

Words, *being but symbols by which a man expresses his ideas,* are an accurate measure of the range of his thought at any given time.   Albert C. Baugh

For years he had been blackmailing the rector, *threatening to publish the facts about a certain youthful escapade of his dead wife.*   Robin G. Collingwood

Adjectival Clauses

Adjectival clauses are less flexible in their positioning than the participial phrase: they must follow their noun. But they too may be either restrictive or nonrestrictive, and they are punctuated accordingly. Restrictive clauses are not punctuated; nonrestrictive ones are set off by commas when they fall inside the main clause, preceded by commas when they fall at the end:[2]

At the apex of the social pyramid, *which was still nominally Republican,* stood the Emperor Augustus.   Robert Graves

All images are symbols, *which make us think about the things they mean.*
                                                                    Susanne K. Langer

Nonrestrictive clauses are sometimes used in a loose sense, to modify not a single noun but an entire idea. Such clauses are introduced by *which,* placed at the end of the sentence or clause they modify, and always preceded by a comma:

Lenin was cruel, *which Gladstone was not.* . . .   Bertrand Russell

---

COMMA WITH ADJECTIVALS
_____

I. Single-word adjectives
   Restrictive: no comma
      The angry man sat down.
   Nonrestrictive: comma(s)
      Angry, the man sat down.
      The man, *angry,* sat down.
      The man sat down, *angry.*
II. Participial adjectival phrases
   Restrictive: no comma
      The man *sitting down* looked angry.
   Nonrestrictive: comma(s)
      Sitting down, the man looked angry.
      The man, *sitting down,* looked angry.
III. Adjectival clauses
   Restrictive: no comma
      The man *who was sitting down* looked angry.
   Nonrestrictive: comma(s)
      The man, *who was sitting down,* looked angry.
_____

---

2. This rule reflects current American practice. Sometimes in older usage all adjectival clauses were punctuated without regard to whether they were restrictive or nonrestrictive in meaning.

▷ The Comma with Adverbials

An adverbial is any word or construction used as an adverb. Adverbials are more flexible in their positioning than adjectivals, modify more kinds of words, and convey a wider range of meanings. Consequently their punctuation is especially variable. In the discussion that follows, advice about using commas with adverbials must be understood as loose generalizations, which skillful writers frequently ignore or adapt to their particular need to be emphatic or clear or rhythmic.

Single-Word Adverbs
When simple adverbs modify verbs, adjectives, or other adverbs, they are not usually punctuated (italics are added in the following examples):

He wept *quietly.*
The people were *extremely* happy.
Everyone was *very deeply* concerned.

Sentence adverbs (those that modify an entire clause rather than any single word) are more frequently punctuated. In composition, sentence adverbs often take the form of connectives, qualifiers, and what may be called "attitudinals" (words like *fortunately* or *unhappily* that express a writer's attitude toward the statement he or she is making). Mostly such words are punctuated, whether in the opening, interrupting, or closing position (italics added):

Further, Hamlet's world is a world of riddles.   Maynard Mack

Unhappily, the gibe has point.   Brand Blanshard

In spite of all these dissimilarities, *however,* the points of resemblance were quite as profound.   Bertrand Russell

But, *luckily,* even at the dreariest moments of our pilgrimage there were compensations.   Aldous Huxley

I missed that class, *fortunately.*   Student

There is, however, considerable variation in punctuating such sentence adverbs. Some (*however,* for example) are always punctuated. With others (*therefore, luckily, fortunately*) the comma(s)—while probably more often used than not—may be omitted if the writer does not like the pause and feels that clarity does not require it.

When the coordinating conjunctions *and, but, for, or* are used to introduce a sentence, they are *not* punctuated, even though they are acting, for all intents and purposes, as conjunctive adverbs:

But we stayed.
NOT   But, we stayed.

Adverbial Prepositional Phrases

In the *first position,* when they open a sentence, adverbial prepositional phrases may or may not be punctuated. Much depends on the conventions regarding specific phrases, on the writer's own preference, and on the need for clarity or emphasis. Some idiomatic phrases are usually followed by commas; this is especially the case with those acting as sentence adverbs signaling logical relationship or attitude *(for example, on the other hand, of course):*

For example, in 1913 there was produced in Great Britain seven billion yards of cotton cloth for export alone.   Carl Becker

Less formulaic phrases are often punctuated or not, according to the writer's sense of rhythm:

In a crude way, Mickey Spillane is something of an innovator.   Charles J. Rolo

Of Pushkin's shorter stories The Queen of Spades is perhaps the most entertaining.   Rosemary Edmonds

However, if there is any chance that an initial phrase may be miscon-nected, a comma should always be used. These two sentences, for instance, would be clearer with commas:

In writing these signals must be replaced by punctuation.

In business machines are built to become obsolete within a few years.

In each case the object of the preposition can be misread as grammatically tied to the following word, as if the writers were talking about "writing these signals" and "business machines."

Within a sentence adverbial phrases are punctuated with great variability. What the phrase modifies, where it is placed, what rhythm or emphasis the writer wants are all important. A key consideration is whether or not the phrase is felt as an interrupter—that is, as intruding into the normal grammatical flow of the sentence. If it is, set off the phrase by commas. Interrupting phrases often come between subject and verb:

Jerusalem, *of course,* contains more than ghosts and architectural mon-strosities.   Aldous Huxley

Barrett Wendell, *in his admirable book on writing,* points out that clearness and vividness often turn on mere specificity.   Brand Bianshard

But they may come elsewhere:

And their former masters were, *from the start,* resolved to maintain the old difference.   Oscar Handlin

Coughlin's activities were clearly, *after Pearl Harbor,* intolerable.   Wallace Stegner

Newspapermen have always felt superstitious, *among other things,* about Lindbergh.   John Lardner

In such cases the writer is seeking clarity or emphasis. The option is not so much whether to punctuate the phrase as where to place it. Any of the phrases in the three examples above could be positioned, and more idiomatically, at the end and would then probably not need commas. But placed where they are, they do require punctuation.

At the close of a sentence or clause, adverbial phrases are not generally punctuated:

The party adjourned *to the kitchen.* . . .   Herbert Asbury

He was quiet and in-dwelling *from early boyhood on.*   John Lardner

Final adverbial phrases may be isolated for emphasis, though the technique quickly loses value if overworked:

They were not men of equal status, *despite the professed democratic procedure.*   Harry Hansen

And why is this picture an absurdity—as it is, *of course?*   George Orwell

Adverbial Clauses
In *initial position,* when they precede the main clause, adverbial clauses are usually punctuated:

If we figure out the answer, we feel devilishly smart; *if we don't,* we enjoy a juicy surprise.   Charles J. Rolo

When the general atmosphere is bad, language must suffer.   George Orwell

A writer has the option of omitting the comma after a short initial adverbial clause if clarity will not suffer. (British writers seem to exercise that choice more often than do Americans):

When he describes the past the historian has to recapture the richness of the moments. . . .   Herbert Butterfield

However, the comma should never be left out if there is any possibility that readers will see an unintended grammatical connection between the last word of the adverbial clause and the first word of the following construction. In the sentence below, for instance, a comma after "sail" would prevent readers from the misstep of thinking the writer is referring to "sail boats":

When you are first learning to sail boats seem to be very cumbersome things.

Adverbial clauses in an *interrupting position* are conventionally punctuated:

The whole thing, *as he himself recognized,* was a clean sporting venture.
P. G. Wodehouse

On occasion, *if no operations were scheduled for the next day,* he would be up early and out on an all-day hunt after getting only one or two hours of sleep.
Ralph K. Andrist

Adverbial clauses in the *closing position* may or may not be punctuated. The primary considerations are clarity and rhythm. A comma generally helps readers follow the grammar, especially before clauses expressing a concession or qualification:

The Supreme Court upheld the conviction, *although the judges could not agree on any one opinion.*
Roger Fisher

Now I seldom cuss, *although at first I was quick to open fire at everything that tried my patience.*
Richard E. Byrd

On the other hand, some writers prefer to omit the comma when the main and the adverbial clauses are both short and unpunctuated within themselves. The comma is often omitted before *because* if the pause might seem overly emphatic:

Locke thought traditional theology worthless *because it was not primarily concerned with truth.*
Paul Johnson

On one occasion, however, a following *because*-clause should be preceded by a comma. This is when it comes after a negative statement and is intended as a straightforward explanation of that statement:

They did not elect him, *because they distrusted him.*

Without the comma such a sentence may be read as an ironic assertion that "they did elect him and certainly did not distrust him."

COMMA WITH ADVERBIALS

I. Single-word adverbs
   A. Sentence adverbs: usually punctuated, whether in the initial, closing, or interrupting position
      However, the people left.
      The people, *however,* left.
      The people left, *however.*
   But there are exceptions
      Fortunately(,) the people left.
      The people *therefore* left.

B. Adverbs modifying verbs and other modifiers: not punctuated unless they are in an unusual position, when a comma may be used for clarity or emphasis.

The people *slowly* left.

EMPHATIC { *Slowly,* the people left.
{ The people left, *slowly.*

II. Adverbial phrase
  A. Initial position: punctuation optional
  On the whole(,) the men were satisfied
  B. Closing position: not generally punctuated, though comma may be used for emphasis
  The men were satisfied *on the whole.*
  EMPHATIC   The men were satisfied, *on the whole.*
  C. Interrupting position: punctuation conventionally required
  The men, *on the whole,* were satisfied.
  The men were, *on the whole,* satisfied.

III. Adverbial clause
  A. Initial position: usually punctuated
  When the sun went down, the women left camp.
  OPTION WITH SHORT, CLEARLY RELATED CLAUSES   *When the sun went down* the women left camp.
  B. Closing position: not usually punctuated, though a comma may be used for emphasis or clarity
  The women left camp *when the sun went down.*
  EMPHATIC   The women left camp, *when the sun went down.*
  C. Interrupting position: conventionally punctuated
  The women, *when the sun went down,* left camp.

▷ Comma with the Main Elements of the Sentence

The main elements of a sentence—the subject, verb, and object—are not separated by commas except under unusual conditions. Very occasionally when the subject is not a single word but a long construction, such as a noun clause, a comma may be put at its end to signal the verb (italics are added in the following examples):

What makes the generation of the '60s different, is that it is largely inner-directed and uncontrolled by adult-doyens.   Time magazine

In such a sentence the comma between the subject and the verb may help readers to follow the grammar.

Commas may also be used with the main elements in the case of inversion—that is, when the subject, verb, and object are arranged in something other than their usual order. Sometimes the pattern is object, subject, verb; if the object is a long construction, a comma may be set between it and the subject:

What he actually meant by it, I cannot imagine.   Aldous Huxley

The most frequent kind of inversion in composition occurs with the idiom "I think" ("I suppose," "I imagine," "I hope" are other variations):

The lectures, *I understand,* are given and may even be taken.   Stephen Leacock

Lenin, on the contrary, might, *I think,* have seemed to me at once a narrow-minded fanatic and a cheap cynic.   Bertrand Russell

In this type of sentence the main subject/verb is the "I think," "I understand." The rest (which contains the key idea) is a contact clause acting as the direct object, telling us what is understood or thought. If the sentence were in straightforward order, no comma would be necessary between the main elements:

I understand the lectures are given. . . .
I think Lenin might have seemed. . . .

But when the "I understand" or "I think" is intruded within the noun clause, the subject/verb must be treated as an interrupting construction and set off by commas.

▷ Comma with Appositives

An appositive is a word or construction which refers to the same thing as another and is (usually) set immediately after it. When appositives are restrictive, they are not punctuated:

The argument *that the corporations create new psychological needs in order to sell their wares* is equally flimsy.   Ellen Willis

In that sentence the clause is in restrictive apposition to the subject "argument"; it specifies "argument," and the noun would be relatively meaningless without it. Notice that the clause is *not* set off by commas. (Sometimes, however, a comma is placed *after* such a clause—though not before—to mark its end and signal a new construction.)

Often appositives are nonrestrictive. In that case they must be punctuated. Usually such appositives follow the noun and should be preceded by a comma (and followed by one if they do not close the sentence):

Poskitt, *the d'Artagnan of the links,* was a man who brought to the tee the tactics which in his youth had won him such fame as a hammer thrower.

P. G. Wodehouse

The newcomers were pagans, *worshippers of Wotan and other Teutonic gods.*   Margaret Schlauch

She was a splendid woman, *this Mme. Guyon.*   W. H. Lewis

Appositives occasionally open a clause or sentence, thus preceding the word to which they are in apposition. Then they must be followed by a comma, as in this example where a series of three appositives precedes the subject ("Bishop Andrewes"):

A gifted preacher, a profound scholar, and a great and good man, Bishop Andrewes was one of the lights of the Church of England.   G. P. V. Akrigg

▷ Comma with Absolutes

An absolute is a construction that is included within a sentence but is not really a grammatical part of that sentence; it serves as a kind of loose clausal modifier.

Nominative absolutes, the most common kind in composition, may precede, follow, or be intruded into the main clause. In all cases they are punctuated (the absolutes are italicized in the following examples):

The savings of the nation having been absorbed by Wall Street, the people were persuaded to borrow money on their farms, factories, homes, machinery, and every other tangible asset that they might earn high interest rates and take big profits out of the rise in the market.   Irving Stone

The bluffs along the water's edge were streaked with black and red and yellow, *their colors deepened by recent rains.*   John G. Neihardt

The official, *his white shirt clinging with sweat to his ribs,* received me with a politeness clearly on the inner edge of neurosis.   James Cameron

Participial and *infinitive absolutes* are also punctuated:

Allowing for hyperbole and halving the figure, that is still one hell of a pile of pulp.   Pauline Kael

To revert for a moment to the story told in the first person, it is plain that in that case the narrator has no such liberty. . . .   Percy Lubbock

▷ Comma with Suspended Constructions

A *suspended construction* occurs when two or more units are hooked grammatically to the same thing. It is really a form of parallelism, but an unusual or emphatic form, which readers may find difficult. Hence such constructions are often (though not invariably) punctuated:

Many people believed, and still do, that he was taking Nazi money to run his machine.   Wallace Stegner

Prescott and Parkman were willing, and Motley reluctant, to concede that the sixteenth-century Spaniard's desire to convert American Indians had not been hypocritical.   David Levin

When the idiomatic phrase *more or less* is treated as a suspended construction, it always requires commas to distinguish it from its more common meaning. Usually *more or less* signifies a qualified affirmation, and then is not punctuated:

He was more or less interested. = He was mildly interested.

But when *more or less* is used in a strict disjunctive sense—that is, to mean either more *or* less, but not both—it must be set off by commas:

It is hard to say whether the payment for votes has become more, or less, important.   Ronald P. Dore

▷ Comma with Dates and Place Names

In American usage, dates are conventionally punctuated like this:

April 14, 1926
April 1926

In European usage the day precedes the month, in which case a comma is unnecessary:

14 April 1926

In those place names that consist of both a local and larger designation (state, region, province, nation), a comma is placed between the two:

London, Ontario
Kittery Point, Maine

The Dash

The dash ought not to be confused with the hyphen. It is a longer mark, and on a typewriter is made either by two hyphens (--) or by a single hyphen with a space on either side (-).

The dash has no function that is uniquely its own. Instead it acts as a strong comma and as a less formal equivalent to the semicolon, the colon, and the parenthesis. As a substitute for the comma, the dash signals a stronger, more significant pause. *For that reason it should be used sparingly,* reserved for occasions when emphasis is really needed.

▷ The Dash Isolating Final Constructions

Dashes force an emphatic pause before the last word or phrase of a sentence:

Our time is one of disillusion in our species and a resulting lack of self-confidence—for good historical reasons.   Barbara Tuchman

So the gift of symbolism, which is the gift of reason, is at the same time the seat of man's peculiar weakness—the danger of lunacy.   Susanne K. Langer

▷ The Dash Around Interrupting Phrases and Dependent Clauses

Dashes may set off dependent interrupting constructions such as nonrestrictive adjective clauses, adverbial phrases and clauses, appositives, and suspended constructions. In such a use, they create emphasis.

After graduation from high school—where he [Charles Lindbergh] once wrote an elaborate and not uncomical satire on the finicky methods of his English teacher— he took three semesters in engineering at the University of Wisconsin, where the only thing that seemed to interest him much was shooting (he made the rifle team).   John Lardner

Occasionally—with a gun in his ribs, another in his back, and a gloating voice saying that in ten seconds he'll be dead—Hammer *does* become a trifle anxious.   Charles J. Rolo

Rotten logs can also be host to the ghostly glow of slime fungus, a plant that creeps— glowing—over the logs or along the ground.   Ruth Rudner

Some of those writers who most admired technology—Whitman, Henry Adams, and H. G. Wells, for example—also feared it greatly.   Samuel C. Florman

Notice, in the last example, that dashes are clearer signals of the grammar than commas would be, since the interrupting series contains commas.

▷ The Dash with Coordinated Elements

As we saw with the comma (page 288), coordinated elements are sometimes punctuated for emphasis. Stronger stress can be attained by using dashes:

We were—and are—in everyday contact with these invisible empires.
                                                                             Thurman Arnold

What the youth of America—and their observing elders—saw at Bethel was the potential power of a generation that in countless disturbing ways has rejected the traditional values and goals of the U.S.   *Time* magazine

Coordinated independent clauses are occasionally separated by a dash instead of the usual comma, but it is worth repeating that the dash is not the conventional stop for such a case and should be employed only when emphasis is necessary:

He was a sad, embittered young man—and well he might be.   Aldous Huxley

Even uncoordinated independent clauses may be punctuated by a dash instead of the conventional semicolon:

Hammer is not just any Superman—he has The Call.   Charles J. Rolo

A town may impose regulation upon the use of trucks which are equipped with loudspeakers—it may, for example, limit the loud playing of music on such trucks.   Roger Fisher

▷ The Dash Introducing a List

The colon conventionally introduces a series of specifics. The dash, how-ever, is employed for the same purpose. The only difference is that the dash is less formal:

In short, says the historian Friedrich Heer, the crusades were promoted with all the devices of the propagandist—atrocity stories, over-simplification, lies, inflammatory speeches.   Morris Bishop

▷ The Dash Around Intrusive Sentence Absolutes

An intrusive sentence absolute is a completely independent second sentence which is stuck into the middle of a containing statement without being syntactically tied to it in any way. Such a construction must be clearly marked, but it cannot be set off by commas, semicolons, or colons, since these stops would imply a grammatical connection between it and the con-taining sentence which does not exist. Parentheses could be used and some-times are; but they are a little formal for this kind of construction, which is colloquial in tone. Here, then, is the one function which belongs pri-marily to the dash:

The opening paragraph—it is one of Pushkin's famous openings—plunges the reader into the heart of the matter.   Rosemary Edmonds

He has never, himself, done anything for which to be hated—which of us has?—and yet he is facing, daily and nightly, people who would gladly see him dead, and he knows it.   James Baldwin

He [the psychoanalyst] tells us—and the notion has gained official acceptance to a limited degree—that crime is not so much willful sin as the product of sickness.   Charles J. Rolo

CHAPTER 33

The Other Marks

In addition to the stops, punctuation marks include the apostrophe, the quotation mark, the hyphen, the ellipsis, the parenthesis and bracket, and the diacritics. We look at these here, along with the related matters of capitalization and underlining.

The Apostrophe

The apostrophe has three main functions: it marks the possessive form of nouns and some pronouns, the contraction of two words, and the omission of sound within a word. It also appears in the plurals of certain abbreviations.

▷ Apostrophe to Show Possession

Common Nouns
In their singular form common nouns that do not end in -*s* or another sibilant add -'*s* to show possession:

the cat's bowl, the girl's hat, the boy's jacket

Singular nouns with a final sibilant also generally add the -'*s* in modern convention:

the horse's tail, the apprentice's job

However, there is a minor variation of usage in this matter. If such a word has several syllables and the final one is unstressed, some writers and editors prefer to drop the -s, using the apostrophe alone to indicate possession:

for appearance's sake OR for appearance' sake

The issue can often be dodged by using an *of*-phrase:

for the sake of appearance

Plural nouns ending in -s (the vast majority) add only an apostrophe:

the girls' books, the mechanics' toolboxes

Those which do not end in -s add -'s:

the men's books, the children's toys

Proper Nouns
Proper nouns that do not have a final sibilant follow the same rule as common nouns:

Sarah's house, Eisenhower's career

With proper nouns ending in sibilants, practice varies. If the noun is monosyllabic, it is conventional to add the full -'s:

Henry James's novels, John Keats's poetry

But opinion differs when proper names have more than a single syllable. Some people prefer -'s, some the apostrophe alone:

Reynolds's paintings OR Reynolds' paintings

However, the -s should be omitted from the possessive of names containing several syllables if it would result in an awkward combination of sounds:

Jesus' ministry NOT Jesus's ministry
Xerxes' army NOT Xerxes's army

When the plural form of a family name is used in the possessive, the apostrophe alone is called for:

the Browns' house, the Johnsons' boat

Pronouns
Indefinite pronouns form the possessive by adding -*'s:*

anyone's, anybody's, someone's, everyone's, and so on

The predicative possessive forms of the personal pronouns, however, do *not* use an apostrophe:

mine, yours, his, hers, its, ours, theirs

Its is especially likely to be misused, probably because of confusion with the contraction *it's* for *it is.* Never use *it's* for the possessive of *it:*

The cat washed its tail.
NOT   The cat washed it's tail.

The possessive of *who* is *whose,* not *who's,* which is the contraction of *who is.*

▷ Apostrophe to Show Contraction

A *contraction* is the coming together of two or more words with the omission of intervening sounds (in writing, of course, the letters). Contractions are common in speech and are permissible in informal writing, though they should be avoided in a formal style. They are most likely with auxiliary verbs and negative words, and in all cases an apostrophe should be placed in the position of the deleted sound or letter:

He'll go. = He will go.
We would've gone. = We would have gone.
They won't go. = They will not go.

Notice that in the last example several sounds have been dropped, but only one apostrophe is used.

The contracted form of the auxiliary *have,* incidentally, sounds exactly like the unstressed *of.* Because of this confusion such constructions as *I could of gone* are sometimes seen. That is not in accordance with formal usage and should be avoided. The proper form is: *I could've gone.*

▷ The Apostrophe to Mark Elision

Elision is dropping a sound from a word. This often occurs in rapid speech *(goin'* for *going)* and was sometimes done in older poetry *(e'en* for *even, ne'er* for *never),* though rarely in modern verse. An apostrophe signals when a sound is elided. Elision is rarely necessary in composition.

▷ The Apostrophe with the Plural Forms of Letters

When letters and numerals are used in the plural, they generally simply add -s:

Learn your ABCs.
The 1960s were a period of great change.

There are, however, three exceptions: (1) capital letters in abbreviations with periods, (2) capital letters that might look confusing with a simple -s plural, and (3) lowercase letters used as nouns:

The university graduated twenty M.A.'s.
He makes his A's in an unusual way.
Mind your p's and q's.

The Quotation Mark

Quotation marks are used with (1) direct quotations, (2) certain titles, and (3) words given a special sense. Quote marks have two forms: double (". . .") and single ('. . .'). Most American writers prefer double quotes, switching to single should they need to mark a quote within a quote. British writers are more likely to begin with single quotes, switching, if necessary, to double. Whether single or double, the quote at the beginning is called an opening quotation mark; the one at the end, a closing.

▷ Quotation Marks with Direct Quotations

A direct quotation consists of the words actually spoken or written by someone other than the writer. It is distinct from an indirect quotation, which reports the substance of what was said or written but changes the words to fit the context—often altering pronouns and verbs:

DIRECT   She said, "We are not going."
INDIRECT   She said that they were not going.

Direct quotations *must be* signaled by quote marks; indirect quotations *must not be.*

Introducing a Quotation
In introducing a quotation the subject and verb of address may precede, follow, or intrude into the quoted matter. The three possibilities are punctuated like this:

She said, "We are not going."
"We are not going," she said.
"We," she said, "are not going."

Notice that the first word of the quotation is capitalized, but that when a quotation is broken—as in the third example—the opening word of the continuation is not capitalized (unless, of course, it happens to be a proper noun or adjective or the beginning word of a new sentence).

Written quotations may be preceded by a comma, or, more formally, by a colon:

Professor Brown writes: "By themselves statistics are rarely enough; they require careful interpretation."

Often written quotations are worked into the text in a smoother manner by an introductory *that*. The *that* requires no stop since it turns the quotation into a noun clause acting as the direct object of the verb; and the first word of the quotation is not capitalized:

Professor Jones writes that "by themselves statistics are rarely enough; they require careful interpretation."

If a quotation is extensive and involves more than one paragraph, it is customary to repeat the opening quote marks at the beginning of each new paragraph. Closing quotes are used only at the end of the final paragraph.

However, extended written quotations are more commonly indented, in which case quote marks are not needed.

Quotation Marks in Relation to Stops
With opening quote marks, a comma, a colon, or any other stop always precedes the quotation mark.

With closing quotes, however, the matter is more complicated. In American usage, commas and periods always come inside a final quote mark; semicolons and colons, outside. This rule applies regardless of whether the stop in question is part of the quotation or not:

She said, "We are not going."
She said, "We are not going," and they didn't.
She said, "We are not going"; they didn't.
She said, "We are not going": why, I wonder?

In the case of question marks and exclamation points, placement depends on whether the stop applies only to the quotation, only to the sentence containing the quotation, or to both. When the quotation is a question (or exclamation) and the enclosing sentence is a declarative statement, the query (or exclamation point) comes inside the final quote mark:

She asked, "Are we going?"

When the quotation is a statement and the enclosing sentence a question, the query is placed outside:

Did she say, "We are going"?

When, finally, both quotation and sentence are questions, the query is inside the quote mark, where it does double duty:

Did she ask, "Are we going?"

Notice that whether it goes inside or outside the closing quotation, the query (or exclamation point) serves as the end stop; no period is necessary.

▷ Quotation Marks with Titles

Some titles of literary works are italicized (in typescript, underlined), others are placed in quote marks. The basic consideration is whether the work was published or presented separately or rather as part of something larger (for example, a magazine or collection). In the first case the title is italicized; in the second, set within quotes. In practical terms, this means that the titles of books, plays, and long poems, such as the *Iliad*, are italicized, while the titles of short stories, short poems, essays, articles in magazines or other periodicals, and the titles of chapters or sections within a book are quoted:

Hemingway's novel *A Farewell to Arms* has been made into a movie.
A Winter's Tale is one of Shakespeare's so-called problem comedies.
"A Rose for Emily" by William Faulkner is a shocking short story.
In *Vanity Fair* Thackeray calls one chapter "How to Live on Nothing a Year."
The finest carpe diem poem in English is Andrew Marvell's "To His Coy Mistress."

The titles of movies are italicized, those of television and radio shows are quoted:

Robin and Marian is an unusual and interesting film treatment of the Robin Hood story.
"Truth or Consequences" was popular both on radio and on television.

Notice that the first word of a title is always capitalized. So are the last word and all intervening words except articles (*a, an, the*), short prepositions, and coordinating conjunctions.

▷ Quotation Marks to Signify Special Meaning

Limited or Technical Meaning
Sometimes a common word must be used in a special sense that applies only within a limited context. To make the limitation clear, it helps to put the word in quotes:

Some years later Eton became the first public school—"public" in the sense that
students were accepted from everywhere, not merely from the neighborhood.

Morris Bishop

Irony

Irony is using a word in a sense very different from—often opposite to—
its conventional meaning. Effective irony depends on the reader's recognizing the writer's intent. Intention should be clear from the context. Even
so, a signal is sometimes advisable. In speech this is given by intonation,
as when we speak the word *brave* in a scornful way to mean "cowardly."
In writing, the signal may be supplied by quotation marks:

The Indians were therefore pushed back behind ever-retreating frontiers. "Permanent" boundaries were established between the United States and the Indians, tribes
were moved out of the United States and established beyond those boundaries.
Again and again the boundaries were violated by the whites.

James Oliver Robertson

Citation Terms

A citation term is a word used to refer to itself rather than to the object or
concept or feeling it conventionally designates. Usually such terms are italicized, but sometimes they are quoted. (They should never be treated both
ways.) The following pair of sentences illustrate the difference between the
same word used first in its conventional sense and second as a citation
term:

A horse grazed in the meadow.
"Horse" is a citation term.

Definitions

When a word is defined, its meaning is sometimes put in quotes, the word
itself being italicized:

Other-directed means "accepting and living by the standards of the social group to
which one belongs or aspires."

Slang and Colloquialisms

It is *not* necessary to place quotation marks around slang or colloquial
expressions, apologizing for them, so to speak. If the term says exactly
what you want to say, no apology is needed; if it does not, no apology
will help.

The Hyphen

The hyphen has two principal functions. It marks the syllabic division of
a word between lines, and it also separates the elements of some compound
words.

▷ The Hyphen to Indicate Division of a Word

When separating a word between lines, you should always place the hyphen at the end of the upper line, never at the beginning of the new line. The word *supper,* for example, must be divided:

sup-   NOT   sup
per   -per

Words can be divided only between syllables. Most of us have only a hazy idea of the syllabication of many words, and it is best to consult a dictionary when you must split a word.

▷ The Hyphen with Compounds

In certain compounds (two or more words treated as one) the hyphen separates the individual words. English does not treat compounds with much consistency. Some are printed as separate words *(contact lens, drawing room, milk shake);* some as single terms *(gunboat, footlight, midships);* and still others are hyphenated *(gun-shy, photo-offset).* Some compounds are treated differently by different writers; you cannot tell how any particular compound is conventionally written without consulting a dictionary or observing how publishers print it.

The examples we just saw are all *conventional compound* words. Another kind exists called the *nonce compound.* This is a construction, usually a modifier, made up for a specific occasion and not existing as a standard idiom. In the following sentence, the first compound is conventional; the other two are nonce expressions:

Old-fashioned, once-in-a-lifetime, till-death-do-us-part marriage. . . .
Leslie Aldridge Westoff

Nonce compounds are always hyphenated.

▷ Other Functions of the Hyphen

Hyphens, finally, have several special applications. When a word is spelled out in composition, the pauses which in speech would separate the letters are signaled by hyphens:

Affect is spelled a-f-f-e-c-t.

If it is necessary to cite inflectional endings or prefixes, they are preceded (or followed) by a hyphen. No space is left between the hyphen and the first or last letter of the cited term:

The regular sign of the plural in English is *-s.*
Anti- and *un-* are common prefixes, while *-ence* is a frequent suffix.

When several different words are understood to be commonly combined with the same final element to form compound words, hyphens are placed after each of the initial elements:

The lemon groves are sunken, down a three- or four-foot retaining wall. . . .
Joan Didion

Parentheses
▷ To Enclose Parenthetical Matter

Parenthetical matter is a word or construction (which may or may not be grammatically related to the rest of the sentence) sufficiently remote in relevance to require a stronger pause than a comma would supply:

Even for those who can do their work in bed (like journalists), still more for those whose work cannot be done in bed (as, for example, the professional harpooner of whales), it is obvious that the indulgence must be very occasional.
G. K. Chesterton

Parenthetical remarks of this sort—which may also be punctuated with dashes—can be a source of interest and variety as well as of necessary information. Moreover, such intrusions loosen the rhythm of a sentence, suggesting more interesting patterns of speech. The effectiveness of parenthetical remarks, however, depends on their scarcity. Using one in every other sentence costs you whatever advantage the device had, and overused parentheses become an irritating mannerism.

When a parenthetical remark comes inside a sentence, any stop that follows it must be set outside the closing parenthesis:

In the last act of the play (or so it seems to me, for I know there can be differences on this point), Hamlet accepts his world and we discover a different man.
Maynard Mack

When a parenthetical remark closes a sentence, the period is also placed outside:

I say only that a considerable number of [TV] set-owners are far from being entirely satisfied (those who are willing to pay and those who hardly ever use their sets).
Gilbert Seldes

However, if an entirely separate sentence is placed within quotes, the period which closes it (or the query or exclamation) must go inside:

Many of winter's plants are partial to the cleared sides of roads. (The roots—which is what most winter foods are—are not subject to the same kind of road pollution as are the leaves.)
Ruth Rudner

▷ Parentheses to Enclose Numbers or Letters Marking a Series

When numbers or letters introduce the items in a list they should be put within parentheses to differentiate them from the text:

We must do three things: (1) study the route thoroughly, (2) purchase supplies and equipment, and (3) hire a reliable guide.

Brackets

Brackets (which look like this:[   ]) are used in composition to enclose within a quotation any words that are not a part of it. Sometimes a writer needs to explain or comment on something in the quotation. The sample sentence by Gilbert Seldes in the section on parentheses contains such editorial addition set within brackets. In the following passage the writer adds a comment within the words spoken by a guide conducting tourists around Jerusalem:

"This area," he would say as he showed us one of the Victorian monstrosities, "this area [it was one of his favorite words] is very rich in antiquity."
Aldous Huxley

Sometimes, too, it is necessary to alter a quotation slightly to fit it into its grammatical context—adding an auxiliary verb or an ending, for instance. Any such addition to the actual quotation must be enclosed in brackets:

Johnson writes that "monkeys . . . [are] held in great esteem by the tribe."

Finally, brackets are used to enclose parenthetical matter within parentheses (though such a labyrinthine style would be, with rare exceptions [of which this is not one], both unusual and annoying).

The Ellipsis

The ellipsis is a series of three dots, or, under certain conditions, four. It is never five or six or any other number. In composition the principal function of the ellipsis is to mark the omission of material from a quotation.

If the deleted matter occurs within the quoted sentence, three dots are used:

Dante, someone has remarked, is "the last . . . great Catholic poet."

Notice the spacing: spaces are left between the preceding word and the first dot, between each dot and the next, and between the last dot and the following word.

If the omitted material includes the end of the sentence and/or the beginning of the next one, four dots are used:

Dante, someone has noted, is "the last great Catholic poet. . . ."

With four dots the spacing is a little different. The first dot, which represents the period of the original statement, is *not* separated from the word it follows, but the spacing between dots remains. Notice too that the ellipsis is placed inside the quote mark.

If the original sentence from which the final words were dropped was closed by a query or exclamation point, the appropriate stop is placed immediately after the final word and is followed by a standard three-dot ellipsis:

It has been asked, "Was Dante the last great Catholic poet? . . ."

It is considered simple honesty to use an ellipsis to acknowledge that you have omitted something from a passage you are quoting. Of course, the omission must not change the substance of what the other writer said, and if you do alter his or her meaning, the use of an ellipsis will not save you from a charge of dishonesty. The same caution applies to adding explanatory matter within brackets: it must not substantially alter the original meaning.

The ellipsis is also used in dialogue to indicate doubt, indecision, weariness, and so on. In the following sentence, for example, the ellipsis signals not an omission of any words but the trailing off of the voice, suggesting the speaker's uncertainty:

She sighed and answered, "I really don't know. . . ."

Sometimes too a writer will use an ellipsis to imply a conclusion which readers are expected to infer for themselves:

And we certainly know what that remark means. . . .

Diacritics

A *diacritic* is a mark placed above, below, or through a letter in order to indicate a special pronunciation. Diacritics are employed because the number of letters in any language is usually fewer than the number of significantly different sounds. Diacritical marks thus supplement the alphabet, enabling a single letter to do the work of two. English, while it certainly has more sounds than letters, has dispensed with diacritical marks except for the diaeresis occasionally seen in words like *naïve* or *coöperate* (meaning that the vowel is to be pronounced as a separate syllable).

But diacritical marks are common in some other languages—the accents grave and acute and the cedilla of French, (` ´ ¸); the umlaut of German (¨); or the tilde of Spanish (˜). When you use a foreign word not yet assimilated into English, reproduce the diacritics that the word has. (If you are typing, it is easiest to put these in with pencil afterwards.)

Underlining

Underlining is the compositional equivalent to italic type. There are several reasons for underlining a word or phrase.

▷ Underline Titles

The titles of newspapers, magazines and other periodicals, books, plays, films, paintings, and long poems are underlined. Titles of works which were not published separately, but rather as part of something else, are placed in quotation marks (these include magazine and journal articles, short stories, short poems, and also radio and television programs). With newspapers the title is what appears on the masthead, except that it is now customary not to italicize an initial article: the *New York Times.*

Names of ships are also italicized, as are the titles of long musical works (symphonies, tone poems, operas; songs and shorter compositions are referred to in quotes).

▷ Underline Foreignisms

Any foreign expression that has not been fully assimilated into English should be italicized:

de trop	(French: "unwanted, in the way")
dolce vita	(Italian: "life that is sweet, easy, enjoyable")
Schadenfreude	(German: "malicious joy at the misfortunes of others")

Because English has always been quick to borrow words from other languages and equally quick to anglicize their pronunciation, it is often difficult to tell whether an imported word is still considered foreign and should be underlined. Few of us think of *delicatessen,* say, as a "German" word or *perfume* as a "French" one, and in normal use these would never be italicized. (They are in the preceding sentence because they are citation terms, not because they are foreign.) But in between such fully accepted terms and plainly alien ones like *Schadenfreude,* many words that have become recently popular in English still have a faintly foreign air: *boutique,* for instance, or *détente.* Editors differ on how to treat such terms. If they are not listed in a standard dictionary, it is never wrong to underline them.

▷ Underline Citation Terms

Words used in self-reference are called *citation terms* and are usually
underlined (less commonly, placed in quotes). In the following pair of sentences, the infinitive to *run* is a citation term in the first, but in the second
it has its conventional sense:

To run is an infinitive.
He wanted to run.

Sometimes citation terms are placed in quotes, but then should not also
be underlined. Underlining—that is, italics—however, is the better choice.

▷ Underline for Emphasis

In manuscripts, underlining stands for italics (as used in the examples that
follow). Underlining (italics) has several purposes. When emphatic underlining is well done, it has the effect not only of drawing attention to key
words, but also of suggesting an actual voice talking to us:

The cause of pornography is *not* the same as the cause of free speech. There *is* a
difference.
                                                             Barbara Tuchman

The church was, in sum, more than the patron of medieval culture; it *was* medieval
culture.
                                                             Morris Bishop

Capitalization

When to use capital letters is a complicated matter; here we mention only
a few common occasions. You will find more thorough discussions in dictionaries and in style books like *The Chicago Manual of Style, 13th Edition*, published by The University of Chicago Press.

▷ Capitalize Titles

The first and last words of a literary title should be capitalized, as should
all words in-between except articles *(a, an, the)*, short prepositions, and
coordinating conjunctions:

The City of Women
The Call of the Wild

However, when an article follows a stop in the title (such as a colon or
comma), it is usually treated as a second "first" word and capitalized:

Charles Dickens, The Last of the Great Men

Remember that the titles of works published or presented separately (books, magazines, plays, long poems, films) are italicized (underlined), while those published as part of something larger are set in quotes (articles, short stories, most poems, and also television and radio programs).

▷ Capitalize the First Word of a Quotation

The opening word of quoted speech is capitalized, whether it begins a sentence or not. However, when a quotation is broken, the first word of the continuation is not capitalized unless it is a proper noun or adjective or begins a new sentence:

He said, "We liked the movie very much."
"We," he said, "liked the movie very much."

With written quotations capitalization of the first word depends on whether the quotation is introduced after a stop or is worked into the sentence as a noun clause following *that*. In the first example which follows, the quotation begins with a capital; in the second, it does not, even though it may have done so in the original:

G. K. Chesterton writes: "This is the real vulgar optimism of Dickens. . . ."
G. K. Chesterton writes that "this is the real vulgar optimism of Dickens. . . ."

▷ Capitalize Proper Names and Adjectives

A proper name is the designation of a particular person, place, structure, and so on. A proper adjective is a modifier derived from such a name.

Specific People
Harry Jones, Mary Winter, C. S. Lewis

When the name includes a particle, the particle should be spaced and capitalized (or lowercased) according to accepted usage for that name:

Gabriele D'Annunzio
Charles de Gaulle

Nouns, verbs, and modifiers derived from proper names are not capitalized when used in a sense generalized from their origin:

Charles Mackintosh   BUT   a mackintosh coat
the French language   BUT   french doors

But if a proper adjective is used in a specialized sense closely related to the name from which it derives, it should be capitalized:

He had a de Gaullean sense of country.

Personal Titles
Capitalize these when they are part of a name but not otherwise:

Judge Harry Jones   BUT   Harry Jones was made a judge.
Professor Mary Winter   BUT   Mary Winter became a professor.

National and Racial Groups and Their Languages

Amerindian   Mexican
Australian   Polish
German   Swahili

Places: Continents, Islands, Countries, Regions, and so on

China, Chinese   North America, North American
Europe, European   Manhattan, Manhattanite
the East Coast   42nd Street
New Jersey, New Jerseyan   the North Pole

When a regional name is a common term given specific application (like the Midwest of the United States), an adjective derived from it may or may not be capitalized. Consult a dictionary or style manual for specific cases:

the Far East, Far Eastern history
the Midwest, midwestern cities

Structures: Names of Buildings, Bridges, and so on

the Brooklyn Bridge
the Empire State Building

Institutions and Businesses

Kearny High School   BUT   a high school in Kearny
Columbia University   BUT   a university in the city
the Boston Symphony Orchestra   BUT   a symphony orchestra
General Motors   BUT   the motor industry

Governmental Agencies and Political Parties

the U.S. Congress   BUT   a congressional district
the Supreme Court   BUT   a municipal court
the Democratic Party   BUT   democratic countries

School Subjects and Courses
The subjects you take in college or high school are not capitalized unless they derive from proper nouns (this means language courses only):